Modern Midrash

SUNY Series in Modern Jewish Literature and Culture
Sarah Blacher Cohen, Editor

Modern Midrash

*The Retelling of Traditional
Jewish Narratives by
Twentieth-Century Hebrew Writers*

David C. Jacobson

State University of New York Press

Published by
State University of New York Press, Albany

© 1987 State University of New York

Printed in the United States of America

For information, address State University of New York Press,
State University Plaza, Albany, N.Y., 12246

Library of Congress Cataloging in Publication Data

Jacobson, David C., 1947–
  Modern midrash.

  (SUNY series in modern Jewish literature and culture)
  Includes index.
  1. Hebrew fiction — History and criticism — Addresses,
essays, lectures. 2. Bible in literature — Addresses,
essays, lectures. 3. Legends, Hasidic — History and
criticism — Addresses, essays, lectures. I. Title.
II. Series.
PJ5029.J3 1986   892.4′35′09382   86-1949
ISBN 0-88706-323-3
ISBN 0-88706-325-X (pbk.)

10 9 8 7 6 5 4 3 2 1

For Jane

Contents

Acknowledgments

This study began with my doctoral dissertation on the retelling of Hasidic tales by modern Hebrew writers, prepared under the supervision of Arnold J. Band. It is to him that I owe my initial interest in attempting to study this phenomenon of the retelling of traditional Jewish narratives by modern Hebrew writers, which is so central to the development of modern Hebrew literature. I am grateful to him for making important comments on the manuscript of the book as it developed, as well as to others for reading the manuscript either in whole or in part and offering valuable suggestions. I thank Max Ticktin for his careful reading of the whole manuscript and for his encouragement. I would also like to express my appreciation to my colleagues at the University of Pennsylvania, Barry Eichler, Judah Goldin, Arthur Green, David Stern, and Jeffrey Tigay, whose comments on those sections of the manuscript related to their fields provided important perspectives on the traditional narratives that I discuss in the book. My students in courses on modern Hebrew literature at the University of Pennsylvania provided me with stimulating forums for trying out my interpretations of the texts discussed in this study. I am also most appreciative of the initial interest and encouragement of Sarah Blacher Cohen, editor of the SUNY Series in Modern Jewish Literature and Culture and of Michele Martin, acquisitions editor of SUNY Press. In addition, I wish to thank the editors of *Hebrew Annual Review* for permission to reprint my article "The Recovery of Myth: M. Y. Berdyczewski and Hasidism" in *Hebrew Annual Review* 2 (1978), 119–30, which appears in revised form as part of chapter one, as well as the editors of *Prooftexts* for permission to reprint my article "The Creative Restoration of Legends in Bialik's 'Megillat ha'esh'" in *Prooftexts* 5 (1985), 191–99, which appears in revised form as part of chapter two.

I wish especially to thank my wife Jane Myers and my children Judah and Miriam for bearing with me and bringing me much joy during the period of the writing of this book. I am most grateful for the role Jane played in editing this book. She read through the entire manuscript offering many perceptive comments that greatly improved its style and content. This book, I am sure, would not have been as effectively written without her help.

Acknowledgment is made to the following sources for permission to reprint materials for this book:

Dvir Co., Ltd. for poetic selections from the translation by Ruth Nevo of "The Scroll of Fire," by Chaim Nachman Bialik, in Chaim Nachman Bialik, *Selected Poems: Bilingual Edition* (Tel Aviv: Dvir and The Jerusalem Post, 1981), copyright 1981 by Dvir Co., Ltd.

ACUM, Ltd. for a selection from the translation by Richard Flantz of "The King," by Shaul Tchernichowsky, in *Anthology of Modern Hebrew Poetry*, edited by S. Y. Penueli and A. Ukhmani, (Jerusalem: Institute for the Translation of Hebrew Literature and Israel Universities Press, 1966), copyright 1966 by Institute for the Translation of Hebrew Literature.

University of California Press for a selection from the translation by Ruth Finer Mintz of "Like This Before You," by Yocheved Bat-Miriam, and for the translation by Ruth Finer Mintz of "Isaac," by Amir Gilboa, in *Modern Hebrew Poetry: A Bilingual Anthology*, edited and translated by Ruth Finer Mintz (Berkeley and Los Angeles: University of California Press, 1966), copyright 1966 by University of California Press.

Shirley Kaufman for her translations of "Saul," by Amir Gilboa, translation copyright 1979 by Shirley Kaufman, and "Brothers," by Dan Pagis, translation copyright 1977 by Shirley Kaufman, in *Voices Within the Ark: The Modern Jewish Poets*, edited by Howard Schwartz and Anthony Rudolf (New York: Avon Books, 1980); and for her translation of "Near," by Abba Kovner, translation copyright 1977 by Shirley Kaufman, in Abba Kovner, *My Little Sister and Selected Poems 1965–1985*, translated by Shirley Kaufman (Oberlin: Oberlin College, 1986).

The Jewish Publication Society of America for the translation by Stephen Mitchell of "Written in Pencil in the Sealed Railway-Car," by Dan Pagis, in Dan Pagis, *Points of Departure*, translated by Stephen Mitchell, (Philadelphia: The Jewish Publication Society of America, 1981), copyright 1981 by The Jewish Publication Society of America.

Robert Friend for his translation of "Autobiography," by Dan Pagis, translation copyright 1977 by Robert Friend, in *Voices Within the Ark: The Modern Jewish Poets*, edited by Howard Schwartz and Anthony Rudolf (New York: Avon Books, 1980).

A Note on Translation and Transliteration

All English translations of passages cited in this work are those of the author unless otherwise indicated. The transliteration of Hebrew and Yiddish is based on the "general" transliteration style for Hebrew and the transliteration style for Yiddish of the *Encyclopaedia Judaica* (Jerusalem: Keter, 1972), 1:90–91, with some modifications. Proper names and other well-known terms are often spelled according to common usage in English, even when this differs from the *Encyclopaedia Judaica* transliteration style.

Introduction: The Development of Modern Midrash in the Twentieth Century

S ince the turn of the twentieth century, Hebrew writers have persisted in publishing retold versions of traditional Jewish narratives. It is the purpose of this study to shed new light on this phenomenon, which has played an important role in the development of twentieth-century Hebrew literature, as well as that of earlier modern Hebrew literature, modern Yiddish literature, and modern Jewish literature in other languages. This study seeks to answer three basic questions: 1. What has motivated so many twentieth-century Hebrew writers to retell traditional Jewish narratives for their readers? 2. What do each of these writers seek to convey by means of retold versions of traditional Jewish narratives? and 3. What is the nature of the dynamic interaction between the traditional and retold versions in each of these writer's works?

In calling this study *Modern Midrash*, the term "midrash" is used to refer to the Jewish tradition of the interpretive retelling of biblical stories that began within the Bible itself, developed in the rabbinic and medieval periods, and, I believe, has continued to the present. As an example of how this tradition has been sustained I would cite the retelling of the biblical account of the binding of Isaac (Genesis 22) by Hebrew writers of rabbinic legend, medieval *piyyut* (liturgical poetry), and modern poetry.

While the story of the binding of Isaac has inspired a variety of interpretations, a number of facts related to its plot and characterization would not be disputed by any reader. The hero of the story is Abraham, who demonstrates his trust in God by obeying His

1

command to offer his son Isaac as a sacrifice. Isaac, the intended victim, plays an essentially passive role in the story. At the moment when Abraham is about to slaughter his son, Isaac's life is spared by an angel of God, who calls on Abraham to sacrifice a ram instead of Isaac.

The postbiblical Jewish tradition of midrash has retold the story of the binding of Isaac in ways that at times significantly contradict these facts. The rabbinic legendary traditions included in the fifth century collection *Bereshit Rabbah* portray Isaac as a hero of equal or near equal stature to his father Abraham. According to one tradition, he is a man of thirty-seven years, who before being bound on the altar gets involved in a competitive discussion with his brother Ishmael over each one's worthiness in the eyes of God. In the course of the argument Isaac declares his desire to be sacrificed to God. He does so because his brother Ishmael had demonstrated his devotion to God by submitting in full awareness to being circumcised at the age of thirteen, while Isaac had not been conscious of his own circumcision when he was eight days old. Isaac therefore sees his own sacrifice as a way to prove his superiority over Ishmael by suffering for God even more than his brother. According to another tradition, when Abraham is about to sacrifice Isaac, Isaac declares his full commitment to playing the role of the victim by urging his father to tie him tightly to the altar. In making this request of his father, Isaac explains that he does not want to squirm out of fear of the sacrificial knife, which might result in Abraham not slaughtering him in the correct place, thereby rendering the sacrifice ritually improper.[1]

Later midrashic works make even more radical departures from the biblical narrative. In a medieval Hebrew liturgical poem by the twelfth-century poet Ephraim ben Jacob of Bonn, Abraham actually slaughters Isaac, Isaac is resurrected, and Abraham then attempts a second slaughter of his son.[2] In a modern Hebrew secular poem by the twentieth-century Israeli poet Amir Gilboa, discussed in greater detail in chapter six, it is Abraham who is slaughtered, while Isaac watches in horror and disbelief, desperately wishing to save his father, but unable to do so.

From a literary point of view, the rabbinic, medieval, and modern authors of these retold versions of the story of the binding of Isaac created new works out of the biblical text in significantly different ways that reflect each period's literary norms and its attitude toward the Bible. Nevertheless, these authors share a common midrashic impulse to use the Bible as a source of characters, plots, images, and themes in order to represent contemporary issues and concerns. For authors of midrash, the way that a biblical text can serve as a meaningful vehicle for the representation of contemporary reality is by transforming it, sometimes even to the point of turning it on its head. Abraham's willingness to sacrifice his son Isaac provided each of these authors with a powerful image for representing issues raised by Jewish suffering in his own day. By means of the portrait of Isaac as a conscious victim eager to prove his worth to God by being slaughtered, the authors of rabbinic legend conveyed the experience of Jews who had been martyred for their faith since the period of the destruction of the Second Temple. These authors needed to transform Isaac, the passive victim, into a more active model of willingness to die for the sake of God.

By portraying Abraham as actually slaughtering Isaac, Ephraim ben Jacob conveyed the reality of the period of the Second Crusade in which he lived, when Jewish fathers murdered their families and then committed suicide rather than submit to forced conversion to Christianity. For a writer so deeply affected by the catastrophic events of the Second Crusade, an Abraham whose hand was stayed before he could slay his son would not do as a meaningful image from the past to convey the experiences of the present. Similarly, for Amir Gilboa, who emigrated from Europe to the Land of Israel before the outbreak of World War II and suffered the loss of his parents, brothers, and sisters who remained in Europe and were murdered by the Nazis, only an actual slaughtering could serve as a representation of contemporary reality. Since it was the son, and not the father, who survived the Holocaust, then in Gilboa's retold version, it had to be Abraham, and not Isaac, who was slaughtered.

At times, rabbinic and medieval midrashic retold versions of biblical stories are presented as exegetical interpretations of passages in the biblical text. Thus, the rabbinic legend about Isaac's willingness to be sacrificed is derived from the author's attempt to understand the first words of the story, *vayehi ʾaḥar hadevarim haʾelleh* (which may be understood to mean: "And it came to pass after these words"). According to the author's exegesis of the verse, the "words" to which the verse refers were those of the competitive discussion between Isaac and Ishmael regarding their relative worthiness in the eyes of God. In Ephraim ben Jacob's liturgical poem, he asserts that his version of the two attempted slaughters of Isaac by Abraham is "well grounded" in the biblical text, for it explains why an angel of God called to Abraham twice at the end of the account in Genesis 22. At other times, rabbinic and medieval retellers of biblical stories make no real claim that there is an exegetical basis for their retold versions. Instead, these authors engage in a process that Alan Mintz refers to as "figuration," in which character types from the past are transformed into new types that reflect the values and experiences of the present. As Mintz points out, the retelling of biblical stories in medieval liturgical poetry is based less on exegesis than is rabbinic midrash and more on figuration.[3] This trend away from exegesis as the basis for the retelling of biblical stories is even more pronounced in modern retold versions of biblical stories, although such works do occasionally appear to draw at least in part on close exegetical readings of the biblical texts on which they are based.[4]

Twentieth-century Hebrew writers have retold not only biblical stories, but other traditional Jewish narratives as well, including legends from apocryphal, rabbinic, and medieval sources, and Hasidic tales. When the whole corpus of retold versions of traditional Jewish narratives by twentieth-century Hebrew writers is taken into account, it may be seen not only as a continuation of the midrashic tradition of the rabbinic and medieval periods, but also as the product of the revival of interest in myths, legends, and folktales that has spread throughout western culture in the past two centuries. Members of national or ethnic groups who have been undergoing a period of cultural redefinition have turned to the traditional narratives of their particular literary heritage as important sources of self-understanding. Such disciplines as anthropology, folklore, and psychology, which began to develop in the nineteenth and early twentieth centuries, have perceived that traditional narratives of all cultures yield universal truths about the nature of human existence of which the modern individual is not always aware. Just as national and ethnic groups and scholars have turned to traditional narratives as a source of truth, so modern writers of belles-lettres have composed mythopoetic works of literature based on traditional narratives for the purpose of exploring cultural and psychological issues. The names of the Brothers Grimm, Hans Christian Andersen, Sir James Frazier, Sigmund Freud, Carl Jung, Claude Lévi-Strauss, William Butler Yeats, James Joyce, Thomas Mann, and André Gide should be sufficient to suggest the wide-ranging influence that this interest in traditional narratives has had on the development of western culture since the nineteenth century.

Twentieth-century Hebrew writers of retold versions of traditional Jewish narratives share with many western writers of mythopoetic works of literature a set of assumptions that underlies their literary creativity. One assumption is that myths of the past are useful as a means to analyze present crises and to explore alternative approaches that might help to resolve these crises. In mythopoetic literature, Henry A. Murray points out:

> [myth] may be most effective when it provides no more than what is necessary in the way of an historical and contemporary perspective — say, a description of relevant antecedent events, of the current crisis, and of the desired outcome.[5]

Another assumption, suggested by Northrop Frye, is that one may discover in the myths of the past a set of cultural values superior to the currently accepted ones. Mythopoetic writers therefore see the mythic world of the past as a source of revolutionary values more appropriate to the cultural needs of their time than are the values of the present.[6] Harry Slochower describes this process as follows:

> In the *re*-creation of the myth by outstanding individual artists, the hero's quest becomes *a critique* of the existing social norms and

points to a futuristic order which is envisaged as integrating the valuable residues of the past and present.[7]

In other words, the retelling of traditional Jewish narratives by modern Hebrew writers involves the creation of counterhistories that reinterpret the myths of the past in an effort to interpret the crises of Jewish modernity and often to justify the kind of radical changes in Jewish culture which they believe to be necessary in the modern period. This mythopoetic literary activity has been paralleled by such phenomena as the counterhistorical reinterpretations of the Jewish past by Zionist thinkers and by the great scholar of Jewish mysticism Gershom Scholem.[8]

In addition to seeing the connections of the retelling of traditional Jewish narratives by twentieth-century Hebrew writers to the premodern midrashic tradition and to modern mythopoetic literature, it is also helpful to note its relationship to the literary phenomenon of "intertextuality" that has received so much recent attention by critics. Theories of intertextuality do not generally focus on the specific phenomenon of the retelling of traditional narratives. Nevertheless, when Julia Kristeva characterizes the poetic text as being "produced in the complex movement of a simultaneous affirmation and negation of another text,"[9] or when Harold Bloom writes, "to live, the poet must *misinterpret* the father [that is, the precursor poet], by the crucial act of misprision, which is the re-writing of the father,"[10] we know that they are analyzing a process of literary creation which is analogous to that of the modern writer retelling the narratives of his cultural tradition.

The reason that the retelling of traditional Jewish narratives by twentieth-century Hebrew writers is related to all three literary phenomena, midrash, mythopoesis, and intertextuality, is that it shares with them a similar purpose. The reteller of traditional Jewish narratives shares with the midrashic exegete, the mythopoetic writer, and the poet engaged in an intertextual struggle with a precursor an attempt to appropriate a text from the past and transform it in order to better understand the experiences of the present. Those who engage in such a process of appropriation and transformation, I would claim, make the most creative and valuable contributions to the vitality of their culture in the present and future.[11]

For the purposes of this study, it is important to distinguish between modern midrashic retold versions of traditional Jewish narratives and other works of modern Hebrew literature that draw on traditional Jewish narratives as a means to illuminate contemporary realities. In order to clarify this distinction, I would propose a system for categorizing Hebrew works related to traditional narratives according to the nature of their relationship to the traditional narratives on which they are based and the contemporary cultural context in which they are written. On one end of the spectrum are collections of traditional narratives which attempt to preserve the plot, characterization, and style of the narratives while making some adjustments to meet contemporary literary norms. The two classic examples of such collections composed in the twentieth century are *Sefer ha'aggadah*, edited by C. N. Bialik and Y. Rawnitzki, and *Mimekor yisra'el*, edited by M. Y. Berdyczewski. Included in this category would be various collections of Hasidic tales presented in a manner that is relatively faithful to the original sources, for example *'Or haganuz*, edited by M. Buber, and *Sifreihem shel tsaddikim*, edited by S. Y. Agnon. On the other end of the spectrum are works of poetry, fiction, and drama which focus on the portrayal of contemporary experience but make significant use of allusions to traditional Jewish narratives as a means to do so. A large proportion of works of belles-lettres by Hebrew writers in the twentieth century fall into this category.

Modern midrash, which consists of retold versions of traditional Jewish narratives, is located in the middle of this spectrum. It maintains much of the plot and characterization in the traditional narratives on which it is based, but it takes great liberty in adding and subtracting aspects of the narratives' content and imaginatively retells the narratives in a more contemporary style. It also takes the form of short stories, novels, plays, ballads, or lyric poems, which, from an aesthetic point of view, have more in common with works of related genres by modern western writers than with the traditional narratives on which they are based. Standing in the middle between works close to the world of the past (those that make up the collections) and works close to the present (which merely allude to the past), modern midrash is a particularly illuminating source of information about the relationship of the modern Jew to the Jewish cultural past and present.

Each Hebrew writer of retold versions of traditional Jewish narratives discussed in this study writes in response to a particular crisis in modern Jewish existence. From an historical point of view, each of these writers belongs to one of four groups which reflect four sets of experiences that gave rise to the crises that elicited their retelling of traditional narratives.

The first group of writers, which includes Micha Yosef Berdyczewski (1865–1921), Y. L. Peretz (1852–1915), Chaim Nachman Bialik (1873–1934), David Frischmann (1859–1922), and Shaul Tchernichowsky (1875–1943), were born in Eastern Europe in the latter half of the nineteenth century and wrote mainly in one or more of the major European Hebrew literary centers Odessa, Warsaw, or Berlin. Two major crises marked the lives of these writers: the failure of the Haskalah (Enlightenment) movement and the violent upheavals of the Russian Revolutions of 1905 and 1917 and of World War I. As youths they shared in the hopes for Jewish revival in the modern era that had been aroused by the Haskalah movement and the beginnings of emancipation for the Jews in the late eighteenth and nineteenth centuries. As they matured, however, they began to question the faith of the previous generation of Hebrew writers, the followers of the Haskalah known as maskilim, in the potential improvement of the Jewish condition in Europe. Whereas the maskilim had assumed that departures from the Jewish tradition through reforms in Jewish education, dress, and other cultural practices would allow the Jews to enter into European society while maintaining their loyalty to the Jewish tradition, this new generation of Hebrew writers saw the increase in anti-Semitism in Europe in the late nineteenth and early twentieth centuries as an indication that European society was unwilling to accept the Jews, even if they were to adopt a more western life style. At the same time, the new generation of writers saw that to the extent that the maskilim were able to enter into western culture, they did not appear to succeed in their attempt to balance their loyalties to western culture and to Jewish culture. Instead, the maskilim and their descendants increasingly attempted to assimilate into the majority culture, even in some cases to the point of conversion to Christianity.

These post-Haskalah writers were caught between their profound disillusionment with the promises of Haskalah and emancipation and the realization that they could never fully return to the world view and practices of the Jewish tradition that had preserved Jewish existence for so many generations. They were attracted at certain points in their lives to at least one of the various political solutions to modern Jewish existence in Europe that were proposed and attempted at the time: political reform, socialist revolution, emigration to America, and the Zionist dream of establishing a Jewish state in the Land of Israel. They doubted, however, whether these solutions would fully resolve all the dilemmas of Jewish existence in the twentieth century. In their later years, the violent upheavals of the Russian Revolutions of 1905 and 1917 and of World War I and the increase in Jewish suffering which accompanied these events aroused in these writers a sense of despair not only about the future of Jewish existence, but also about the future of that western civilization on which Jews had placed so much hope for redemption.

Each of these writers sought in traditional Jewish narratives sources of vitality that would inspire the revival of their people, who appeared to be on the road to physical and spiritual extinction. In response to the failure of the Haskalah movement, Berdyczewski and Peretz retold tales of the religious revival movement of Hasidism that arose in the late eighteenth and early nineteenth centuries. In so doing they provided contemporary interpretations of Hasidism that would point the way to the revival of Jewry at the beginning of the twentieth century. The zaddik, the hero of the Hasidic tale, emerged in these modern versions as a model for the modern Jewish writer who was seeking a way to build a new culture on the ruins of the decaying Jewish tradition.

In response to his sense of the deteriorating physical and spiritual condition of European Jewry at the time of the Russian

Revolution of 1905, Bialik turned to legendary accounts of the destructions of the First and Second Temples and the building of the Second Temple to express his grave doubts about the possibility of reviving his people. In retelling these legends, he transformed the priestly heroes who discovered the original fire of the sacrificial cult at the time of the dedication of the Second Temple into a self-portrait of himself as a poet and collector of classical Jewish texts so desperately seeking to rekindle the spirit of the people.

Frischmann and Tchernichowsky responded to the effects of World War I and the Russian Revolution of 1917 on European Jewry by looking to biblical characters who defied God as models of how Jews might pursue radical alternatives to traditional Jewish culture as well as to the barbaric degeneracy of western civilization that they were witnessing at the time. For Frischmann, the models were those who rebelled against the authority of God in the period of the wanderings of the Israelites in the wilderness but were ultimately defeated. Tchernichowsky's hero was King Saul, whom God chose to be the first king of ancient Israel and then abandoned because he was insufficiently obedient to the divine will. By identifying with these heroic biblical defiers of God who were successful in only a limited way, these writers conveyed their realization that their attempts to play a role in the radical cultural renewal of the Jewish people would most likely be opposed by forces that would deny them the complete fulfillment of their dreams.[12]

Yocheved Bat-Miriam (1901–1980) belongs to a second group of writers who were born in Eastern Europe at the beginning of the twentieth century and emigrated to the Land of Israel in the 1920s and 1930s, where they lay the groundwork for their newly adopted country to succeed Europe as the center of modern Hebrew literature.[13] It was the hope of this first generation of Hebrew writers living in the Land of Israel that the fulfillment of the Zionist dream would resolve for once and for all the crises of modern Jewish existence by providing for the physical security of the Jews and by developing a modern Hebrew culture that would create the balance between western culture and Jewish culture that had eluded the Haskalah. The works of these writers, however, reflect the fact that they brought with them from Europe many of the cultural issues with which European Jews had been struggling and that they were not able to find in the Land of Israel easy solutions to these issues.

Bat-Miriam was preoccupied with psychological issues stemming from the transition of Jewish culture from tradition to modernity, as well as from the experience of emigration to the Land of Israel. In her poetry she portrayed the male and female biblical characters Adam, Eve, Abraham, Hagar, Miriam, and Saul as representatives of the struggle of modern Jewish men and women to find national and personal liberation in a time of cultural transition despite the limitations of human existence. Some of these characters represent the poet herself whose special insights provide for modern Jews ways to deal with the difficulties aroused by the cultural and psychological issues of their time.

The third group, the poets Amir Gilboa (1917–1984), Abba Kovner (1918–   ), and Dan Pagis (1930–1986), are Holocaust survivors who came to Israel in their youth either shortly before or after World War II and lost many of their relatives and friends in the war. In those poems on which this study focuses these poets drew on biblical accounts of potential or actual violence (Cain's slaying of Abel, the binding of Isaac, and the defeat and death of Saul). In these poems, in which the biblical characters represent either victims or survivors of the Holocaust, the poets attempt to communicate to those not directly affected by the war the painful personal experiences of those who were. In so doing these survivor poets seek to define the cultural role that they might play in contemporary Israel.

The fourth group of writers, which includes Nissim Aloni (1926–   ), Moshe Shamir (1921–   ), and Amos Oz (1939–   ), were born in the Land of Israel before the establishment of the State of Israel. These writers were only indirectly touched by the experiences of the European-born writers. Their writings published since the establishment of the state reflect their realization that many of the dilemmas of modern Jewish existence experienced by their parents and grandparents in Europe will not be resolved simply by accomplishing the Zionist goal of establishing a sovereign Jewish state in the Land of Israel. In fact, they conclude, the establishment

of that state has created a whole new set of painful political and
cultural issues that make these writers uncomfortable in their role as
citizens of Israel.[14] In works of fiction and drama they deal with their
crisis of confidence in Zionism by retelling stories of abuses of power
by political leaders of ancient Israel — Rehoboam's strengthening of
the yoke of royal power over the people following the death of his
father Solomon; David's adultery with Bathsheba and his murder of
her husband Uriah; and Jephthah's sacrifice of his daughter — as a
means to explore the limitations placed on the life of the individual
Israeli by abuses of governmental power in Israel. In each work the
writer identifies with a hero: for Aloni it is Jeroboam, who led a
rebellion of ten tribes against the rule of Rehoboam; for Shamir it
is Uriah, the victim of David's crimes; and for Oz it is Jephthah, who
grieved over his self-imposed obligation to sacrifice his daughter.
These heroes represent the writers' own role as alienated critics of the
culture and politics of contemporary Israel and their painful choice
to cast their lot with the fate of a country that so far has not provided
for them the means to complete personal fulfillment.

I have divided this study of retold versions of traditional Jewish
narratives into two parts. Part I, whose title "Secular Scripture" is
borrowed from Northrop Frye, includes retold versions of Hasidic
tales, legends, and biblical stories by the writers Berdyczewski,
Peretz, Bialik, and Frischmann. These works have in common an
apparent attempt on the part of the author to create for the early
twentieth-century European Jewish reader a kind of secular scripture which, if not intended to replace the religious narratives of the
past, has an air of sacred authenticity that demands it be taken
seriously as the basis for new cultural traditions. The neo-Hasidic
tales of Berdyczewski and Peretz were collected under the titles *Sefer
ḥasidim* (*Book of Hasidim*) and *Ḥasidut* (*Hasidism*), respectively, as if
they were published to replace the view of Hasidism put forth by the
collections of Hasidic discourses and tales published by the Hasidim
themselves. The retold versions of legends by Bialik discussèd in this
study are contained in a prose-poem titled "Megillat ha'esh: me-
'agaddot haḥurban" ("The Scroll of Fire: From the Legends of the
Destruction"). The use of the word *megillah* (scroll) in the title imme-

diately associates the work with the five scrolls of scripture tradition-ally read in the synagogue on Jewish holidays, and particularly with *Megillat ʾEikhah* (The Scroll of Lamentations), which is read on the fast day of the Ninth of Av in commemoration of the destructions of the First and Second Temples. By asserting in the subtitle that the work contains a selection of legends about the destructions of the Temples, the author suggests that his versions of the legends have an importance equal to that of the legends found in traditional collec-tions. Frischmann called his series of stories *Bamidbar: maʿasiyyot bibliyyot (In the Wilderness: Biblical Tales)*. The title implies that these stories are the folktales of the biblical period that were not collected in the canon of the Bible but should have been.[15]

Part II, titled "Biblical Archetypes and the Modern Jewish Experience," includes works published, in most cases, after those discussed in Part I: poems by Tchernichowsky, Bat-Miriam, Gilboa, Kovner, and Pagis, and works of drama and fiction by Aloni, Shamir, and Oz. These authors continue the literary tradition of modern midrash without attaching to their works the air of sacred authenticity that Berdyczewski, Peretz, Bialik, and Frischmann attached to theirs. While the authors discussed in Part II do not attempt to write a secular scripture, their works are nevertheless closely tied to the traditional narratives they retell as sources of archetypal characters and situations that add a meaningful dimen-sion to what each author wishes to say about the crises of Jewish existence in the twentieth century.

Part I
Secular Scripture

Chapter 1

Neo-Hasidic Tales:
Micha Yosef Berdyczewski
and Y. L. Peretz

The Hasidic legend . . . came to life in narrow streets and small, musty rooms, passing from awkward lips to the ears of anxious listeners. A stammer gave birth to it and a stammer bore it onward — from generation to generation.

I have received it from folk-books, from note-books and pamphlets, at times also from a living mouth, from the mouths of people still living who even in their lifetime heard this stammer. I have received it and have told it anew . . . as one who was born later. I bear in me the blood and the spirit of those who created it, and out of my blood and spirit it has become new. I stand in the chain of narrators, a link between links; I tell once again the old stories, and if they sound new, it is because the new already lay dormant in them when they were told for the first time.[1]

This passage from the introduction to Martin Buber's collection of retold versions of Hasidic tales *Die Legende des Baalschem (The Legend of the Baal Shem [Tov])* (1907) reflects an approach that pervades the work of most writers who have engaged in the modern midrashic retelling of Hasidic tales. He declares that although the Hasidic tales he is retelling were originally told about a century ago, there is a contemporary relevance in what they teach that makes them of great importance to the reader of his day. The problem with them, however, is that they have been told in such awkward forms that they are not accessible to the twentieth-century reader.

17

The task of the reteller of Hasidic tales, Buber therefore believes, is to convey the truths of the Hasidic tales in a new idiom that will convey their relevance to the present. Buber is very careful to assure his readers of the validity of this enterprise of retelling Hasidic tales by asserting that as one who is linked by blood and spirit to the original tellers of Hasidic tales, he is not changing the essence of the Hasidic message, but merely carrying on the tradition of transmitting it from generation to generation. As one can see from comparing the retold versions in this collection and in Buber's earlier collection *Die Geschichten des Rabbi Nachman (The Tales of Rabbi Nachman [of Bratslav])* (1906) with the original versions, Buber felt that the fulfillment of this task could be accomplished only by making significant departures in plot, characterization, and description. Several years prior to the publication of Buber's German collections of retold versions of Hasidic tales, Hebrew and Yiddish writers had already begun to publish their own retold versions of Hasidic tales written in the same appreciative spirit as those written by Buber. While they shared a linguistic affinity with original Hebrew and Yiddish Hasidic tales, these Hebrew and Yiddish retold versions were often as different in form and content from their sources as were those of Buber.

Hebrew retold versions of Hasidic tales, on which this study focuses, may be best appreciated by viewing them as one stage in the publication, since the early nineteenth century, of narratives by Hasidim and non-Hasidim portraying the Hasidic way of life.[2] The first collections of narratives based on the Hasidic way of life were published by Hasidim. One, titled *Shivḥei habesht (In Praise of the Baal Shem Tov)*, contains tales told about the founder of Hasidim, Israel Baal Shem Tov and his early followers. The other, titled *Sefer sippurei ma'asiyyot (The Book of Tales)*, contains tales told by the great-grandson of Israel Baal Shem Tov, Nachman of Bratslav. As far as scholars have been able to determine, the Hasidim refrained from publishing any additional collections of tales for several decades.

Meanwhile, satirical works portraying the life of the Hasidim were published by followers of the Haskalah movement, who bitterly criticized the Hasidim as the traditional Jews most adamantly opposed to the reforms in Jewish culture advocated by the Haskalah. As the nineteenth century progressed, some of the opposition to Hasidism by maskilim began to soften. One of the first signs of this change of attitude was the publication of the work *Shalom 'al yisra'el* (*Peace Upon Israel*) (1868–1873), by Eliezer Zweifel, defending Hasidism as a legitimate trend within Jewish culture which was not necessarily opposed to the ideals of the Haskalah. There is evidence that in the second half of the nineteenth century some maskilim turned from the satirical portrayal of Hasidic life to become involved in the anonymous publication of collections of Hasidic tales which gave the impression of being of authentic Hasidic origin.

When toward the end of the nineteenth century Hebrew writers became disillusioned with the teachings of the Haskalah, including its early opposition to Hasidism, a decisive trend was established in Hebrew literature, beginning in the 1890s, in favor of the positive evaluation of Hasidism which had begun among the later maskilim. This trend, which has come to be known as neo-Hasidism, included essays, stories, retold versions of Hasidic tales, anthologies, and historical studies in which writers turned to Hasidism as a source of values which might serve as the basis for meeting the cultural needs of the present. Of this large body of Hebrew neo-Hasidic literature, the concern of this study will be with retold versions of Hasidic tales. The two most important early collections of neo-Hasidic literature, including such retold versions of Hasidic tales, were published in Warsaw at the turn of the twentieth century: *Sefer ḥasidim* (*The Book of Hasidim*) (1900), by Micha Yosef Berdyczewski, and *Ḥasidut* (*Hasidism*) (1901), by Y. L. Peretz.[3]

The ways in which Hasidism was significant for Berdyczewski and Peretz differed according to their backgrounds, personal experiences, and cultural concerns. Berdyczewski was raised in a Hasidic family in Medzibezh, Podolia, and as a youth was attracted to the Haskalah. In rebellion against his upbringing, he sought to expand his intellectual horizons by pursuing courses of study in a number of institutions: the yeshiva of Volozhin, the rabbinical seminary and the university in Breslau, and universities in Berlin and Berne. He gradually emerged as a leading Jewish cultural figure who wrote in Hebrew, Yiddish, and German in a variety of literary areas: fiction; essays on contemporary cultural and literary issues and on Jewish history; the collection, editing, and rewriting of Jewish myths, legends, and folktales; and text criticism and interpretation of the Hebrew Bible and the New Testament. He spent the final years of his life in Berlin and Breslau. Peretz, on the other hand, grew up in Zamosc, Poland in a non-Hasidic traditional Jewish family which provided tutors for him in both traditional Jewish and European secular studies. He eventually settled in Warsaw, where in his writings and his association with other writers he emerged as a very influential force in the development of modern Hebrew literature, and even more so of modern Yiddish literature.[4]

Peretz did not share either Berdyczewski's intimate familiarity with the Hasidic world or his youthful need to rebel against it. Furthermore, Hasidism played a different role in the development of each writer's literary activity. For Berdyczewski, Hasidism was a source from the past of cultural trends which he was seeking to reveal in his historical scholarship and in his fiction and essays on contemporary Jewish life. Peretz, on the other hand, saw Hasidism as a source of the aesthetic vision which guided the direction he sought for the development of Hebrew and Yiddish literature in his day. Both writers, however, considered the Hasidic tale as a basis for the creation of a myth of modern Jewish existence that would suggest a solution to the crises of that existence at the turn of the century.

Berdyczewski's Two Worlds

Berdyczewski's appreciation of Hasidism stemmed from his sense that European Jewry was facing a crisis that threatened the very existence of the people. In an essay titled "Setirah uvinyan" ("Destruction and Building") (1897),[5] he declares that due to both external and internal pressures on the Jewish people of his time, they have arrived at a point where "two worlds meet: existence or nonexistence." The choice he saw before the people was thus: either to die as "the last Jews" or to be reborn as "the first Hebrews."[6]

Berdyczewski's understanding of this crisis of his time is based on an interpretation of Jewish history since the destruction of the Second Temple in 70 C. E. that was strongly influenced by the writings of Friedrich Nietzsche.[7] In Berdyczewski's view, with the destruction of the Second Temple the heroic ancient Hebrew people lost its sovereign political status and became a passive and culturally degenerate Jewish people. While as Hebrews thay had related "to the world and to life in a natural manner,"[8] as Jews they became slaves to the spirit: their natural human drives were perverted by an excessive involvement with the spiritualized Judaism of the rabbinic period.

This perversion of the natural drives of the people has led, Berdyczewski maintains, to the current division of the people into three camps:

> We are torn to pieces. The one extreme forsakes the House of Israel and moves on to the alien world, offers up to it the creativeness of its soul and spirit, and gives up to it its best energies; the other extreme, the pious group, still dwells in its dark alleys, observing and keeping what it has been commanded. The enlightened ones, those who steer the middle course, are two-faced: semi-occidental in their life and thought, and Jews in their synagogues. The vital forces are dissipated, and the nation is falling into ruins.[9]

Faced with the extreme alternatives of the spiritualized life of rabbinic Judaism and the more natural life of the gentiles, the assimilationists have chosen the latter, the traditional Jews have chosen the former, and the maskilim have attempted to strike a compromise.

Berdyczewski believes, however, that none of these groups provides a viable alternative to the impending cultural death of the Jewish people. A cultural renaissance can come about only by means of a transvaluation of those values (*shinnui ha'arakhim*) on which Jewish culture has been based since the rabbinic period. Only through such a radical rejection of rabbinic Judaism, he argues, will the Jewish people rediscover the connection which the ancient Hebrews had with all of nature and life. The choice is up to the people: either to acquiesce in the death of the Jewish people, or to create a new Hebrew people liberated from the shackles of the rabbinic tradition.

While Berdyczewski saw the culture of the ancient Hebrews as the main source for the kind of cultural values that would have to replace the values of rabbinic Judaism, he came to believe around the turn of the century that he had found a source for those values in the more recent movement of Hasidism.[10] Berdyczewski explained his appreciation for Hasidism in the introductory essay of his collection of neo-Hasidic writings, *Sefer ḥasidim*, titled "Nishmat hasidim" ("The Soul of Hasidim").[11] He writes that as a youth he had rejected the Hasidism in which he had been raised because he perceived that in its attempt to attain spiritual purification, it was opposed to life. He embraced instead the idealogy of the Haskalah, which emphasized involvement in the physical world in opposition to the spiritual demands of Hasidism. Eventually, however, he came to realize that at least in the early period of Hasidism, the purpose of the spiritual demands was not to oppose life, but rather to enable people to attain the spiritual heights which the fullest involvement in life can offer. This new realization moved him to a nostalgic re-evaluation of Hasidism:

> Therefore, I look longingly to the beautiful period of the days of Hasidism, for in that exalted period I find life lived from the depths of the heart, a poetic and lofty life. . . . a life of Life.[12]

Berdyczewski was particularly impressed by the success of Hasidism to attract Jews to new revolutionary values that challenged those of the rabbinic Judaism of their day. He describes the contrast between traditional Jewish pietists and the new Hasidic man who emerged at the time of the rise of Hasidism as follows:

> In the midst of the people of the old group which preceded Hasidism, people sitting wrapped in their old prayer shawls, and on Minor Yom Kippur [a fast day observed the day before the new moon] which occurred during the beautiful spring days crying over the "exile of the *shekhinah*," or blackening their teeth in fasting

for the sins they have sinned against God . . . and if we introduce into this world one of the first Hasidim, standing upright, with the spirit of life in him, a spirit which penetrates the world open before him in all its breadth and depth, then he will be like a king among troops, like a man with the wreath of God on his head among those who sit in darkness. The latter are afraid of desecrating the holy, while he even does profane actions with the purity of holiness.[13]

In contrast to the ascetic approach of those who followed rabbinic Judaism, in his relationship with the world this new Hasidic man was able to discover a path to spiritual exaltation by transcending his sense of himself as a separate entity and perceiving that he, the world, and God are one. Such a spiritual experience was best achieved by the Hasid when he would leave the city to re-establish the "thread which connects the human being with nature:"

Not in masses of people, in a large community, will he fulfill his spiritual needs, but rather in complete isolation, there far from the noise of life and the mob, there where he dwells alone, there he finds himself, there he is what he really is . . . and this existence, which is dependent on *ʾein sof* [infinite God] and His spirit which unifies all, he feels within himself and from himself, from the life which is around him, from the inanimate and the vegetation, from the speech of the animals and the birds, and even from the song of the trees and rivers.[14]

By the beginning of the second decade of the twentieth century, Berdyczewski's attitude toward Hasidism had undergone considerable revision. Instead of viewing Hasidism as an attractive alternative to the choice between rabbinic Judaism and assimilation, he came to the conclusion that Hasidism, even in its earliest teachings, contained the same spiritually sterile values that he had criticized in rabbinic Judaism. In an essay titled "Harḥavah vetsimtsum" ("Expansion and Contraction") (1913), [15] he reviewed passages from early Hasidic texts, primarily *Shivḥei habesht* and two collections of teachings attributed to the Baal Shem Tov, *Keter shem tov* (*The Crown of a Good Name*) and *Tsavaʾat harivash* (*The Will of Rabbi Israel Baal*

Shem), and concluded that the cultural solutions he had so enthusiastically found in Hasidism at the turn of the century had never in fact been there. Instead, Hasidism had always been ascetic, law-bound, detached from nature and life, overly particularistic, and as unable to achieve a synthesis of spirit and life as rabbinic Judaism had been. Even so, Berdyczewski did not completely abandon his interest in Hasidism in his later years. He even included Hasidic tales in the collections of legends and folktales which he published then. In the last two decades of his life, however, he increasingly looked to the period of ancient Israel as the main source of vitality for the Jews of his time.

In the first story in the collection *Sefer ḥasidim*, "Shnei ʿolamot" ("Two Worlds"),[16] Berdyczewski expressed his early positive evaluation of Hasidism by retelling the first tale in *Shivḥei habesht*.[17] The original version of the tale recounts that before Israel Baal Shem Tov was born, his father Eliezer was taken captive and sold into slavery in a gentile land. During his captivity, Eliezer maintained his identity as a pious Jew and eventually rose to the rank of adviser to the king of the land. On the merit of Eliezer's observance of the Jewish tradition in captivity, Heaven enabled him to return home, and his wife gave birth in their old age to Israel Baal Shem Tov.

In the course of the narrative, the narrator of the tale alludes to three biblical heroes who shared a fate similar to Eliezer: Joseph, Esther, and Daniel. Like Eliezer, these heroes lived in exile, rose to political power, and yet maintained their identification with the people of Israel. The hero to whom the narrator most frequently alludes is Joseph, who is praised by the rabbinic and mystical traditions for having resisted the sexual temptations of Potiphar's wife, just as Eliezer resisted the temptation to have sexual relations with the wife given to him in exile.[18] These allusions suggest that the temptations and dangers facing Eliezer were just as great as those facing these biblical heroes, and that he remained just as brave, wise, and loyal to his faith and people as did these heroes. Such a man would certainly be considered to be a worthy father of the founder of Hasidism.

One can discern in this tale a relatively pure form of a plot structure which is quite common in traditional narratives.[19] This plot structure is based on the themes of descent and ascent, in which the hero descends to a lower world, where his identity becomes confused and his actions restricted, following which he rediscovers his true identity, his freedom is restored, and he ascends from the lower world back to the world from where he had descended. Eliezer is taken captive from the Jewish world and is forced to descend to the lower world of slavery among the gentiles, where his identity as a pious Jew is in grave danger. Eventually, he rises in status within the gentile world and is finally able to return to the higher Jewish world, where his freedom to live the life of a pious Jew is once again unrestricted. He is a hero because he is able to maintain his true identity as a pious Jew in a gentile world, where other lesser Jews would be tempted to abandon their identities and assimilate.

This plot structure is quite an appropriate one for a story about the father of the founder of Hasidism, for it reflects the plot structure of the central myth of Hasidism on which, as Yosef Dan has noted,[20] numerous Hasidic tales are based: the descent of the zaddik (the spiritual leader of the Hasidic community) for the purpose of ascent (*yeridah tsorekh ʿaliyyah*). As the hero of this myth, the zaddik descends from his spiritual heights in order to redeem the sparks of holiness trapped in the evil shells and to raise those sparks to their source in the divine light. In so doing, the zaddik contributes to the process of *tikkun ʿolam*, or restoration of the unity of the cosmos.[21]

"Shnei ʿolamot," Berdyczewski's rewritten version of the first tale in *Shivḥei habesht*, closely follows the mythic plot structure of the Hasidic tale on which it is based. In his version, however, Berdyczewski makes use of this mythic plot structure to create a myth of modern Jewish existence. Berdyczewski does so by reinterpreting the three situations of the original version in which Eliezer finds himself during the process of descent and ascent: his situation before his descent, his situation in the lower world of slavery among the gentiles, and his situation after he has ascended to the world from which he had been taken captive.

In the description of Eliezer before he descends he is portrayed as a pious traditional Jew who is careful to fulfill his obligations to God as well as to his fellow human beings. As the description proceeds, the reader begins to realize that in contrast to the positive portrayal of Eliezer in the original version of the story, Berdyczewski raises serious doubts about the character of Eliezer. The main flaw in his character lies in his inability to grasp the realities of human existence. He lives with his wife "far from the city dwellers in a small inn" (p. 23).[22] His home is described as being filled with "peace and tranquility" (p. 23). However, the narrator points out, in the world outside of Eliezer's home there is no peace. In the ships which sail on the river near Eliezer's home two types of people travel: "sheep-people" and "wolf-people" (p. 23). Eliezer and his wife are completely unaware that human existence consists of a constant struggle between wolf-like aggressive people and sheep-like passive people. Significantly, the only member of their household who is aware of this dichotomy of human existence is a servant whose status is based on a dichotomy: he is "half-slave" and "half-free" (p. 23). It is this servant who must brave the dangers of the outside world to accompany the guests of the inn as they travel on the road leading to and from the inn.

Eliezer's illusion of peace and tranquility is disturbed only by his realization that the *shekhinah* is in exile. His method of dealing with this problem is to practice acts of ascetic mourning:

> And at midnight, at the time when the whole world rests from the vexations of the day, he goes up onto the roof, rolls in the dust, and cries over the exile of the *shekhinah* (p. 23).

We know from Berdyczewski's essay "Nishmat ḥasidim" how negatively he viewed this ascetic type of behavior by traditional Jews. The story portrays this ascetic mourning negatively by showing that it has no effect on the exile of the *shekhinah* or the Jewish people. On the contrary, it puts Eliezer in a vulnerable position analogous to that of passive sheep among aggressive wolves: he is kidnapped by gentile robbers and is forced into slavery in a foreign land. Even his God is powerless to help him: He merely roars like a lion, "Woe to the children who have been exiled" (p. 24).

Eliezer's second situation, as a high minister in the court of the king, is portrayed more positively. While serving in that court he preserves certain aspects of his identity as a traditional Jew, especially in his observance of the Sabbath and the dietary laws. He does, however, abandon his ascetic practices, and he ceases to relate passively to the world. He uses his political power to make important contributions to his newly adopted land:

> And God is with him. In everything he does he succeeds. And the land is blessed because of him — all of the enemies which rise against it are defeated — quiet, without fear, and fruitful (p. 25).

Instead of living in an illusion of tranquility, Eliezer has now come to learn how to create tranquility by becoming actively involved in the real world.

This portrayal of Eliezer in his second situation alludes to the identity of the maskil who, while attempting to maintain his ties to the Jewish tradition, has begun to involve himself in gentile European culture and to make significant contributions to it. Since the portrayal of Eliezer's character in the second situation is a more positive one than that of Eliezer in the first one, the reader might infer that Berdyczewski prefers the maskilic identity over that of the piously ascetic traditional Jew. Eliezer, however, is not completely satisfied with his new identity. His mourning over the exile of the *shekhinah* has been transformed into mourning over the destruction of Jerusalem, as well as a longing to return to his wife and home. Furthermore, the dichotomies of human existence that characterized his earlier situation have been replaced by the dichotomy of a dual identity which is symbolized by his clothing: "under his purple garment he wears sackcloth" (p. 25). Outwardly he appears to identify as a member of the upper classes of the land, yet within himself he remains a Jew living in exile. This description of Eliezer's identity corresponds to that of the two-faced compromising maskil that Berdyczewski condemns in his essay "Setirah uvinyan."

The transcendence of the dichotomies of Eliezer's existence as a traditional Jew and as a maskil is achieved in the story only in the identity of his son, Israel, who is born to Eliezer after he is liberated from the land of his captivity and returns home. In transcending all dichotomies, Israel arrives at the true experience of peace and tranquility which had eluded his father Eliezer as a traditional Jew and as a maskil. The narrator's description of Israel's way of relating to the world closely resembles Berdyczewski's description in "Nishmat ḥasidim" of the Hasid standing alone in nature, sensing his oneness with the world and with God, although in this passage Berdyczewski speaks more of Israel's sense of a life-force than of the spirit of God:

> Within the simple life he dwells, and in the purity of wholeness he lives. In everything around him, in everything, in everything he hears as if life is speaking, as if it is expressing itself powerfully. In the heaven above, as well as the earth below, in the silence of the mountains and the waves of the river, even there in the depths of his heart, he hears the sound of life and its reverberation (p. 26).

The Hasidic myth of the descent and ascent of the zaddik embodied in the tale of Eliezer in the original Hasidic version has been reworked by Berdyczewski into a myth of modern Jewish existence. Such a myth is meant to function as a description of the crisis of modern Jewry and as a suggestion of a solution to that crisis. Berdyczewski transforms the original tale of Eliezer's descent to the threatening world of the gentiles into the story of the transition of the modern Jew from the perverted values of traditional Judaism to the inadequate compromise solution of the Haskalah. It is this transition which has led to the cultural crisis in which Jews find themselves at the turn of the century. According to Berdyczewski, the desired outcome of this crisis would be the birth of a neo-Hasidic generation of people who would transcend the dichotomies which plagued traditional Judaism and the Haskalah and would achieve a sense of inner integration and oneness with the world.

In the final passage of the story, Eliezer contemplates his impending death:

> A kind of sad restfulness fills the heart of the old man who is going to eternity when he sees the *two worlds* touch [or: kiss] each other . . . . He knows that this little son of his will rise to greatness and will surely be a lamp for Israel; yet now, when he is still young, he will be abandoned and alone. Suddenly, his lips whisper, "My son, behold I see that you will light my lamp; remember that God is with you" (p. 27).

The "two worlds" can be interpreted as the two worlds of Eliezer's finite existence on earth and his eternal existence in heaven, in line with the image found in rabbinic literature of the two worlds touching, or kissing, at the moment of death.[23] It can be shown, however, from Berdyczewski's reference to "two worlds" in his essay "Setirah uvinyan" that this image had another set of associations for him. In that essay, the two worlds are those of "existence or non-existence," the new Hebrew people or the old Jewish people. These two worlds are radically opposed to each other: the world of the Jewish people must be destroyed so that on its ruins will be built the new world of the Hebrew people. In the story, however, the transition is a more harmonious one. In Eliezer's mind the two worlds touch, or kiss: Eliezer, symbol of traditional and maskilic Jews, calmly accepts and affirms the validity of the new Hasidic identity of his son Israel.

Berdyczewski's hope is that just as in the eighteenth century Hasidism was able to convince large numbers of traditional Jews to adopt its revolutionary set of cultural values, so might traditional Jews and maskilim of the early twentieth century find in the values and world view of Hasidism a basis for a neo-Hasidic cultural renaissance. When they do, Berdyczewski's myth of modern Jewish existence will have reached its conclusion. The Jewish people will have then transcended the dichotomies of its perverted identities and returned to the ancient Hebrew people's truly harmonious relationship with nature and with life.

Peretz's Birds and Parchment Scrolls

Peretz was attracted to Hasidism because he found in it an expression of the inner truths that he sought, as a writer, to uncover for other Jews. These truths, he believed, could be discerned in his day only by the artist who, unlike others, was not blinded by outer reality:

> But people seek to see through the eye of the artist, and the eye of the artist sees reality not as it is, but rather in a much more realistic way, for he sees its inner content, he sees its relationship to the world and its dependence on the soul of the world, and on that which transpires beyond the surface of the world.[24]

This neoromantic approach to literature was one of the most significant contributions Peretz made to the development of Hebrew and Yiddish literature at the end of the nineteenth and beginning of the twentieth centuries.

Peretz's readers had generally been influenced by the anti-Hasidic attitude of the maskilim and the traditional opponents of Hasidism, the mitnagdim. In order to convince his readers of the value of Hasidism as an expression of inner truths, Peretz needed to change their negative attitude toward Hasidism. Some of the stories in his collection of neo-Hasidic stories *Ḥasidut*, which also appeared in Yiddish versions in Peretz's collection *Khasidish*, focus on the possibility of transforming a negative perception of Hasidism into a positive one by seeing beyond the outer shabby appearance of Hasidism to the truths of its inner content. In one story, for example, "Bein shnei harim" ("Between Two Peaks")[25], in a confrontation between a cold, overly intellectual, law-bound mitnaged rabbi and his former student, who had become a warm, more emotionally oriented Hasidic zaddik, the narrator affords the reader two ways of viewing a scene of Hasidim singing before their rebbe (as they would call the zaddik):

> On the meadows with their sparkle, groups of Hasidim were strolling. The satin caftans and even those of cotton — the old and

ragged, as well as the new ones — were glittering like mirrors. And the little fires which surged between the grasses would tease and touch and be reflected from the holiday garments. It seemed as if lights were dancing around every Hasid with exaltation and tenderness. And all of the Hasidim gazed — with wonderfully thirsty eyes — up at the rebbe's porch. I could feel these eyes draw sustenance from the rebbe's face. The more of this radiance they drew, the higher rose their song. Higher, always higher — ever more joyously, ever more holy.

Each of these groups sang its own song. But all of their tunes, all of the voices, mingled in the air. A single melody that rose to where the rebbe stood, as if all of his disciples were singing one song.

And all things sang. The skies were singing, the celestial spheres, and the earth beneath. The spirit of the world was singing. Now everything was song.[26]

This idyllic scene of unity among the Hasidim and between the Hasidim and the world is suddenly shattered by the mitnaged rabbi's call to refrain from singing and fulfill the obligation to engage in the traditional evening prayer:

The veil fell back over my eyes. An ordinary sky above. And below — everyday pastures, commonplace Hasidim in their torn caftans. Limping fragments of old songs. The little sparks extinguished.[27]

By presenting the more negative view of the Hasidim, which was brought on by the mitnaged rabbi's call to prayer, as if it were seen through a veil Peretz is saying to his readers that while from their mitnaged-like maskilic point of view Hasidism may appear to be worn-out and uninspiring, from his deeper more discerning point of view, it is in fact a source of great spiritual exaltation.

Just as he was concerned with how to change his readers' view of Hasidic life in general, as a reteller of Hasidic tales Peretz felt the challenge to transform those tales into stories whose value his readers could appreciate. One example of a story in which he tried to meet that challenge is "Ha'ofot vehagevilim" ("The Birds and the Parchment Scrolls"), a retold version of a dream-tale told by Nachman of Bratslav. At the beginning of the story the narrator discusses his role as a reteller of Hasidic tales:

> And when I wish to give the public the privilege and to republish [the tales], I feel in my heart a great trembling. I know that at this time it is practically impossible to tell those tales that are about different people and in a different language. And I doubt if I am worthy to tell them or if the generation is worthy to hear them . . . the world seeks entertainment and vanities like the "Broder Tales" [of popular Yiddish folk singers] and is not at all concerned about its soul, and does not absorb that which is inner, but only sees that outer shell, and does not have the understanding to discover the inner kernel . . . . But, be that as it may, one must rescue the precious pearls from the sand (p. 83).[28]

The narrator, whose views would appear to reflect those of Peretz the author, is uncertain how the Hasidic tales will be received, for he sees that the modern Jews around him are more attracted to superficial forms of entertainment, and they have lost an appreciation for the inner truth of the Hasidic tale. To them, it has an ugly form, and they have therefore rejected it. It is thus the role of the reteller of Hasidic tales to rescue each tale by retelling it in such a way as to demonstrate its beauty and its truth to the modern reader.

The dream-tale of Nachman of Bratslav, which Peretz retells, is found in *Ḥayyei moharan* (*The Life of Our Teacher Rabbi Nachman*) (1874). The work contains a biography of Rabbi Nachman of Bratslav written by his disciple Nathan of Nemirov, as well as tales composed by Nachman and dreams of Nachman which he recounted to Nathan.[29] The dream on which Peretz's story is based was told by Nachman to Nathan in 1807 after Nathan had recited the prayers for the sanctification of the moon by himself. Nachman introduced his account of the dream by declaring to Nathan, "Had you been joyous, it would have done the world a lot of good."[30] In the dream, Nachman observes a large troop of soldiers followed by birds flying behind them. When Nachman inquires of a fellow bystander what the role of the birds is, he is told that they can help the soldiers in battle by giving off a poisonous fluid that would kill the enemy troops. When he observes the birds landing and walking on the ground, he is informed that they are gathering round things which serve as the source of their poison liquid. Then Nachman enters a small, dark room with no windows in order to hide from the scene he has just witnessed. The birds follow him into the room, and he tries to shoo them away, but he is unsuccessful. Soon after their arrival, the birds die of a pox which it turns out was the source of their poison fluid. Nachman prays to God to save him from dying of the stench of their dead bodies. God answers Nachman's prayer by healing the birds, who fly out of the room joyfully. The dream ends with Nachman joining in a great shout of "Mazal tov!"

This dream-tale is different from most Hasidic tales in that it is not a tale told *about* a zaddik, but rather one told *by* a zaddik about himself in the form of a narration of a dream. The assumption behind Nachman's recounting of the dream and its subsequent publication by Nathan was that the inner life of the zaddik had a spiritual significance which it was important to share with his disciples, for the subconscious wishes and fears of the zaddik's dream tell much about the role of the zaddik in the world.

It is important to note the context in which Nachman recounted this dream. The prayers for the sanctification of the moon, which Nathan had just recited, are traditionally said in a joyous mood during the early part of the month in the Hebrew lunar calendar, usually after the conclusion of the Sabbath. The prayers are preferably said in a group, or at least with one other person, for they call for an exchange between two worshippers, with one saying, *shalom 'aleikhem* ("peace unto you"), and the other responding, *'aleikhem shalom* ("unto you peace"). Nachman's comment to Nathan, "Had you been joyous, it would have done the world a lot of good," could be understood as a rebuke directed at Nathan for violating the practice and spirit of the sanctification of the moon prayers by reciting them alone and not in the proper joyful mood.

Arthur Green, in his biography of Nachman, discusses Nachman's very strong tendency throughout his life to sadness and depression. Green attributes Nachman's depression to intense guilt feelings related to his sexual desires. Nachman was frequently tormented by the doubts which his sexual desires aroused about his claim that he was the leading zaddik of his generation:

> Out of his own struggle with this passions, he had come to determine that absolute victory over those passions was the defining characteristic of the true *zaddiq*. Yet here he was claiming to be the greatest of all the *zaddiqim*, indeed the only true *zaddiq ha-dor* [zaddik of the generation], still secretly torn by his own inner conflicts, and feeling that his claim to leadership was, on some level, nothing but a lie . . . . What he sought was perfection, and perfection meant the overcoming of *desire* itself.[31]

The conflict within Nachman influenced him to approach the issues of sexual purity and joy in a manner which was not fully in the spirit of the teachings of his great-grandfather, the Baal Shem Tov:

> Just as his own sadness led him to challenge the Baal Shem's teachings on the easy accessibility of joy, so his own battles with sexual guilt caused him to return to the pre-Hasidic emphasis on purity in this area.[32]

Nevertheless, Nachman was known to have urged his disciples to seek what the Baal Shem Tov had taught, the worship of God through joy, even if it appeared to them that *he* was depressed. In Nachman's apparent rebuke to Nathan before recounting the dream, the zaddik is suggesting to his disciple that the latter's lack of joy has taken something from the world, that one of the great struggles of Bratslav Hasidim must be to overcome sadness and be joyful in order to contribute to the restoration of the unity of the cosmos. As Nachman taught in another context:

> The main thing is that one must struggle with all one's strength to be joyous always. It is the nature of man to be drawn into malancholy and sadness, because of the things that happen to him; every man is filled with sorrows.[33]

It is not known when Nachman dreamed this dream. It is known, however, that the winter of 1806 to 1807, when he recounted it to Nathan, was a very trying period for him, and the dream very well may reflect his mood at that time. During the years 1804 to 1806, Nachman performed a series of acts which strongly suggest that he believed he was in the process of playing a central role in the coming of the Messiah.[34] Nachman was very fearful that his messianic activities at that time might harm himself or others both physically and spiritually. He concluded that one of his granddaughters became ill in the spring of 1805 with "measles or the pox"[35] as a result of his messianic endeavors. When his infant son, who he believed would play a central role in the messianic era, died in the summer of 1806, Nachman concluded he had failed in his endeavors. It was at that time that Nachman began to tell his now famous tales, later collected in *Sefer sippurei maʿasiyyot*, apparently "seeking in the world of fantasy and imagination the redemption history had failed to provide."[36]

This dream may have been a response to Nachman's sense of failure at that time. The image of the battle of the soldiers aided by the birds may reflect Nachman's messianic struggle against the forces of evil. As in the tale of Eliezer in *Shivḥei habesht,* images of descent and ascent lie at the heart of this dream-tale. The birds descend from their flight to walk along the ground. They also descend into a situation in which their very existence is threatened: the fluid that they give off to kill the enemy is the result of an illness they have contracted which threatens their lives. Nachman, in turn, also endangers himself, first by getting close to the battle, and then by entering the room in which he is afraid he might die from the stench of the dead birds. These images of descent are then followed by images of ascent: the birds are cured of their illness and joyfully fly back up to the heavens, and Nachman, who is rescued from death, shares in their joy.

In terms of the Hasidic myth, the dream is an expression of the descent of Nachman into the realm of the evil shells in order to raise the divine sparks to their source in infinite God and thereby bring about the restoration of the unity of the cosmos. It is a dangerous path in which Nachman and those who accompany him in the descent might lose their lives. The illness of the pox which endangers the birds may reflect his granddaughter's illness and the death of his son at the time of his messianic activities. Given what is known of Nachman's preoccupation with sadness and of his statement to Nathan before recounting the dream, it would appear that the descent into depression is seen here as one of the necessary dangerous paths of the zaddik in order to raise depression to joy and thereby contribute to the restoration of the unity of the cosmos.

Nachman's descent may also reflect his role in the restoration of the souls of sinners to a state of purity *(tikkun neshamot)*. As a part of his messianic endeavors he had tried to achieve the restoration of the souls of his disciples through their repentance from sin, and as a zaddik he considered it his responsibility to restore the souls of other sinners, living and dead, as well, in order to bring about the restoration of the unity of the cosmos. In Jewish literature birds often symbolize souls. Thus Nachman's way of relating to the birds by expressing concern but also by running away from them and trying to shoo them away suggests his ambivalent feelings about his role in the restoration of souls. Nachman cares about the sinners, but he is also afraid that he will be dragged down into the mire of their existence.[37]

In the dream, Nachman and the birds recover from the dangerous depression, or perhaps the sinful condition, into which they had descended, and the narrative concludes with the joyous shout of congratulation said by Jews on such occasions as a marriage or the birth of a child: "Mazal tov!" In telling this dream to Nathan, Nachman shared with his disciple his deepest anxieties about the struggle of the zaddik in his descent into depression and into the realm of evil and his desire, if not his faith, that he would be able to ascend to joy and purity and thereby contribute to the restoration of the unity of the cosmos. The defeat of the previous summer became, in his dream, a messianic victory for Nachman.

In Peretz's retold version of this dream-tale, "Ha'ofot vehagevilim," the narrator's introductory remarks on the retelling of Hasidic tales are followed by a description of the atmosphere in which Nachmanke, the Yiddish familiar form of the name by which the narrator calls Nachman, tells the tale. It is Saturday night, following the conclusion of the Sabbath, the time when Nachman of Bratslav most likely recounted his dream to his disciple Nathan. Just as Nachman of Bratslav struggled against personal sadness and depression and urged his disciples to be happy, so in Peretz's story Nachmanke's community is fighting a battle against sadness, with Nachmanke in the lead. Gradually, Nachmanke overcomes his depression by asserting his faith in himself as the "leader of the world" (*manhig ha'olam*), an expression which echoes Nachman of Bratzlav's reference to himself as "the zaddik of the generation" (*tsaddik hador*).

Nachmanke tells his disciples of an experience he once had of being immersed in the depths of a depression in which it appeared to him that the *shekhinah* had disappeared so that he was unable to perceive the soul present in everything in the world. He describes this depression to his disciples as a kind of wandering in a wilderness. This wandering represents feelings of alienation from others that prevent people from helping each other to transcend the depression:

> For the wilderness is large, very large, and twice as many as went out of Egypt, myriads of people wander in it, but each one wanders by himself, not meeting any fellow human being. A person walks on a confused path and hears the voice of a human being pleading for his life from another confused path, and he does not draw near to him to grasp his hand. On the contrary, he flees from the voice, which seems to him to be the voice of a wild beast (p. 88).

Nachmanke points out that although both the Hasidim and the mitnagdim may experience such a wandering-like depression, the wandering of the mitnaged is qualitatively different from that of the Hasid:

> Is it possible that the mitnaged does not wander? Of course he too wanders, but he wanders not on account of himself but on account of others — on account of some book or some legal authority. For

his part, he has no intention of wandering. And wandering is a
result only of intention . . . . The mitnaged proceeds on a path
paved from eternity, and does not turn right or left from the paved
path, and if the path itself is slightly crooked — "our fathers"
sinned, those who paved it (pp. 86–87).

The mitnagdim are unable to discern the inner soul of the
world, not because of some personal experience of the disappearance
of the *shekhinah,* but rather because they rely too heavily on traditional authority. When they realize that the tradition is keeping them
from discerning the truth, they merely blame the ways of the past
without trying to change tradition to make it more in keeping with
the truth. According to Nachmanke, while even the Hasidim may
find themselves in the wilderness of depression, their leader the
zaddik knows how to rescue them from the bookish tradition-bound
orientation of the mitnagdim and lead them back to a sense of happiness and acceptance in the experience of community.

Following these introductory comments by Nachmanke on
depression, which parallel Nachman's admonition to Nathan to
be happy, Nachmanke turns to telling the tale which is based on the
original dream-tale of Nachman of Bratslav. Like Nachman in the
original dream-tale, Nachmanke follows a flock of birds and inquires
about them. He learns that they are hopping on the ground because
their wings are stuck to their bodies, and they are thus unable to fly.
He also learns that the birds are on their way to battle against "a very
old house." The king of the birds explains the reason for the battle
to Nachmanke:

> In generations past, birds were hunted in the forests and brought
> to that house and placed in cages to sing at mealtimes. And during
> many generations of living in narrow cages without being able to
> fly in them and to use their wings, the wings became smaller and
> dried out, and the descendants of the caged birds inherited from
> their ancestors dry wings (p. 93).

The birds, the king continues, now want to take revenge by destroying the house which was the cause of their inability to fly. The king's

account of the past history of the birds constitutes the first part of a myth of modern Jewish existence which Peretz, like Berdyczewski, creates out of the Hasidic tale he is retelling. The house symbolizes the Jewish tradition, which in ancient times captured the Jewish people, symbolized by the birds, forcing them into the confines of the tradition and thereby repressing within them the ability to feel or act freely. The current generation of birds in the story symbolizes the maskilim who now wish to take revenge by attacking and destroying the tradition which has so severely limited them and their forebears.

Nachmanke runs ahead of the birds to warn the inhabitants of the house of the imminent attack. In the house he enters a room:

> and there were in that room three windows: before him, to his right, and to his left, but no light penetrated the windows, even though it was the middle of the day, for the window which faced east and the window which faced to the left were sealed, and on the window which faced to the right was spread a thick black curtain. And only a small red lamp was affixed to the ceiling in the middle and it projected a dark reddish light on the faces of people standing around a table under the lamp arguing. And in front of each of them were placed old parchment scrolls with seals of red wax (p. 94).

This room, which corresponds to the room in the original dream-tale into which Nachman fled to hide, calls to mind a small Eastern European traditional Jewish *beit midrash* (prayer and study room). The window to the right covered with a black curtain resembles the holy ark which contains the Torah scrolls; the small red lamp hanging from the ceiling resembles the eternal light; and the people standing around a table arguing before old parchment scrolls resemble traditional Jews reading from the Torah scrolls and engaging in discussions over details of Jewish law. Significantly, the atmosphere of the room is one of darkness, mourning, and gloom, and the room is cut off from the light of the outside world.

Nachmanke learns that the people in this room are fully aware of the threat to their existence by the birds who have set out to battle them. The people, he discovers, are arguing about how to respond to this threat. A number of suggestions are put forth: fight against the birds, seek a compromise with them, open up the house and let the birds enter, or abandon the house and become like the birds. All of these suggestions reflect options that Peretz is exploring in his myth of modern Jewish existence for a possible rapprochement between the opposing camps of the traditional Jews, symbolized by the people in the room, and the maskilim, symbolized by the birds. Finally, a most radical proposition is put forth: if they would burn the parchment scrolls, the people would be able to grow wings and join the birds in a flight to freedom. Several of the people do proceed to act on this proposition and set their scrolls on fire, whereupon an old man jumps up, and roaring like a lion, calls them traitors and then extinguishes the lamp. At that point, Nachmanke flees, as he puts it, "from [these] human beings who dwell in darkness" (p. 96).

The debate among the traditional Jews has reached an impasse. The polarization between those who want to aid the maskilim in destroying the tradition and those who consider any change in the tradition to be traitorous has prevented the Jewish people from finding a means to a rapprochement between these two extremes. Like a number of tales told by Nachman of Bratslav, Peretz's version of the dream-tale does not have an ending. When Nachmanke is asked by one of his disciples what the end of the tale is, Nachmanke sighs and states that "the end has not yet occurred: the birds . . . . which do not yet fly and do not walk but only hop have not yet reached the house" (p. 97). Since Peretz is living at a time when the battle between traditional Jews and maskilim has not been concluded, he does not really know what the end of his myth of modern Jewish existence will be: whether the maskilim will succeed in destroying all vestiges of traditional Judaism in an attempt to liberate the Jewish people from the shackles of the past, or whether some form of rapprochement between the tradition and the Haskalah will be found.

The meaning of Peretz's myth of modern Jewish existence may be fully understood by discerning the connections among the three parts of the story "Ha'ofot vehagevilim:" the narrator's comments on his role as a reteller of Hasidic tales, Nachmanke's introductory comments on depression, and the tale which Nachmanke tells. It is clear from the comments by the narrator and by Nachmanke that for Peretz, of the three major groups of Jews in his day, the mitnagdim, the maskilim, and the Hasidim, the first two share a common set of deficiencies which can only be corrected by turning to the truths of the third. The maskilim and the mitnagdim share a superficial approach to the world which leads to sadness, loneliness, and alienation: the maskilim, to whom the narrator refers, have embraced popular secular culture, and therefore can no longer appreciate the inner truth of Hasidism, while the mitnagdim, to whom Nachmanke refers, are too tied to the errors of tradition to perceive this inner truth.

While these introductory comments reflect a lack of sympathy on Peretz's part for maskilim and mitnagdim, in his version of Nachman's dream-tale he expresses a more understanding view of these groups. The maskilim are presented as birds whose ancestors have been cruelly confined, and the mitnagdim are presented as people who are hopelessly confused. By presenting these groups as suffering, Peretz modifies the disdain for them expressed by the narrator and Nachmanke and portrays the conflict between them as a misfortune of the people which calls for a constructive solution. That solution would appear to come from Peretz as a neo-Hasidic writer, who, like Nachmanke in the tale, seeks to serve as an intermediary between the maskilic Jews who want to fly to freedom and the Jews who want to remain in the "old house" of the tradition. It is his role to prevent the total rejection of the tradition by the misguided maskilim by presenting to his readers a new understanding of Hasidism. This new understanding will provide modern Jews with a sense of the hidden dimensions of human existence and a sense of community that will heal them both of their anger toward the tradition for limiting them and of the radical alienation from which they suffer as a result of their abandonment of traditional Jewish culture.

Each of the retold versions of Hasidic tales by Berdyczewski and Peretz that have been discussed reflects each writer's relationship to the crisis of Jewish culture at the turn of the century and how he arrived at a neo-Hasidic solution to that crisis. In "Shenei ʿolamot" Berdyczewski retells the tale of Eliezer, father of the Baal Shem Tov, who had to struggle to maintain his Jewish identity while living as a captive in gentile cultural surroundings. It is clear that Berdyczewski identifies with Eliezer's struggle, which in the retold version he transforms into a sense of being caught between two worlds: the limiting world of the Jewish tradition and the liberating world of gentile culture. In the final section of the story, Berdyczewski expresses his discovery that instead of having to choose between a torturous loyalty to the Jewish past or a liberating abandonment of Jewish culture for the culture of the gentiles, Jews could choose a third alternative: a spiritual rebirth effected by a new appreciation of what Hasidism has to offer the modern Jew.

The hero of the tale which Peretz retells, Nachman of Bratslav, is involved like Eliezer in a personal struggle in which he is ultimately successful. What apparently attracted Peretz to Nachman's dream-tale, however, was the portrayal of Nachman as a bystander to a battle with a relatively passive role in the successful conclusion of the story. For Peretz, whose less strictly traditional upbringing eliminated the need for him to experience the conflict between tradition and modernity as a personal struggle, Nachman was an apt symbol of the role he played as a concerned observer of the conflict in Jewish culture between traditionalists and modernists. Most likely he also identified with Nachman of Bratslav as a teller of complex symbolic tales which, like Peretz's own neoromantic stories, attempt to make people aware of the inner kernel of truth that lies beneath the surface of reality. It was in this role of writer that Peretz hoped to heal the rift between tradition and modernity among the Jews of his time.

Both of these retellers of Hasidic tales were most attracted to Hasidism's discovery of a sense of the inner unity which underlies existence. Such a discovery, they believed, enabled the Hasid to live life freely and joyously to the fullest extent without arbitrarily imposed traditional cultural restraints or the alienation of contemporary cultural life. The Hasidic tales they retold demonstrate how selective and reinterpretive Peretz and Berdyczewski were in their presentations of Hasidism to the modern reader. Neither Eliezer nor Nachman were struggling with how to overcome the alienation of modern existence. Furthermore, the heroism of each of these zaddikim consisted of their ability to control their sensual desires, not their ability to be free to enjoy them. Eliezer's refraining from sexual relations with the wife given to him in captivity brought him the reward of the birth of his son Israel Baal Shem Tov. The narrator also declares that Eliezer's lack of desire or pleasure in the sexual relations he had with his wife before the birth of the Baal Shem Tov was further reason for rewarding him. The nightmare struggles of Nachman of Bratslav's dream may be seen as symbolizing the depression which was the result of his attempts to struggle against his own sinful sensuality and that of his disciples in order to achieve the restoration of his and their souls. Nevertheless, since many Hasidic texts did teach that the profane pleasures of life may be used to serve God, Berdyczewski and Peretz could find justification in transforming the figure of the zaddik from the hero of the Hasidic myth of battle against cosmic evil to the hero of a myth of modern Jewish existence who would show the way to a life-affirming synthesis between the rebellious call to freedom of modernity and loyalty to the Jewish tradition.

Chapter 2

The Creative Restoration of Legends: Chaim Nachman Bialik

In a public talk to the teachers of Tel Aviv in 1933, a little more than a year before his death, Chaim Nachman Bialik reflected on the meaning of one of his most enigmatic works, the prose-poem "Megillat ha'esh: me'aggadot haḥurban" ("The Scroll of Fire: From the Legends of the Destruction").[1] In that work, published nearly three decades earlier in 1905, Bialik had retold legends of the destructions of the First and Second Temples and the dedication of the Second Temple in the days of Ezra and Nehemiah and had woven those retold legends into a narrative whole. One of the issues that Bialik raised in his talk was the nature and meaning of his retold versions of legends in "Megillat ha'esh:"

> Did I intend that "The Scroll" be an allegory, or merely a reworking of various legends like the melting and remolding of metal, like the transmigration of souls? In other words: did I also synthesize the material, did I also introduce contemporary meanings, or did these meanings sprout spontaneously out of the creative restoration *(tikkun yetsiri)* of the material?[2]

It is clear from Bialik's discussion of the work that he believed his reworked legends did more than just describe the experiences of the Jewish people's ancient past in a new form. He believed, rather,

45

that he had submitted the legends to a process of "creative restoration" which allowed them to convey the meaning of contemporary Jewish experience as well. Bailik's use of the term *tikkun* (restoration), with its kabbalistic and Hasidic associations of restoration of a sinful soul or restoration of the unity of an imperfect world, is significant. This term implies that he saw this process of creative restoration as a transformation of legends of the past with the purpose of restoring them so that they would be relevant and meaningful for the contemporary Jew.[3]

This process of creative restoration involved a synthesis of images from the poet's own personal experience and from the legends he retold. In his talk Bialik referred to two personal experiences, one as a child and one as an adult, which played a role in the genesis of "Megillat ha'esh." The childhood experience was the first fire he witnessed in his life. Bialik had been born in Radi, Volhynia, in 1873 and had moved with his family at the age of six to live just outside the nearby town of Zhitomir. The family moved so that his father could take a job as a saloon keeper after having failed in his attempts to earn a living in Radi in the trading of timber and the milling of flour. Bialik's father died about a year after the move, when Bialik was only seven. About half a year after his father's death, a house caught on fire in Bialik's neighborhood in the middle of the night:

> I was yet a boy of seven and a half, and suddenly at night — we lived outside of town and my mother was a widow with little children — we awoke startled and went out and found the house caught on fire. Tongues of fire flames broke out and made a powerful impression on me. All the neighbors, of course, removed the contents of the house. That was the first fire of my life, and no other fire . . . . has made a greater impression on me than this one. It was in the middle of the night, and it seemed to me that truly the world was being destroyed. There were a plain, a field, a synagogue, cries, but it was all also a kind of game for me. I remember that I took great joy in the scene, but that together with the joy there was also the fear of God. When I wrote ["Megillat ha'esh"] before me were revealed the trees which were dry and had been burned by a great power in a great fire storm, while of everything that had been destroyed only piles of embers remained.[4]

Bialik was eventually entrusted to the care of his paternal grandfather, a traditional Jew with little sympathy for the young Bialik's growing interest in Haskalah and European culture. In 1890, Bialik convinced his grandfather to allow him to study in the yeshiva of Volozhin, which Bialik chose because of its reputation as a relatively modern one. Having found the yeshiva to be too traditionally oriented for his own tastes, Bialik left it and moved to Odessa, where he began to write and publish poetry. He spent several years away from Odessa working first in his father-in-law's timber business and later as a teacher. In 1900, he returned to live in Odessa.[5]

It was in Odessa that Bialik underwent the second experience which played a role in the genesis of "Megillat ha'esh:" the rebellion on the ship Potemkin in the Odessa harbor in 1905:

> The days were those of a great storm in Odessa, the days of the Potemkin rebellion, and the air was greatly electrified. The winds were stormy, and the temperature was high, and perhaps this too was a cause of my unrest. It would appear that this was an incidental matter of no consequence, but I remember how from such an inner storm and an inner heat I approached the writing of ["Megillat ha'esh"]. I was fully stirred up by the firing of the cannons, by the rumors captivating everyone's attention each day. Of course, I participated with the public in this storm. It was impossible to sit tranquilly. Nevertheless, I found free time in the midst of this confusion to remain in my room and occupy myself in writing ["Megillat ha'esh"].[6]

Bialik's inner agitation at the time of the Potemkin rebellion reflected the conflicting feelings of hope and despair which he and other Hebrew writers had during the Russian Revolution of 1905. Among these writers, the events of the time were viewed in two ways. According to Jacob Fichmann, who experienced the events of the Potemkin rebellion together with Bialik, the rebellion raised great expectations of a successful revolution which would bring about a significant improvement in the condition of Russian Jewry:

> All the days that the rebels' ship was anchored in the waters of Odessa, the city was saturated with fear and curiosity. During the

day people would gather . . . and observe the gigantic dark form which crouched like a large beast in the water, no one knowing what it was plotting to do. Several times we would stand with Bialik in the city park in the evening and see the mysterious ship standing in the multitude of its lights and prophesying destruction to the trembling city, but something new as well: liberation and the beginning of a new life.

Masses of people left the city that summer, and those who remained went around like shadows. However, with this there was throughout a mood of exaltation. It was clear that the country was facing great and decisive events, and the rebellious ship which cast its shadow on the horizon of the blue sea attracted attention as the symbol of the destruction of the evil regime; and greater than our concern for the welfare of the city was our concern for that of the ship, whose red flag waved as a sign of the tidings of freedom for the enslaved peoples of Russia.[7]

At the same time, there was a growing sense of despair among these writers about the future of Jewish life in Europe. Pogroms against the Jews were continuing to erupt in Russia, and the Jews of Europe appeared to be hopelessly divided into a variety of political persuasions, each claiming to have discovered the path to physical security for the Jews. The disillusionment of many European Jews with the values of traditional Judaism had still not been replaced with viable alternative cultural values. Bialik and his fellow Hebrew writers were particularly troubled by what appeared to them as a growing lack of interest by European Jewish intellectuals in modern Hebrew literature as a vehicle for the expression of cultural values relevant to their needs.[8]

The two personal experiences cited by Bialik in his talk — the destruction by fire of the house in his childhood town and the shelling of Odessa by the Potemkin — were dominated in his memory by images of fire, water, dryness, and barrenness, all associated with upheaval and destruction. The house was destroyed by a fire which was perceived by the orphaned child as a fire storm bringing about the destruction of the world. This fire resulted in a scene of scorched trees and embers. During hot stormy summer days a ship at sea fired cannons in an attempt to overturn established authority. The emotions which were associated in Bialik's memory with these experiences ranged from exaltation to despair: the child's joy and fear of God and the adult's hope for liberation and sense of doom.

Among the legends which Bialik retells in "Megillat ha'esh," two legends featuring images of fire, water, dryness, and barrenness are of central importance: a legend about the holy sacrificial fire hidden at the time of the destruction of the First Temple and rediscovered at the time of the building of the Second Temple, and a legend about Judean males and females taken captive in ships by the Romans to serve as prostitutes after the destruction of the Second Temple. Out of Bialik's synthesis of the images of fire, water, dryness, and barrenness, taken from his personal experiences and from ancient legends, emerged "Megillat ha'esh" as a myth of modern Jewish existence. In this myth, Bialik sought to convey to his readers his understanding of the crises of his time.

Hidden Fire and Captives

The legends that play a major role in "Megillat ha'esh" each come from two major sources, and it is likely that Bialik drew on both of the sources for each of the legends.[9] The legend of the hidden fire is found in the apocryphal book of II Maccabees as well as in the early medieval historical narrative *Josippon.* The source in II Maccabees is a letter from the Jews of Judea to the Jews of Egypt following the victory over King Antiochous. In that letter the Jews of Judea seek to establish the legitimacy of the new holiday of Hanukkah as a celebration of their victory and to convince their brethren in Egypt to begin observing the new holiday. They base the legitimacy of the new holiday on the connection they see between the rededication of the Temple in their day and the building and dedication of the Second Temple in the days of Ezra and Nehemiah.

The Jews of Judea recount in the letter how according to legend at the time of the destruction of the First Temple and the Babylonian exile, the priests were ordered by the prophet Jeremiah to hide fire from the sacrificial altar in a dry well. When Nehemiah was allowed to lead the people back from captivity to Judea, he sent the priests who had hidden the fire to retrieve it. Instead of fire, the priests found a thick liquid in the well. They sprinkled the liquid on the wood of the altar, and when the sun came out, the altar burst into flame. The first sacrifice in the newly rededicated Temple was then performed with this fire that originated in the First Temple. By using the original fire of the First Temple the religious authenticity of the Second Temple cult was established as a continuation of the First Temple cult. (II Maccabees 1–2:18).

Although the version of the legend found in *Josippon* is based on the account in II Maccabees[10] and follows its plot structure, it differs from the version in Maccabees in a few details. In this later version, it was Jeremiah himself, together with other prophets of his day, who had hidden the fire of the sacrificial altar in a well. An elderly priest, who remembered where Jeremiah had hidden the fire, led the other elders to the well, where they discovered the thick liquid. When they informed Ezra of their discovery, Ezra instructed the priests to go down into the well and take the liquid back to the altar. As soon as the liquid was thrown onto the altar, the sacrificial fire began to burn. The fire became so great that the priests had to flee the Temple. After the fire spread throughout the Temple, purifying all of the holy objects in it, it receded and was limited to the altar.[11]

The legend of the Judeans taken captive by the Romans after the destruction of the Second Temple is also found in two sources: the Babylonian Talmud (Tractate *Gittin*) and the midrashic collection *ʾEikhah Rabbah*.[12] In the talmudic version it was four hundred boys and girls who were taken captive, and in the midrashic version it was an unspecified number of men and women of the nobility of Jerusalem. In both versions they were being taken by ship to be used as prostitutes in Rome. When they realized for what purpose they were being taken captive, they discussed among themselves what the proper religious response to their situation should be. On the basis of their interpretation of a verse from Psalms, they decided that their response should be to commit suicide by jumping into the sea and thereby choose martyrdom rather than allow themselves to be forced into prostitution. They felt assured by their interpretation of the verse that in so doing they would be rewarded with eternal life in paradise. In both versions it was the females who set the example for the males to reject a life of forced prostitution. In the talmudic version, after the interpretation of the verse was made, it was the girls who first jumped into the sea; in the midrashic version, even before the interpretation was made, it was the women who first declared their unwillingness to submit to a life of prostitution.

The legends of the hidden fire and the Judean captives both contain images of fire, water, dryness, and barrenness which are also present in Bialik's memory of his personal experiences of the childhood fire and the Potemkin rebellion. In the legend of the hidden fire the priests find the sacrificial fire when they descend into a dry well and remove a liquid which is transformed into fire. This fire appears (according to the version in *Josippon*) to be on the verge of destroying the Temple, just as fire had destroyed the Temple in the past, but in fact it serves to purify the Temple and re-establish the sacrificial cult. In the legend of the captives, the Judean males and females are traveling by ship to their place of exile and decide to jump into the sea. Their descent into the sea (which Bialik may have connected in his imagination to the descent of the priests into the well in the legend of the hidden fire) ends the captives' lives in this world, but it also provides a kind of ritual purification through immersion in a body of water which saves the captives from sexual defilement and gains them entrance into eternal life in paradise.

These images of fire, water, dryness, and barrenness function in a paradoxical manner in these legends. In a time of rebuilding (in the legend of the hidden fire), the well, which appears to be dry and barren, leads to a renewed vitality by yielding the liquid which turns to fire, and the fire, which appears to be destructive, leads to a renewed purification. In a time of destruction (in the legend of the captives), the waters of the sea which destroy the lives of the captives when they drown also cause them to rise in their spiritual status to that of martyrs. In both legends the paradoxical nature of the images conveys the ultimate triumph of hope and faith over a situation of potential defeat and despair. In his retold versions of these legends, Bialik made use of the paradoxical nature of these images to express the struggle in his own soul between despair and hope as he tried to determine whether twentieth-century Jewish existence was headed in the direction of destruction or renewal.

Bialik's retold version of the legend of the hidden fire begins with the act of saving the fire of the sacrificial altar after the destruction of the Temple. In that version the fire is saved by the young guardian angel of tears of sorrow, who flies down to the altar and saves fire from the last burning ember so that it is not lost to God's people forever. He brings the fire to a desert island and prays to God to keep it burning. God responds to the angel's prayer by placing the morning star to guard the fire until it is clear what will ultimately happen to it.

The transformation of the savior of the fire from the priests and prophets of the original versions of the legend into this angel of sorrow reveals a need on Bialik's part for a hero not modeled on either of these two main types of religious leaders of ancient Israel. It would appear that this angel of sorrow represents the poet himself, who is filled with sorrow as he lives through the period of his people's potential physical and cultural destruction, yet still seeks a way to preserve the vital power of the people before it is completely destroyed. Unlike the prophets and priests of the original versions of the legend, who hide the fire as an act of faith that the Temple will ultimately be rebuilt and the fire will again burn on the altar, the angel is not sure of the fate of the fire. Even God Himself appears to be unsure as He appoints the morning star to watch over the fire until its fate becomes clearer.

The poet, represented by the angel, and the vital powers of the people, represented by the fire, experience the similar fates of being overwhelmed by sorrow and barrenness. The fire is preserved not in the potentially reviving liquid of the dry well of the original versions, but in an utterly barren desert. Moreover, when the angel comes into contact with the fire, he is not, as one might expect, rejuvenated by his contact with the fire. Unlike the prophet Isaiah, who was purified of sin by having his lips touched by a coal from the fire of the Temple

(Isaiah 6:6-7), and unlike the Temple in the hidden fire legend, which was purified by fire, the angel in Bialik's version is wounded by the fire and brought even deeper into sorrow.

In the original versions of the legend, the restoration of the fire to its proper role in the life of the people depends on the return of the people to Judea, where the priests will rediscover the fire and re-establish the sacrificial cult. In Bialik's version the restoration of the fire depends on the ability of the poet to transcend the despair which has overwhelmed the vital forces of the people and restore the power of those forces. Bialik turns at this point to the retelling of the legend of the captives, in which he puts forth a fuller explication of the nature of the despair which has overwhelmed him as well as the vital forces of the people. He then resumes the retelling of the hidden fire legend, in which he suggests the process by which he might transcend that despair and emerge as the hero who would lead the people in attempting to restore the power of those forces.

Although Bialik's retold version of the legend of the captives follows the basic plot structure of the original versions of the legend, his version differs significantly in a number of areas: the nature of the suffering which the enemy inflicts on the captives, the sources of truth to which the captives turn in order to find a solution to their plight, the motivation of the captives for committing suicide by drowning, and their fate following their drowning. While in the original versions, the male and female captives are brought by ship to Rome to be forced into prostitution, in Bialik's version "two hundred [male] youths and two hundred maidens" are brought by ship by a nameless enemy to a desert island to be killed in a most cruel manner:

> [The enemy] determined to put an end to them in the desert by way of a lingering death from hunger and thirst. He stripped them naked and left them on the desert island, the [male] youths on one side of the island and the maidens on the other, and abandoned them there.
>
> The vile enemy said: "If they cross over their calamity will be doubled! They will get lost on the desert island, and will be unable

to see or find each other, till their spirits flag and their hearts
wither and the light of their eyes is extinguished; and with only a
step between them, and their hands stretched out to each other —
their faces will suddenly twist, their knees buckle and they will fall
to the ground, dying an atrocious death on an iron earth beneath
a copper sky, without one iota of comfort or love" (p. 140)![13]

Instead of being forced into a life of sexual promiscuity, as the
captives in the original versions of the legend were supposed to be,
the captives in the retold version are forced into an ascetic life of star-
vation, physical separation between the sexes, and spiritual emptiness. Bialik has turned the nature of the persecution on its head: the
captives' plight is not a forced defilement of their physical drives in
a way which violates their religious values, but rather a denial of all
fulfillment of their physical drives.

The captives are linked to the holy fire of the hidden fire legend
in that they are exiled to the same desert island where the angel has
sought to preserve the fire. The captives do not, however, discover
the holy fire which would restore their vital forces to them. Instead,
they gradually descend into a physical and spiritual death.

While the captives in the traditional versions of the legend
discover the solution to their dilemma by interpreting a scriptural
verse, the male youths in the retold version turn instead to another
source: a wondrous person (*'ehad peli'*), who reflects their inner feelings and has the power to guide them. Actually, when one of the
male youths looks carefully at the wondrous person, he sees not one
but two figures: a fair youth (*'elem rakh*) and a man of terror (*'ish
'eimot*). It is unclear at first to the male youths which of these figures
is the wondrous person who might lead them out of the suffering of
their exile.

The choice of which aspect of this two-sided wondrous person
to follow becomes clear when the male youths arrive at a great river,
where the man of terror sings to them "the song of hate and annihilation" (*shirat hamastemah vehakillayon*). This song expresses the anger
and despair of one who can no longer find meaning in life and therefore feels both an urge to destroy the world and a longing for death:[14]

Asleep, deep and black the depths of Abaddon
weaving the enigma of death . . .
In its depths the world's affliction sinks like a stone
and the world's cry for help . . .
And where is salvation?
She plays the harlot to heaven and its God,
adorns herself with drums and dances on hilltops to the stars.

.   .   .

From the depths of Abaddon raise me the song of
destruction black as your heart's burnt out brand;
carry it through the nations, disperse it among the
        rejected of God,
pour its coal upon their head.
With it you will sow ruin and devastation upon your fields
and upon every man.
If your shadow falls upon the lily in your garden, it will
        blacken and die;
if your glance falls upon the marble of your sculptured
        contrivance, it will break like clay;
and laughter you will have, laughter as bitter as gall, cruel and
        killing.

.   .   .

This is the song of fury—
the flames of the stake created it
on the night of ire
from the blood of babes and the old
from desecrated corpses and the jewels of temple virgins
slain in the field . . . (pp. 144–48).[15]

The man of terror calls the river on whose bank the male youths
stand Abaddon (from the Hebrew root ʾ-b-d, connoting loss and
destruction). The river symbolizes his absolute despair which comes
from the realization that all the solutions that have been proposed to
alleviate human suffering have failed. Out of this realization he concludes that the only adequate response to suffering is for the victim
to smash the idols of false solutions, angrily destroy the world of the

powerful oppressors, and then descend into the attractive realm of self-destruction and death in the waters of the river Abaddon.

The fair youth, who is the opposite aspect of the wondrous person, asks the male youths if they are familiar with his alternative vision, "the song of comfort and redemption" *(shirat hanehamah veha'aharit)*. The male youths, however, are not interested in his song, for they have already given themselves fully to the despair of Abaddon.

Moved by the song of the man of terror, the male youths experience not only a wish to die, but also a strong desire to hate and destroy in order to overcome their suffering. They express a roaring rage in which they convey their attempt to recover the vitality they had lost as a result of the destruction of the Temple and their exile to the desert island. In so doing, however, they discover not the original holy fire whose restoration is a prerequisite for true revival, but rather a black fire of destruction and death.

When the captives in the original versions of the legend jump into the sea, they do so with the firm faith, substantiated by scripture, that they are fulfilling God's will and that they will be rewarded with eternal life in paradise. In the retold version, however, the death of the captives by descent into water is not portrayed as a meaningful act of martyrdom. After the conclusion of the man of terror's song of hate and annihilation, the male youths suddenly catch a glimpse of the maidens, from whom they had been separated, walking along a mountain top. The maidens, portrayed as pure angelic figures and as suffering victims wearing Christ-like crowns of thorn, blindly descend to their death in the river Abaddon. In contrast to the original versions of the legend, in which the males see the females' willingness to commit suicide as a positive example, the male youths in the retold version cry out to the maidens to prevent them from unwittingly falling into the water. As the maidens begin to fall into the river, the male youths jump in and attempt to save them. The water, however, sweeps the male youths down to their death at the bottom of the river. There, ironically, they meet the maidens for the first time since having been so cruelly separated from them by the enemy.

In the original versions of the legend, the captives achieve a spiritual victory as the destructive waters of the sea are transformed into a means for their purification. The captives thereby rise to the status of martyrs and deprive their captors of the opportunity to impose suffering on them. In the retold version, the enemy is handed a great victory as the waters of the sea become the means for the self-destruction of the male youths and maidens. It turns out that neither the maidens' passive acceptance of suffering nor the male youths' despair and angry rage is a true path to redemption after the destruction. The captives therefore find neither the renewal of vitality nor the purification achieved by the priests who re-established the sacrificial cult at the beginning of the Second Temple period and by the captive martyrs following the destruction of the Second Temple. Instead, the black fire of their anger destroys them, and they drown in the waters of their passivity and despair.

Since by retelling the legends of the hidden fire and the captives in "Megillat ha'esh" Bialik is attempting to convey his understanding of the crises of modern Jewish existence and the nature of his despair over those crises, it is important to understand the contemporary meaning of each aspect of these retold versions. One approach, advanced by Bialik himself in his talk on "Megillat ha'esh" and later developed by Lahower and Fichmann, would be to interpret the work as a statement on issues of Jewish national existence. According to this approach, the division between the sexes and the opposing figures of the fair youth and the man of terror represent conflicting responses on the part of European Jews to the crises of the early twentieth century. The maidens symbolize traditional Jews who accept their suffering in a silence based on blind faith in supernatural messianic redemption. The male youths stand for the more secularized Jews who are seeking alternative responses to the current suffering of the Jews. The maidens' fall into the river Abaddon symbolizes the self-destructive willingness of traditional Jews to submit to martyrdom, while the jumping of the male youths into the river represents the desperate, futile attempts of secularized Jews to save themselves and traditional Jews from destruction by nontraditional means: assimilation, political reform, socialist revolution, or Zionism.

According to this national approach, the division of the wondrous person into two figures, a fair youth and a man of terror, symbolizes two attitudes of secular Jews in Bialik's day toward the gentiles who are causing the Jews to suffer. The man of terror embodies an attitude of hatred toward the gentiles and a desire to seek revenge against them for Jewish suffering, either by engaging in the revolutionary upheaval of gentile society or by assimilating into gentile society and gradually undermining it from within. The fair youth embodies an attitude of love and a desire to work more constructively toward the redemption of the Jews by peaceful means. The deaths of the maidens and the male youths who follow the path of the man of terror convey Bialik's conviction that neither the traditional Jews' passive ideal of martyrdom nor the secular Jews' more activist ideals hold out much hope for the future of Jewish existence.

The cause of Bialik's despair, however, is not only that the Jews of his time have arrived at a dead end in their responses to the contemporary crises, but also that the legends of the past can no longer serve as sources of meaning for the modern Jew. Just as the priest and the prophet of the hidden fire legend could no longer serve as models of heroic leadership that could restore the people to its original vitality, so the martyrs of the legend of the captives can no longer serve as models of heroic response to the crises of physical and cultural destruction. Modern Jews have lost their faith in revealed scripture, and therefore they must turn to a variety of less reliable human interpretations of events, as represented by the two aspects of the wondrous person, which divide them and do not lead them to a positive and creative response to their situation.[16] Finally, since modern Jews no longer find meaning in acts of martyrdom, if they choose to commit suicide, either in a physical or cultural sense, that act can only be seen as one of meaningless self-destruction.

Bialik's Personal Despair and the Search for the Hidden Fire

Bialik retold the legends of the hidden fire and the captives not only as a reaction to the national crises, or to the failure of legends of the past to convey meaning in the present, but also as a reaction to a personal psychological crisis as well. Strauss and Kurzweil, among others, have demonstrated that the key to understanding this crisis is in images of separation between males and females and between the holy and the erotic in "Megillat ha'esh." It is significant that Bialik transformed the suffering of the Judean captives in the traditional legend from forced prostitution to forced separation between the sexes. By means of this transformation Bialik expresses his belief that the enemy of the Jews in modern times is not only the gentile who physically attacks the Jews but also the Jewish tradition that has mandated a separation between the sexes in religious life. This traditional separation of the sexes, he believes, is based on a misguided ideal of sacrificing the erotic for the sake of the holy and has destroyed the individual Jew's soul.[17]

Bialik's personal struggle with the conflicts aroused by having been raised with this ideal, which he considered to be so misguided, becomes clear in the passage following the deaths of the male youths and maidens. In this passage, the fair youth, who is the only survivor of the captives' mass suicide, makes an autobiographical confession. In his talk on "Megillat ha'esh" Bialik refused to interpret this passage for his audience because he considered it to be too private to share with a large group of people.[18] While this refusal to interpret the passage points to the essentially personal meaning of the fair youth's confession, Bialik was also careful to point out in his talk that he shared this experience with many of his generation who had the same religious upbringing as he had.

The confession of the fair youth draws on images from the legends retold by Bialik in "Megillat ha'esh" as well as experiences of Bialik's life. In this confession, made to "a lonely sad-eyed girl" (p.150), the youth relates his struggle to resolve the tension in his life between the physical and the spiritual. As a child, the youth had been both at one with the God of the earth, whom he loved, and in fear of the God of the heavens. He learned how to resolve this tension between himself and the God of the heavens from the sad-eyed girl, who had appeared to him bringing a "hidden light" (p. 152), which allowed him to love not only the physical aspects of life represented by the God of the earth, but also the spiritual dimensions of life represented by the God of the heavens. This vital and unconflicted approach to life would appear to correspond to the life of the people in the retold versions of the legends of the hidden fire and the captives before the destruction of the Temple reduced them to despair and spiritual emptiness.

This ability to unify the physical with the spiritual was undermined following the death of the youth's father and the youth's abandonment by his mother, when an old Nazirite offered him a home to replace the one he had lost.[19] This event in the youth's life corresponds both to the exile of the captives after the destruction of the Temple and Bialik's removal to his grandfather's house after his father died. Like the enemy in Bialik's retold version of the captives legend, the old Nazirite forced the youth into a life of ascetic repression of his physical drives. In the spirit of traditional Jewish teachings as understood by Bialik, the Nazirite sought to suppress the erotic aspects of the youth's life so that the youth might draw closer to the holiness of God.

The youth's response to this repression of his physical drives was similar to that of the male youths in the retold version of the captives legend: just as the persecution of the enemy drove the youths to despair and to a raging, self-destructive expression of power, so the youth would find himself consumed by the fire of sexual passion while at the same time fearful of and angry at the old Nazirite who sought to restrict his erotic enjoyment.

Until the time of his confession, the youth has been unable to discover a way to resolve the tension between the physical and the spiritual in the way that the girl had shown him. The youth therefore searches for the holy fire which has been hidden since the destruction of the Temple. He hopes thereby to heal the conflicts of his own soul as well as to play the role parallel to the priests in the hidden fire legend who restore the people to their original religious vitality. When the morning star leads him to the place where it has been watching over the hidden fire, the youth rises up to seize it and appears to be on the verge of finding in it the redemption he had sought for himself and for his people. Suddenly, however, the image of the girl appears to him from the river Abaddon, and just as the captive male youths had jumped into the river after the captive maidens, so the youth, erotically attracted to the girl, jumps into the river while holding onto the holy fire.

By jumping into the river Abaddon, the youth destroys himself as well as the holy fire, which is extinguished forever. The youth's descent into the river re-enacts the conclusion of Bialik's retold version of the captives legend and also provides a conclusion to his retold version of the hidden fire legend. This concluding act, however, is radically different from the conclusions of the captives legend and the hidden fire legend in their original versions. Instead of the ascent of the captives' souls to eternal life, the youth appears to have met only physical death in the river. Instead of the rekindling by the priests of the holy fire of the sacrificial cult from the liquid of the well, the fire is extinguished in the waters of the river Abaddon. The youth's destructive act is more final than the destruction of the Temple in the original legends, for now the possibility of eternal reward for martyrdom and the possibility of continuing the sacrificial cult with the original holy fire have been permanently eliminated.

At the end of "Megillat ha'esh" the fair youth actually survives his descent into the river. However, unlike the miraculous spiritual survival of the captives or the miraculous physical survival of the hidden fire, the youth's survival hardly constitutes a victorious restoration of vitality. He is cast up onto dry land to wander among his people in exile "like an ancient legend and like a prophecy of the future" (p. 170). In this new identity he represents the role which Bialik assumes as a collector and restorer of legends and as a prophet-like poet offering both rebuke and comfort to the people.

As constructive a role as he may play as a restorer of legends and as a poet, Bialik is never able fully to transcend his despair over the national and personal destruction he has experienced. This is clear from the portrayal of the youth at the end of "Megillat ha'esh," who, realizing that he is powerless to rebuild that which has been destroyed, descends into a lonely despair which he believes is shared by the world as a whole.

The angel of sorrow, who like the fair youth represents the poet, had tried following the destruction of the Temple to preserve the vital holy fire. That attempt has failed. The angel therefore concludes "Megillat ha'esh" by tipping tears of sorrow into the dawn. For Bialik, the dawning of a new era does not bring the light of redemption, but rather the tears of silent despair. Bialik's role as restorer of legends and poet has some merit as a last desperate attempt to revive the people. At this time of national and personal crisis, however, his overwhelming despair forces him to call into question the hopes aroused in his day for a true and lasting revival of the Jewish people.

Chapter 3

Biblical Tales of the Wilderness:
David Frischmann

I n a series of essays published in the years 1920 to 1921, in which
he made his last major assessment of modern Hebrew literature,
David Frischmann complained bitterly of the slavish and inauthentic
imitations of European romantic poetry, which he believed plagued
Hebrew letters in his day:

> Our writers have lost almost completely any sign of ability to
> express anything of *their own* which took place within their heart
> and which *their own lives* brought about, but rather they live in an
> alien world, and so they express daily only that which comes to
> them from the outside . . . . They write evening, morning, and
> noontime about women and about beauty and about love and
> about longings — but I suspect somewhat that they do not "long"
> at all, but rather they are actually proper, good, and nice boys,
> whose faces for the most part still blush from embarrassment when
> they have to sit alone in the presence of a young woman with
> whom they are not familiar.[1]

Frischmann went on to declare that while certain European peoples
provided the proper cultural setting for the emergence of great erotic
poetry, it was inconceivable that the traditional Jewish culture in
which the Hebrew writers of his day had been raised could produce
such poetry:

> Is there any possibility that we would find it, or even any example
> of it, among sick and impoverished people whose boys sat and rot-

ted for hundreds and thousands of years in their schoolrooms and houses of study until the skin on their flesh itself began to resemble the dry parchment upon which they wasted their days and nights, and not only that, but now we must decide in addition that a miracle has happened to them and all that great and new abundance of life came suddenly to these dry bones unintentionally and overnight? — I do not believe it; I do not believe it; I do not believe it.[2]

Frischmann's dissatisfaction with the Hebrew literature of his day stemmed not only from the inability of modern Hebrew writers to incorporate authentically in their writings the experiences of European writers with a less repressed upbringing, but also from their inability to convey the Jewish experience itself in an aesthetically sophisticated manner:

We still do not have the poet whose wings have spread to the extent that he would have the power to rise to the writing of our folk epic. We do not yet have even the poet who could write our novel. We are still in diapers.[3]

Frischmann challenged the Hebrew writers of his day to create works of literature that were the aesthetic equal of the best of contemporary European literature, that incorporated a wide range of human experience, but that also conveyed an authentic portrait of the experiences of the Jewish people.[4] Frischmann's dream that modern Hebrew writers would produce literary works embodying a creative synthesis of the European and Jewish cultures was the product of his life-long involvement in both of these cultures. Frischmann was born in Zgierz, Poland, to a family of well-to-do merchants and grew up in Lodz, Poland. While his parents were traditional in their practice of Judaism, they encouraged their son's study of modern European culture as well as of traditional Jewish culture. He spent most of his adult life in several centers of Hebrew and Yiddish literature and of European learning: Warsaw, St. Petersburg, Moscow, Berlin, and Breslau. In the course of his life he demonstrated his commitment to three major areas. He immersed himself in European culture by receiving a university education and by associating with gentile and Jewish figures of German literature. He contributed to the development of a sophisticated modern Hebrew literature by writing essays, stories, and poems and by editing Hebrew literary journals. He also strove for the expansion of Jewish cultural horizons by publishing great works of European literature in his own Hebrew translations of those works.

At the very time that Frischmann was issuing his call for literary expressions that were a synthesis of the European and Jewish cultures, he had recently undergone experiences which led him to historical conclusions that belied his hopes for such a cultural synthesis. At the outbreak of World War I, Frischmann was visiting Berlin and was arrested as an alien. After his release from prison, he returned to his home in Warsaw. Fearing a German invasion of Poland, he fled to Odessa. Following the February 1917 revolution in Russia, he was invited to be the chairman of the editorial board of the important Hebrew publishing house of Stybel in Moscow. He was forced, however, together with the publishing house, to leave Moscow and relocate to Warsaw in 1919 as a result of the opposition to Hebrew which arose in the aftermath of the Bolshevik Revolution of October 1917.[5]

The events of World War I and the Bolshevik Revolution, which Frischmann had witnessed first hand, called into question his faith in the viability of European culture as well as his faith in the potential integration of the Jew into that culture.[6] In passages interspersed throughout his series of literary essays, he recalled the breakdown of German and Russian culture in the cataclysmic events since 1914 and the persistence of anti-Semitism which accompanied those events. In one passage he wrote of the mass hysteria of the German people at the beginning of World War I:

> It was in the early days of the war — and even now all the sinews of my heart tremble as I remember these beginnings. It was the end of July and the beginning of August in the year 1914, and by chance I was living in Berlin, and whoever did not see with his own eyes what was going on in this thriving and contented city and how suddenly a whole nation became crazed and suddenly cast off culture from itself like a person casting off a narrow collar, and

how every throat shouted in the streets and how every eye was
filled with blood and hatred and murder and how even delicate
virgins were transformed overnight into she-wolves in the forest
yearning for the dead bodies of the enemy to be impaled and mortally wounded and piled high — such a person has never seen such
an awesome power at the moment it breaks out of its restraints. No
one could possibly forget those days. In the middle of the streets
masses stood day and night and moment by moment new masses
were added, and they raged and shouted loudly and ceaselessly:
"War, war! We want war! The war was forced upon us, and now
we will show them! We will smash at one and only one blow into
tiny pieces those weak-kneed lovers of concubines, the French! We
will attack Russia and in three weeks wipe those liquor drinking
barbarians from the face of the earth until there is no remnant of
them! We will blow at the nation of shopkeepers, England, and it
will be no more! No one will stand up to us! We are we!" . . . And
what they did then to every foreigner or whoever was thought to
be a foreigner no one could imagine: such an unfortunate person,
if they recognized him, could no longer be sure of his life.[7]

Frischmann believed that the war cries of the masses were
orchestrated by their political leaders in order to create a national
mood disposed to war. What was perhaps even more disheartening
to Frischmann than the war fever of the masses, however, was what
he described as the absence in Germany of any significant opposition
to the war. Even the social democrats, who would have been expected
to champion peace in order to maintain the world-wide solidarity of
the laboring masses, and even the intellectuals, who would have been
expected to oppose the horrors of war to preserve the values of a cul-
tured civilization, joined in the chauvinistic war cries.

In another passage, Frischmann reacted with equal disgust to
the excesses that were the result of the Bolshevik Revolution, which
eventually forced him and his employer to move from Moscow to
Warsaw:

It was not the revolutionaries who took matters into their hands,
but some mixed multitude ('erev rav), . . . who overnight were suddenly transformed into revolutionaries, remnants of the gen-

darmerie that remained after [the overthrow of Czar] Nicholas . . .
robbers and murderers who were released from prison . . . and
owners of brothels, thieves who formerly had done their deeds in
secret at night and now did them openly by day, all of these captured the "revolution" and they stuck the "Marseillaise" into their
throats, since they smelled here a piece of fat, and it was they who
defeated the movement. Not only that, but we saw another interesting and natural accompaning phenomenon: those same
unruly refugees (*pelitei ha'asafsuf*), with the loftiness of the revolution in their throats and seventy-seven abominations in their
hearts, as soon as they broke into the sanctuary of the revolution,
they arrived immediately at a very terrible and dangerous invention: when they saw any true revolutionary, they would attack him
en masse, loudly declaring him to be a "counterrevolutionary," and
they would push him aside from the mainstream so that he would
not disturb them.[8]

As in Germany in 1914, so in Russia in 1917, Frischmann saw the
highest values of a culture destroyed as the violent upheavals of
World War I and the Bolshevik Revolution unleashed the worst
impulses of the masses. Frischmann's personal experiences as a
persecuted alien in Germany in World War I and as a counterrevolutionary advocate of Hebrew culture in Bolshevik Russia undoubtedly added to his pain as he witnessed the failure of nationalism in
Germany and the failure of socialism in Russia.

Frischmann was also greatly pained by the persistence of anti-
Semitic impulses among the masses of Europe. He recounted in one
passage his experience of attending a Russian production of Shakespeare's play *The Merchant of Venice*, in which the actor who played
Shylock the Jew portrayed the character

in a manner which aroused particular horror so that as I sat my
teeth chattered throughout the play, and I was afraid at every moment that this realism would capture the hearts of the sensitive
Russian audience sitting with me, which when it identified my
[Jewish] nose would attack me a bit and make for me a small
pogrom or would at least break a few of my bones.[9]

In the Wilderness

During the years 1918 to 1922, at about the same time that Frischmann was publishing his final assessment of the state of modern Hebrew literature and the historical realities of Europe, he published a series of seven stories based on biblical accounts of the life of the Israelites in the wilderness after their exodus from Egypt. He conceived these stories as part of a series titled *Bamidbar: ma'asiyyot bibliyyot* (*In the Wilderness: Biblical Tales*), of which he had previously published two stories.[10] When first published, each story in the *Bamidbar* series began with the same introduction. In the collected edition, that introduction became the introduction for the entire series:

> My mother received these words from her mother, and her mother from her mother, her grandmother from her grandmother, and her grandmother from her grandmother, generation from generation — and my mother transmitted the words to me.[11]

The stories in the *Bamidbar* series are thus presented by the narrator as part of an oral tradition that has been maintained and transmitted by women since biblical times as an alternative to the male oral tradition recounted in the written Torah of Moses and the oral Torah of the rabbis.[12]

The introduction raises an interesting question regarding the identity of the narrator of each of these stories. Since the stories purportedly belong to a strictly feminine tradition, the narrator may be a woman who has received the tradition passed on by women since biblical times. Another possibility is that for the first time in history, the division between the male-dominated tradition and the female-dominated tradition has been removed and that finally in the modern period a man, the narrator, has been told this tradition by his mother. Either way, it is significant that the narrator has concluded that the time has come to publish for both men and women the content of this feminine tradition.

By referring to these stories in the subtitle of the series as *ma'asiyyot bibliyyot* (biblical tales), Frischmann is making an important statement about their nature. The term *ma'asiyyot* (or *mayses* in the Yiddish pronunciation of the word) referred in Frischmann's time to folktales. His use of the term *ma'asiyyot* suggests a link between the folk wisdom of the tales which were circulating among the Jewish masses of his time and that of the alternative feminine tradition of his biblical tales. It is as if he were saying that from biblical times to the present there has always existed a folk tradition based on a point of view which was different from that of the established cultural norm. Frischmann's use of the Greek term *biblia* as the basis for his adjective *bibliyyot*, rather than a Hebrew term for the Bible such as *mikra'* or *tanakh*, suggests that the author's approach to the biblical text draws not only on traditional Jewish interpretations, but also on the modern scholarship of gentile scholars, who had begun to study the Bible in a scientific and critical manner. While there is an affinity between the retelling of biblical stories in traditional midrash and what Frischmann is doing in the *Bamidbar* series, by choosing the term *ma'asiyyot bibliyyot* he is also clearly emphasizing the affinity of these stories with folktales and with modern biblical scholarship. The term *ma'asiyyot bibliyyot*, with its Hebrew and Greek components, embodies as well the very ideal of the synthesis of the Jewish and European cultures which Frischmann pursued.

For the most part, the stories in the *Bamidbar* series are not actually based on the plot of a biblical story. Since Frischmann was interested in creating an antiestablishment set of traditions about the period of the wilderness, he avoided retelling the major events of the Israelites' wanderings. When he did base a story on one of these events, he created a new story which purportedly took place at the time of one of the major events but with main characters and plots that were largely the product of his imagination. These new stories were generally about characters unfamiliar to the readers of the Bible, as if Frischmann had discovered neglected aspects of biblical life that reflected the concerns and values of the common Israelite not dealt with in the stories told by the cultural establishment.

He based some stories on hypothetical situations given in passages of biblical causistic law that state if a certain situation arises the Israelites are to execute a particular legal procedure. He turned to such hypothetical situations of causistic law to uncover the experiences of the common Israelite that the cultural establishment did not deem worthy to be the subject of a story, but only as an example to illustrate a point of law.[13]

One story, based on the account of the man who gathered wood on the Sabbath (Numbers 15:32–36), comes closest of all the stories of the *Bamidbar* series to being a retold version of a biblical story, in that the plot and main character of the original version of the story are the basis for Frischmann's version. In this one biblical text Frischmann discovered a story which narrates an event but also resembles a passage of causistic law about the life of the common people, since the actual event of gathering the wood led to the promulgation of a law by God that the punishment of such a violation of the Sabbath is death.

The period of the Israelites' wanderings in the wilderness is presented in the *Bamidbar* series as a time when life was lived in a fuller and more intense way than it is in the time of the contemporary narrator. The narrator of one story, for example, declares:

> In those distant days the sun burned seven times more powerfully than now, and the wilderness was seventy-seven times more awesome and bigger than now, and love was thousands of times stronger and stormier than now (p. 118).[14]

In another story, the narrator connects the strength and intensity of the wilderness with a greater drive for freedom than is found in his day:

> In those days the wilderness was yet seventy times stronger and more awesome than now, the mountains were seventy-seven times harder and more solid than now, and man was stronger and harder and loved rebellion and opposed and smashed and hated every yoke seven hundred seven times more than now (p. 74).

Such comments by the narrators of the stories place the human issues of the stories in a kind of mythic dimension in which super heroes of ancient times interact with a world more intense and better than the one known today. It is as if the narrator is saying that he is bringing the reader back to some sort of beginning of time before the world and humanity had deteriorated to its current fallen state. The narrator also recounts why and how the fall occurred, so that the reader can understand his experiences as a modern person struggling with the results of that fall. The struggles of the ancient past are seen, thus, as both the origin of, and a powerful representation of, the struggles of the present.[15]

Frischmann was attracted to the wilderness as a point of mythic origins since it was located outside of the Land of Israel and resembled the diaspora experience of the Jews of Europe. In order to emphasize that resemblance, Frischmann changed the details in the Bible that portrayed the wilderness as a temporary dwelling place of the Israelites to be followed by their eventual settlement in Canaan. In Frischmann's stories, instead, the people seem to be spread out and settled into fairly permanent communities and towns outside of the land. Frischmann's portrayal of the wilderness period as a relatively stable one which corresponded to the later European diaspora experience was in keeping with his reluctance to fully endorse the Zionist belief that the future of the Jews was to be in the Land of Israel and his stated preference to see the Jews as a model of a non-nationalist people, whose revival would ideally take place in the diaspora.[16]

As in his later essays, Frischmann expresses in the stories of the *Bamidbar* series his dream of a diaspora Jewry pursuing the ideal of a creative synthesis of the European and Jewish cultures. Like the essays, however, these stories also reflect Frischmann's concerns about the dangers inherent in the Jews' rebellion against their culture and their attempt to embrace European culture. Such actions would mean not only the sacrifice of their own identity and expose them to a culture hopelessly mired in anti-Semitic attitudes, but also involve them in a culture which, since the outbreak of World War I, had undergone a process of degeneration. In some stories, in fact, it appears that Frischmann sees in these two cultures certain shared deficiencies that constitute hindrances to the achievement of a creative synthesis of the two cultures. He finds, in particular, that both cultures suffer from a lack of proper balance between the rule of law and the needs of the individual and a problematic relationship with the erotic dimension of life.

The Dream of Cultural Synthesis

The first story in the *Bamidbar* series, "Meḥolot" ("Dances"), published several years before the main body of stories, expresses Frischmann's longing for the creation of a synthesis of the Jewish and European cultures. The story takes place before and during the time of the Israelites' worship of the golden calf during Moses' forty-day absence from their midst on Mount Sinai (Exodus 32). An Israelite woman named Timna falls in love with a man named Put who belongs to the mixed multitude of non-Israelites who left Egypt together with the Israelites at the time of the exodus. Timna and Put have a passionate love affair, during which Put gives Timna a ring to express his great love for her. One day, for no apparent reason, Put disappears from the Israelite camp. Despite the fact that many Israelites assume he has done so because he is tired of Timna and has decided to return to Egypt, Timna maintains her faith in Put. For her, the ring he has given her is concrete proof that he is devoted to her and will eventually return.

When the Israelites decide to fashion and worship a golden calf because they have lost faith in a God who can only be heard and not seen and in a leader who has absented himself from the community, Timna reacts in an ambivalent way. At first, when gold is collected to make the calf, she refuses to give up the ring which is the token of the love between herself and Put. Suddenly, however, without realizing what she is doing, Timna is caught up in the frenzy of the people and throws the ring into the collection.

During the celebration around the golden calf, Timna interrupts the dancing of the women to begin her own dance. In her dance she expresses the inner conflict she has experienced since Put left her: whether to remain loyal only to herself, to maintain her loyalty to and trust in Put, or to transfer her loyalty from Put to the god of the golden calf by sacrificing to it the ring Put had given her.

At the climax of her dance, Timna transcends this conflict by discovering her own personal revelation of unity in one God:

> And her soul and her chosen one [Put] and her ring and her life and God were assimilated together suddenly and were mixed together and merged and became one thing, and she could no longer distinguish among them: her soul ceased to be within her and entered her chosen one; her chosen one ceased to be and entered the ring: the ring ceased to be and became life for her; life ceased to be and became God (p. 24).

In this story of Timna at the time of worship of the golden calf, Frischmann suggests a correspondence between her situation and that of European Jewry in his day. Timna is faced with two alternatives: to remain loyal to the non-Israelite Put or to join in the communal religious celebration around the calf. Similarly, the Jew of Frischmann's day is faced with a choice between his attraction to European culture and the demand of the traditional religious community to follow its ways.

Just as neither alternative faced by Timna is without its problems, so is neither alternative faced by the modern Jew without its problems. The Israelite religious community tends to allow itself to be so caught up in religious frenzy that it ignores the needs of people. For example, Timna's suffering is ignored because the people are so stirred by the events of the revelation at Sinai. Later, at the time of the gathering of the gold to fashion the golden calf, a woman takes a gold flute with which her sick child is playing and contributes it to the collection. This abandonment of human needs for the sake of ritual acts is for Frischmann a serious defect in the ways of the traditional Jews of his day.

Another problematic aspect of the Israelite religious alternative is the apparent abandonment of them by their God, which undermines their faith and leads them to worship a false god. Similarly in Frischmann's day, in the midst of the suffering of the Jews at a time when traditional religious belief had been subjected to strong contemporary skeptical challenges, it is difficult for the Jews to maintain the traditional relationship of faith and trust between themselves and God.

The alternative of following Put, while attractive to Timna, is not without its problems. Just as the Israelites feel they have been abandoned by God and thus must worship a false god, so Timna is abandoned by Put and is left only with a ring to which she can be loyal. Frischmann's portrayal of this sudden unexpected abandonment suggests that the relationship of the modern Jew to European culture is fraught with uncertainty because given the persistence of anti-Semitism, it is not clear how committed the peoples of Europe are to the Jews and to their continued existence. It is significant that Timna is more steadfast in her faith in the lover who *has* actually abandoned her than the Israelites are in the God who has only apparently abandoned them. Somehow it is easier for modern Jews to maintain their faith in what European culture has to offer them, even in the face of signs that European gentiles are not willing to accept them, than it is for them to maintain their faith in the traditional God of Israel.

Timna's response to the choice between the religion of Israel and the culture of the gentiles is to choose a third path — that of a synthesizing vision embodied in art. Her dance constitutes an aesthetic expression of the conflict within her soul between loyalty to the Israelite community and loyalty to the gentile Put. It also expresses her ability to transcend the problematic limitations of foreign cultures as well as those of the religion of Israel to discover a universal God of all the earth who apparently represents the breakdown of distinctions between cultures which is a prerequisite for a creative synthesis of those cultures. Her discovery is presented as a revelation to the Israelites. As the people "fell back and stood at a distance" (Exodus 20:15) when they experienced the revelation at Mount Sinai, so the people are greatly overwhelmed when they experience Timna's revelation:

> And the dance became stronger and stronger, and the storm became greater and greater, and the wildness became greater and greater. And a great trembling seized the whole people around,

and each one cast aside his drum and flute, and they were moved to flee for their lives (p. 24).

Following this flight of the people from her revelation, Timna falls to the ground dead.

As a writer Frischmann identifies with Timna. Like his heroine, he sets for himself the role to achieve in the aesthetic unity of a literary work a synthesis of the European and Jewish cultures which will be of greater value to the Jews than either culture is on its own. Nevertheless, both the flight of the Israelites from Timna's revelation and Timna's death at the end of the story point to Frischmann's doubts about the viability of his role as an artist and his suspicion that his vision will ultimately perish unheeded by the Jews.

Rebellion Against the Law

In the later stories of the *Bamidbar* series, Frischmann continues to make his claim that traditional Jewish culture is a hindrance to the realization of his vision of cultural synthesis. He locates the inability of the Jews to respond positively to his vision in their having been subjected to the limitations of an overly law-bound culture since the days of the giving of the Torah in the wilderness. He expresses in these stories the need to rebel against the laws of the Torah, which are arbitrarily and insensitively enforced in situations where the needs of life contradict the requirements of law. He also expresses his belief in the need of the Jew to join with his gentile fellow European in rebellion against the unjust power wielded by European governments. Nevertheless, as much as he makes clear his support for the struggle to liberate the individual from the arbitrary power of the law in the Jewish and European societies, Frischmann also suggests that there are potential pitfalls in the rebellion of the individual Jew against traditional Jewish and contemporary European law.

In the story "Hamekoshesh" ("The Gatherer of Wood"), Frischmann retells the story of the man found gathering wood on the Sabbath who, in accordance with God's decree, is stoned to death by the Israelite community (Numbers 15:32–36). In Frischmann's version, the story is told in the context of the attempt by the priestly religious establishment to impose the new laws of the Torah on a free-spirited people. Despite all of the priests' efforts, the people refuse to submit to the law, for:

> the people were still like the spirit of the wilderness, free of spirit, fully strong, unaccustomed to a yoke, so the words came only to their ears but did not touch them inside (p. 62).

During this period of the promulgation of the Torah laws, a new law is enacted: observance of the seventh day as a day of rest, with death as the penalty for its violation. Although the priests keep enumerating the details of the Sabbath law to the people, they refuse to take it seriously and merely laugh and shrug their shoulders.

In the context of this struggle between the priests and the people, the gatherer of wood is portrayed by Frischmann as less of an active rebel against the law than an innocent victim of a confused period of transition from a free-spirited era of Israelite history to a law-bound one. In Frischmann's version, the gatherer of wood is a poor laborer with a sick wife and four small children. He is only vaguely aware of this new law of the Sabbath, and thus he thinks nothing of going out on the seventh day to gather wood to make a fire for his sick wife. He is given the name Gog, which may allude to the wars of Gog and Magog in biblical and postbiblical literature. With this name Frischmann suggests that in violating the Sabbath law the hero of the story is an unwitting participant in a great social upheaval that has the potential of being parallel to the cataclysmic events prophesied for the end of days.

When Gog is caught violating the Sabbath, he is brought before the priests, who, like Moses in the original version of the story, are unsure what to do with him. At first, they favor leniency, for after all *they* had not observed the Sabbath only a short time ago, before the law was enacted. On second thought, however, they decide to detain him until they can consult with the high priest Phinehas, who declares that Gog must suffer the ultimate punishment of death in order to teach the people that they are obligated to observe the Sabbath. With great pomp and ceremony Gog is led to his death by stoning. Phinehas cries out that Gog must be put to death, and the people cry out in a ritualistic response, "He shall surely be put to death! He shall surely be put to death!" (p. 69).

In this version of the story of the gatherer of the wood on the Sabbath, Frischmann shows that the conflict between the needs of the people and the demands of the religious establishment in his day is not a new one: it goes back to the original imposition of the law on the people in the wilderness. His distaste for this imposition is clear from the changes he makes as he retells the original version of the story. Unlike the original version, Moses is virtually absent in Frischmann's version, as is God, and Phinehas is portrayed as the high priest, instead of Aaron, who is the high priest in the original version. Whatever positive associations the reader may have when he thinks of God, Moses, and Aaron are eliminated in Frischmann's portrayal of Phinehas and the priests, who have arbitrarily forced a new set of laws on the people and then have insisted on enforcing those laws despite the actual needs of people. Although at first the priests recognize the absurdity of treating the Sabbath as a binding law allowing for no extenuating circumstances, since no Israelite had observed it until recently, in the end they follow the fanaticism of Phinehas (known in the Bible for his zealous punishment of the Israelite man and the Midianite woman in Numbers 25:7–9).

What may even be more disturbing to Frischmann than the insensitivity of the religious leadership in biblical times, which has carried over to his own time, is the willingness of the people to allow themselves to be swept along by the fanaticism of their religious leaders and to abandon their commitment to freedom in the name of upholding an arbitrary divine law. At the end of the story, the narrator tells of Gog's young daughter's joining in the communal stoning of Gog, unaware that she is helping to kill her own father. The daughter's betrayal of the father serves as an apt image to portray the Jewish community's betrayal of the individual in its insistence on upholding the insensitive authority of their religious leaders.

Whereas the hero of "Hamekoshesh" was the passive victim of the law-bound Israelite culture, the hero of another story in the series, "Sorer umoreh" ("The Rebellious Son"), actively rebels against the legal authorities of that culture. Based on the hypothetical situation in Deuteronomy 21:18-21 of the son who rebels against his parents' authority, the story is about Kehat (or Kohath, the name of the grandfather of the rebel Korah in Numbers 16), who rebels not only against his parents but also against the laws of the Torah.

The principles which form the basis of Kehat's rebellion are such obviously anachronistic projections of modern concerns onto biblical times that it is clear he represents the young Jew of Frischmann's day who opposes the abusive power of Jewish communal leaders as well as that of the governments of Europe.[17] His challenge to the authority of Moses and Aaron strongly resembles the rebellion of his grandson Korah, yet is portrayed far more sympathetically than the rebellion of Korah is portrayed in the Bible. For Frischmann, the rebellious son and Korah of biblical times are not the evil destroyers of the social order that they appear to be in the Bible. Instead, they are the ancient models for the Jewish rebels of his day who challenge the destructive power of Jewish and gentile leaders.

When the priests and the officers proclaim the law of the military draft (Deuteronomy 20:1-9), Kehat takes a position which echoes modern pacifism, declaring:

> What do we need an army for? What do we need to fight for? Why should a person rise up against another person and murder him and spill his blood on the ground without purpose? We will not go! We will not go! (p. 74).

He also assumes a modern socialist stance, stating:

> There is no property and no acquisition, no master of property and no lord of acquisition! All that exists on the face of the earth belongs to all who dwell on earth, and everyone may take it! (p. 76).

This stance leads him to act like a Robin Hood figure, stealing from the rich to give to the poor.[18]

In an anarchistic spirit, Kehat views laws of war that justify murder and laws of property that hurt the poor as arbitrary impositions on the natural freedom of the people by those who wish to rule over them. He refuses to accept the leadership of Moses and Aaron and accuses them of using their power for personal gain. When Moses and Aaron declare that they have not taken one animal from an Israelite, Kehat sarcastically cites specific examples of times when Moses and the priests persecuted the poor by taking not one but many of their animals in the name of the law.

Kehat also reaches the conclusion that life is absurd and without meaning, and thus he sees no reason to honor the father and mother who brought him into this meaningless existence. He feels no debt of gratitude to his father, who he believes fathered him only because of a need to fulfill his sexual desires. One day, when his father rebukes him, Kehat curses him and strikes his mother, in direct violation of biblical law (Exodus 21:15, 17).

Like the rebellious son described in the causistic law passage in Deuteronomy 21, who is described as "a glutton and a drunkard," Kehat decides that if life is meaningless, he should at least pursue hedonistic delights. He surrounds himself with the riffraff of the Israelites, and together they constitute a subversive force which challenges the injustices of the established leadership of Israel.

In order to preserve their power and to crush the subversion, the leaders of Israel go to Kehat's parents and convince them to bring Kehat to justice in accordance with the law of the rebellious son. Like the punishment of Gog in "Hamekoshesh," the judgment and punishment of Kehat is portrayed as an act of uncivilized mass hysteria on the part of the people. All of the Israelites, including even the poor people whom Kehat has defended in the past, are caught up in the frenzy of the execution, as it is accompanied by pomp and ceremony and the sounds of trumpets, rams horns, and drums:

> And a kind of drunkenness passed through the camp. A lust arose like Sheol, and the people smelled blood. (p. 82).

As the priests cry that the people must eliminate evil from the nation, the people stone Kehat to death.

Kehat is portrayed in the story as the offspring of an Israelite man and a Hittite woman. As in "Meḥolot," non-Israelites who become a part of the Israelite camp represent the introduction of gentile cultural influences into the culture of Israel. While it is suggested that Kehat's rebelliousness may be traced in part to the gentile influence of his Hittite mother, it is she who makes the accusation against her son, and later it is she who is the first to cast a stone at Kehat when he is put to death. Her national identity seems to be responsible for her desire to destroy her offspring:

> And in her eyes lighted a foreign, strong, and great desire, and her spittle dripped from her mouth, and those who saw her suddenly remembered the Hittite women who eat the flesh of their children and lick their lips with pleasure (p. 81).

Here Frischmann is pointing to the paradoxical nature of the modern Jew's relationship with European culture: it is very alluring but also very dangerous. While European culture provides new and exciting ideas for the Jew that form the basis for his rebellion against the Jewish and gentile cultural establishments, that same European culture is also capable of turning against the Jew and destroying him because he has challenged the cultural norm.

Eros in Jewish and European Cultures

In some of the stories in the *Bamidbar* series, Frischmann explores the problematic position of the erotic in modern times. While the historical context of the stories is ancient Israel, it would appear that Frischmann is writing about opposing tendencies in the contemporary Jewish and European cultures. In one story, he focuses on the effects of the overly restrictive approach to the erotic traditional religion. In another story, he indicates his recognition of the dangers inherent in the less restrictive approach to the erotic of modern culture.

The story "'Ir hamiklat" ("The City of Refuge") tells of a character of Frischmann's imagination who was the first to commit unintentional murder and thereby to avail herself of one of the cities of refuge constructed in accordance with biblical law (Numbers 35:9–34). When the cities are first established the Israelites are portrayed as naively convinced that it will never be necessary to make use of them:

> And the people enjoyed telling each other in a mocking way, "Surely these three cities will be desolate and will disappear from the face of the earth before a murderer will come to dwell in them. For there is no murderer in Israel, and there will never be in its midst any murderer (p 125).

One day a teenage woman named Noah, who is destined to destroy the Israelites' naive illusion, arrives in their camp. When asked of her origins, she declares, "My father is the wilderness, my mother the plain" (p.117). In fact, the narrator relates, she had been born to poor working class parents who had died among those stricken by the plague sent by God to destroy those who ate too many quails (Numbers 11:31–35). Noah had then raised herself in the wilderness.

As a product of parents who rebelled against God to fulfill their sensual desires, and as a child of the wilderness, Noah relates to her sexuality in a manner that is oblivious to any moral or societal restraints. All the Israelite men are attracted to her, and she allows any man who wishes to do so to have sexual relations with her. She pays no particular attention to the man lying with her, and she laughs loudly, not seeing her action as sinful in any way. It is particularly satisfying to her to have sexual relations with the riffraff of Israel rather than with the aristocracy. When she is not engaged in sexual relations with the men, she plays with snakes in an obviously erotic manner.

There are certain disturbing aspects to the arrival of this wild teenage nymphomaniac in the Israelite camp. The men's fascination with Noah is portrayed as a dangerous intoxicating cup of poison passing through the camp. Noah also displays disturbing narcissistic tendencies:

> And at times a strong desire flared up in her suddenly to kneel on her knees and kiss in the mirror of water all of her flesh, all parts of her body, and all of her skin (p. 120).

Furthermore, it turns out that Noah's happiness is disturbed at certain moments when she is alone and she sees her lovers and the gifts they have given her as a burden. At those moments her heart feels empty, and she is full of longing:

> like the tract of salty land between Paran and Tophel, which has never been rained upon, thirsty for the gift of dew (p. 121).

Noah begins to realize that her thirst is for access to the holy. One day she feels a powerful desire to enter into the tabernacle, where she sees a young priest exhorting the people to observe the laws of sexual purity. Soon after they get to know each other, the priest and Noah feel a strong attraction to each other. Each finds in the other the aspect of life which he or she has been missing: for Noah the priest provides the opportunity to have contact with the holy, and for the priest Noah provides the possibility of transcending the biblical perception of sexuality as profane.

The problem in their relationship is that Noah and the priest each see themselves as unworthy of approaching the other: each perceives the other to be on a much higher level of holiness. The priest feels that it is he who is profane and Noah who is the truly holy one. He therefore abandons the priesthood so that he can partake in the sanctified sexuality which he sees in their relationship. Noah, on the other hand, refuses to have sexual relations with him. As much as she longs to be with him, she is unable to do so because she feels that he is too holy and she is too profane.

One day the dead body of the priest is found floating in a river. Noah realizes that the priest has committed suicide in his despair at ever being able to fulfill his desire for her. Although she did not actually murder him, Noah presents herself at the gate of Gezer, one of the cities of refuge, as an unintentional murderer.

The story "'Ir hamiklat" represents the conflict between holiness and sexuality which Frischmann discerns as central to Jewish culture since biblical times. The extreme poles which the young priest and Noah represent — holiness and sexuality — are two experiences for which Jews long, but which they have been taught to see as opposed to each other. The assumption in Jewish culture has been that women represent the sexual side of life and men represent holiness. Men and women each long for the other side, yet they are unable to achieve together an integration of those two sides. Neither extreme is desirable: Noah's sensuality leads to narcissism, and the priest's holiness leads to excessive self-control and sexual frustration.

The priest's suicide and Noah's self-imprisonment in a city of refuge suggest Frischmann's pessimistic assessment of the potential for achieving the integration of sexuality and holiness in Jewish culture. Not only does the priest die, but Noah indicates that she prefers to remain in the city of refuge for the rest of her life rather than return to the culture in which sexuality is seen as too profane to be integrated with holiness.

As critics have noted, the plot and characterization of "'Ir hamiklat" parallel that of the late-nineteenth-century French novel *Thaïs* by Anatole France, which Frischmann translated into Hebrew.[19] In that work, an ascetic monk living in the Egyptian desert in the early days of Christianity is attracted to a sexually liberated actress and courtesan named Thaïs. The fate of their relationship closely resembles that of the priest and Noah in Frischmann's story. Just as the priest abandons the priesthood for the sake of Noah and Noah in turn withdraws from life into the city of refuge, so in France's novel, the monk descends into the realm of sexuality as a result of his attraction to Thaïs, and she in turn rises to the realm of holiness as a result of her contact with the monk and enters a convent. This synthesis of the biblical passages concerning the city of refuge, the European novel *Thaïs*, and contemporary Jewish experience provides a good example of the kind of literary expression of the synthesis of the Jewish and European cultures which Frischmann

advocated. Frischmann's allusions in his story to France's novel suggest his awareness of the difficulty of integrating holiness and sexuality as one which also concerned Christian culture.

If Frischmann is keenly aware of the problems arising from a
traditional culture's exaggerated preoccupation with restricting sexuality and its inability to integrate holiness with sexuality, he also
indicates in the *Bamidbar* series that the lifting of restrictions on sexuality can lead to a serious moral problem for a culture: the sexual
abuse of women by men. The story "'Eglah 'arufah" ("The Heifer
Whose Neck Was Broken"), in which Frischmann expresses his concerns about sexual abuse, is based on two consecutive passages of
causistic law: the ritual declaration of innocence over a heifer whose
neck has been broken by a town near where a slain body has been
found (Deuteronomy 21:1–9) and the obligation to allow a foreign
woman taken captive in war to lament the loss of her family for a
month before marrying her (Deuteronomy 21:10–14).

The story begins with a description of a war between the Israelites and the five kings of Midian. The Israelite men are portrayed
as bloodthirsty and unrestrained in their efforts to loot the cities of
Midian:

> Then they pursued all the survivors of the war, every male, and
> destroyed them and slew them and did not leave even one. After-
> ward, intoxicated by blood, they entered the abandoned cities and
> searched every house and every hiding place and dragged out the
> rest of the survivors from every hiding place . . . but the women
> of Midian and their children and all their animals and livestock
> and weapons they took, the gold and the silver and the copper and
> the iron, the tin and the lead, all of these they took with them and
> brought them to the plains of Moab by the river Jordan near
> Jericho (p. 103).

The Israelite men lust for Midianite women, and therefore when
these captive women are put up for sale, there is much interest on
the part of the men. A priest exhorts the men who purchase these
women to obey the law to allow a captive foreign woman to mourn

her family for a month before taking her as a wife. Some listen to the priest, while others ignore him.

A priest named Elizaphan purchases a captive Midianite woman named Hoglah, but finds it most difficult to curb his passion for her and wait the required month to exercise his legal prerogative to marry her. He spends the first three weeks after purchasing Hoglah trying to convince her to have sexual relations with him, but each time he does so, she resists, for she is still in mourning for her childhood sweetheart who has been killed in the war between the Midianites and the Israelites.

Finally, at the beginning of the fourth week of Hoglah's captivity, Elizaphan decides to disobey biblical law and to disregard Hoglah's feelings, and he forces her to have sexual relations with him. Elizaphan's rape of Hoglah is portrayed as if it were an improper sacrifice of "strange fire" (*'esh zarah*) upsetting the order of the law as well as the order of nature:

> In his eyes burned a strange fire . . . . And the night was very dark.
> Outside a storm raged and the wind whistled from the mountain
> and was like a wail. The dogs barked. The foxes wailed all night
> (p. 111).

Hoglah fights back by scratching Elizaphan's face and poking at his eyes, but finally she succumbs. The next day Hoglah is missing from the Israelite camp, and a while later her dead body is found. Since it is not known who has murdered her, the community performs the ritual declaration of innocence over a heifer whose neck has been broken.

The breaking of the heifer's neck and its use in the ritual declaration of innocence are portrayed as a symbolic re-enactment of the rape of Hoglah by the priest Elizaphan. The shedding of the heifer's blood and the pouring of it into the river are described in great detail. When Elizaphan joins in the ritual declaration of innocence, at first his voice is inaudible, for he knows he is responsible for her death. A moment later he recovers and rationalizes his murder of

Hoglah with the thought, "Was she not merely a heifer whose neck was broken?" (p. 114).

"'Eglah 'arufah" reflects Frischmann's concerns about the relationship between sex and violence in the male psyche since biblical times, the abusive ways that men treat women, and the ways that religious and political institutions have sustained this abusive power of men over women and encouraged acts of violence. The shedding of blood in war and in ritual sacrifice, he is saying, are related to sexual passion in the male psyche. Although the law seeks to protect women from the violent sexual power which men wish to impose on them, it does not fully succeed in doing so. Religious ritual is then used to cover up the guilt of the men and to confirm their right to make women into sacrificial victims of male sexual passion.

In recalling Frischmann's references in his later essays to the irrational release of violent passion among the masses of Germany at the beginning of World War I and the masses of Russia at the time of the Bolshevik Revolution, it may be inferred that in this story Frischmann is attempting to demonstrate that there is a link between the disintegration of moral restraints on sexuality and the disintegration of moral restraints on violence in his time. Taking into account both "'Ir hamiklat" and "'Eglah 'arufah," it is clear that Frischmann was not comfortable with either the restrictive attitude of traditional culture nor with the freer attitude of modern culture toward sexuality. His dream appears to have been to create a synthesis of the traditional attempts to sanctify sexuality and the modern tendency to lift traditional restrictions so as to liberate human sexual expression.

In the *Bambidar* series Frischmann draws on biblical texts that tell of the promulgation of the law and of rebellion against that law in the wilderness of Israel's wanderings in order to express his understanding of conflicts central to modern European Jewish existence: Jewish culture versus European culture, law versus freedom, and control versus license in sexual relations. In these stories Frischmann conveys his longings for ideal liberating ways to resolve these conflicts. The attractiveness of such gentile characters as Put ("Meḥolot") and Hoglah ("'Eglah 'arufah") to Israelite characters represents the Jews' longing for entrance into the attractive European culture. The rebellion of Kehat ("Sorer umoreh") serves at least in part as a model of the attempt to release the stranglehold of the law on life. The passionate love affairs of Timna and Put ("Meḥolot") and Noah and the priest ("'Ir hamiklat") are an expression of the beauty of human sexual love that transcends cultural restrictions. Conversely, those forces which attempt to interfere with the Jewish striving for contact with gentile culture, freedom from law, and romantic love are seen by Frischmann as destructive forces: the idolatrous Israelites who seek to undermine Timna's faith in Put ("Meḥolot"); Phinehas the priest, who cannot forgive Gog's violation of the Sabbath ("Hamekoshesh"); the authorities who defeat Kehat's rebellion ("Sorer umoreh"); and the teaching that it is necessary to restrict sexuality to achieve holiness which interferes with the relationship between Noah and the priest ("'Ir hamiklat").

Often in these stories, however, it is the striving for a liberating way which carries within it the seeds of its own destruction. Those who strive for a life closer to gentile culture are abandoned and sometimes even destroyed by it: Put of the mixed multitude leaves Timna for no apparent reason ("Meḥolot"), and Kehat's Hittite mother is the first to denounce and stone him ("Sorer umoreh"). Sexual passion, when left unchecked, becomes a powerfully destructive force in such a male-female relationship as that of Elizaphan and Hoglah ("'Eglah 'arufah").

Furthermore, the authorities who, by upholding the law appear to be opposed to the freedom of the individual, are at times more sensitive and morally responsible than the individuals who are subject to their power. Biblical law in fact does seek to curb the destructive excesses of the individual and protect the weak from the powerful. When Elizaphan defies the law of the captive woman ("'Eglah 'arufah"), it is clear that the purpose of the law may be to function at times as a curb which is necessary to effect true freedom and justice in society.

Although the communal leaders are often the ones who rob the people of their freedom and lead them to abandon the free way of life to which they are naturally inclined, the people in these stories appear frequently to be the ones who are responsible for their own abandonment of freedom. While the initial instinct of the people is not to accept the newly promulgated laws of the Bible, they are easily persuaded to join with the authorities in punishing the rebels against the law ("Hamekoshesh" and "Sorer umoreh").

Frischmann's versions of biblical texts in the *Bamidbar* series constitute a radical reinterpretation of the biblical origins of the Jewish people. According to normative Jewish tradition these texts affirm the values of loyalty to Jewish, as opposed to gentile culture, of the primacy of the law over the inclinations of the individual, and of the need to control sexual passion. Frischmann has created an alternative tradition which affirms values relevant to his existence as a modern Jew: the legitimacy of being attracted to gentile culture; the right of the individual to assert his needs over the demands of the law and the abuses of legally constituted authorities; and the positive nature of sexual expression.

Nevertheless, Frischmann's radical critique of traditional Jewish values is tempered by the realization that the drive to rebel against the norms of the tradition can easily lead to self-destruction. Frischmann's biblical rebels are portrayed in a sober light based on the experiences of the author and the Jewish people in the early twentieth century. In the end, Frischmann is unable to endorse fully the cultural revolution which he is proposing. He is all too painfully aware that the realities of gentile anti-Semitism destroy the rebel who leaves Jewish culture as well as those who remain loyal to it. He is also aware of the tendency of individuals to inflict pain on others in the name of personal freedom. Finally, he knows all too well the inclination of the masses to abandon their natural instinct of freedom and act as corruptly as the authorities against whom they should rebel.

Part II

Biblical Archetypes
and the
Modern Jewish Experience

Chapter 4

The Life and Death of King Saul: Shaul Tchernichowsky

I do not know why, but I have always held a grudge in my heart against all those of our people who were famous as holy and good, despite all the evil that they did, and I thought that those who wrote our history hid much from us in order to justify them and condemn others.

And thus I always sided with King Saul. And perhaps the name was a factor.[1]

In this passage from an autobiographical statement by Shaul Tchernichowsky the poet declares his commitment to re-evaluate the traditional version of Jewish history and to discover instead an alternative version more suited to contemporary values. His reference to "holy and good" characters whose evil deeds were played down by the Jewish tradition undoubtedly includes King David. It disturbed Tchernichowsky that despite such morally questionable acts as his adulterous relations with Bathsheba and his arrangement of her husband's death, David was still hailed by Jewish tradition as a great hero. On the other hand, Tchernichowsky believed, Saul, the first king of ancient Israel, who was succeeded by David, was wrongly maligned by the tradition which viewed Saul as a God-forsaken failure.[2]

During a period which spanned most of his literary career, Tchernichowsky wrote five ballads retelling events from the life of Saul as recounted in I Samuel.[3] In these ballads the poet sought to change the negative image of Saul in Jewish tradition. As he indicates in his autobiographical statement, Tchernichowsky, who saw himself as a namesake of the first king of Israel, identified with King Saul. Thus in his portraits of the king in these ballads, the political triumphs and failures of Saul represent the poet's sense of his own triumphs and failures as well as those of the Jewish people in their struggle to revolutionize the Jewish present on the basis of a radically new understanding of the Jewish past.

These ballads about Saul were written during three different periods of Tchernichowsky's life. The poet's choices of what event in Saul's life to retell and how to portray Saul correspond directly to the set of concerns which most preoccupied him at the time that he wrote each poem. He was raised in the village of Mikhailovka, Russia, in a family that provided him with a traditional Jewish as well as a modern Russian education. At the age of fourteen he went to Odessa and eventually became part of the literary scene in that center of modern Hebrew letters. It was there that in his late teens and twenties Tchernichowsky wrote his first two ballads about Saul: "Be'eindor" ("At En-dor") (1893) and "'Al ḥorvot beit-shan" ("On the Ruins of Beth-shan") (1898).

Excluded from admission to medical school in Russia, Tchernichowsky pursued his medical studies in Germany and Switzerland and then returned to Russia to practice medicine. During World War I he served as a physician in the Russian army. After witnessing the devastating effects of the war and of the Bolshevik Revolution, he left Russia in the 1920s and for about a decade lived mostly in Germany, where he wrote the third ballad on Saul, "Hamelekh" ("The King") (1925). The last two ballads, "'Al harei gilboa'" (On the Mountains of Gilboa") (1929) and "'Anshei ḥayil ḥevel" ("A Band of Stalwart Men") (1936), were written shortly before and after Tchernichowsky's emigration to the Land of Israel in 1931, where he pursued his medical and literary careers.[4]

In the two ballads of the Odessa period, "Be'ein-dor" and "'Al ḥorvot beit-shan," Tchernichowsky's reinterpretation of the life of Saul reflects the radical approach to Jewish history which he had begun to take in his youth. This approach was based on a Nietzschean view of the decline of Israel not unlike that which Berdyczewski held at the time. That view is most forcefully put forth in Tchernichowsky's poem "Lenokhaḥ pesel ʾappolo" ("Before a Statue of Apollo") (1899), which begins with a paean of praise to the life-affirming qualities of ancient Greek culture as embodied by the god Apollo. The poet puts forth the claim in this poem that these praiseworthy qualities of ancient Greek culture had also been the driving force behind the culture of ancient Israel, at least through the period of the Israelites' conquest of Canaan. He mourns the fact that subsequently the Jewish tradition confined the youthful spirit of ancient Israel in the later biblical, rabbinic, and medieval periods. This confinement, he feels, has resulted in the Jews being an old and sick people worshipping a weak and aged God. In the concluding lines of the poem (probably the best known passage of his poetry), the poet expresses his disgust at the decline of the people, who have tied up "the God of the conquerors of Canaan"[5] with phylactery straps. For Tchernichowsky the phylacteries and all they had come to symbolize as a sign of the covenant between God and Israel are merely concrete manifestations of the ways that the biblical and rabbinic traditions limited the original vital spirit of the people and its concept of God.

When Tchernichowsky returned to the poetic retelling of the story of Saul's life in his German period in the poem "Hamelekh," his approach to history was deeply affected by the traumatic events of World War I as well as the Bolshevik Revolution and its aftermath in the Russian Civil War. He conveyed his reaction to those events in two sonnet cycles, "Lashemesh" ("To the Sun") (1919) and "'Al hadam" ("On the Blood") (1922).[6] "Lashemesh" begins with a passage from the Mishnah which quotes a declaration made by the priests during the celebration of the Sukkot festival in the Second Temple in Jerusalem:

> Our ancestors who were in this place stood with their backs to the
> Temple of God facing the east and prostrated themselves to the sun
> in the east (*Sukkah* 5:4).

The declaration, which is based on the prophet Ezekiel's condemnation of sun worship (Ezekiel 8:16), goes on to state that in contrast
to the pagan practices of the past, the Israelites of the Second Temple
period worship only one God. Tchernichowsky, who has deleted the
affirmation of monotheism in the mishnaic passage, makes clear in
the course of the sonnet cycle that he views the sun worship condemned by the prophets and priests as superior to the monotheistic
worship in the Second Temple. As he did in the 1890s, Tchernichowsky continues to oppose what he perceives as the confinement
by the biblical and rabbinic traditions of the life-affirming qualities
which had found expression in the pagan impulses of ancient Israel.

In the aftermath of World War I, however, Tchernichowsky is
desperately driven to search for life-affirming cultural values not
only to revive a degenerate Jewish culture, but a degenerate European culture as well. Like Frischmann, who was writing at the same
time, Tchernichowsky sees as much to criticize in post-World War I
European culture as he does in traditional Jewish culture. He writes
of himself as a poet feeling out of place in a period of cultural
decline, for he alone is in touch with the vital forces of the ancient
past. He wonders to himself, "Have I arrived too early or has the
Rock [God] created me too late?"[7], that is, is it too late for him to
play a role in restoring the European and Jewish cultures to the
vitality of the pagan past, or is there yet hope of restoring that vitality in the future?

In the sonnet cycle "'Al hadam," Tchernichowsky reacts to the
evil inclination of humanity revealed in the violent events that he
had recently witnessed by declaring his disillusionment with all past
attempts to redeem humanity, be they prophecy, rational philosophy,
or politics. The only hope for the redemption of humanity can come,
he believes, from the artists and poets of the time.

Tchernichowsky's final two poems based on the life of Saul, "'Al
harei gilboa'" and "'Anshei ḥayil ḥevel," reflect his preoccupation

with the violent struggle between Jews and Arabs over the Land of Israel in the late 1920s and 1930s. During this period of his emigration to the Land of Israel, Tchernichowsky expressed in his poetry his enthusiastic support for Zionism as a concrete expression of the spirit of Israel's ancient pagan past. At the same time, particularly after his emigration, when he began to experience first hand the violent struggle over the land, he expressed in his poetry his anguish at the bitter price the twentieth-century "conquerors of Canaan by storm" were paying to fulfill the Zionist dream. In the poem "Re'i, 'adamah" ("See, Land") (1938) the poet addresses the Land of Israel, which has received the dead bodies of too many young Jews who have died in the struggle over the land. As proud as he is of the sacrifices of these youths, which he believes will lay the groundwork for the eventual establishment of Jewish sovereignty, the poet undermines his own pride by declaring how wasteful their deaths have been.

The Death of Saul

Four of the five ballads about Saul, the first two and the last two, focus on the period shortly before, during, and after the death of the king. Only the middle poem, "Hamelekh," portrays Saul at the height of his powers. This curious preoccupation on Tchernichowsky's part with the death as opposed to the life of Saul indicates the extent to which the poet felt himself and his people struggling with the forces of death, be they degenerate tendencies in traditional Jewish culture or the desire of their enemies in Europe or the Middle East to destroy them.

In the poem "Be'ein-dor," Tchernichowsky retells the story of Saul's raising of the ghost of the prophet Samuel from the dead shortly before the king's final battle against the Philistine enemy (I Samuel 28). In the original version of the story Saul has lost his nerve as he contemplates the impending battle. The death of Samuel had removed from Saul any hope of a reconciliation between himself and God, who had already declared His rejection of Saul as king. Saul senses that the divine assistance necessary to win the battle against the Philistines is being denied him, for he is unable to receive a message from God by means of dreams, oracles, or prophets. He finally feels that he has no choice but to violate his own interdiction against consulting ghosts. He disguises himself by wearing different clothes and goes to En-dor to seek the aid of a woman who consults ghosts to raise the ghost of Samuel from the dead, so that the prophet can advise him how to deal with the enemy. When he is brought back to the realm of the living, Samuel angrily declares that Saul is no longer worthy of God's aid because he had sinned against God by not fulfilling the commandment to destroy all of Amalek when he spared the life of the Amalekite king Agag (I Samuel 15).

While the biblical version of this story confirms the validity of God's rejection of Saul, it also evokes a large measure of sympathy for the king. Saul is portrayed as weak from the fast he has undertaken in preparation for raising Samuel from the dead and hopelessly terrified by the ghostly revelation of the prophet. In addition, the woman who consults ghosts and Saul's courtiers express a concern for the king's physical and mental state that the reader comes to share as well. In his version Tchernichowsky denies the validity of God's rejection of Saul and greatly outdoes the biblical author in evoking sympathy for Saul.

In the first part of "Be'ein-dor," the poet describes Saul's journey to En-dor and his entrance into the woman's house in much greater detail than is found in the original version. In describing the house, Tchernichowsky creates a mysterious and magical atmosphere of a boiling cauldron, snake-like billowing smoke, and dancing creatures of darkness that corresponds to the inner turmoil of the king.[8] The imagery conveys as well the severely weakened state in which Saul finds himself. The different clothes which Saul puts on to disguise himself in the original version are transformed in Tchernichowsky's version into a description of Saul as "without bow or javelin." Saul has now lost the power that these weapons of war give to a person in order to defend himself against his enemies.[9] Awaiting the apparition of Samuel's ghost, Saul stands within a magical circle anointed with sulfur in a state which is very far from that of the days of his power that followed his being anointed with oil by the prophet.

Saul then begins to recall his childhood whose idyllic pastoral setting contrasts markedly with his situation as a failed king facing impending death. Instead of the images of inner turmoil, limitation, and powerlessness which fill Saul's present consciousness, Saul's memory of his youth is characterized by images of his strength, tranquility, and serenity in a world of limitless fields and heavens. In his childhood, cattle, not creatures of darkness, danced before him. Shade *(tsel)* was provided for him not by the elusive spirit of Samuel whose shadow *(tsel)* he had asked the woman to reveal to him, but rather by the more concrete and reliable terebinth.

Tortured by his inability to return to his youth, Saul is suddenly confronted by the ghost of Samuel, who, as in the original version, rises angrily from the dead. The king and the prophet engage in a dialogue which draws on Samuel's rebuke of Saul in the original version. However, the issue discussed in this confrontation between king and prophet is somewhat different from that discussed in the original version. In the Bible, Saul wants advice from Samuel on how to deal with being attacked by the Philistines and with being abandoned by God. Samuel replies that Saul is being punished by God, who will have him defeated and killed in battle so that David may succeed him as king. In Tchernichowsky's version, while Saul is concerned about the battle with the Philistines and God's abandonment of him, the central issue that he raises is why Samuel took him from the idyllic pastoral setting of his youth to be a king destined to lose his power, happiness, and sanity. Samuel's response in Tchernichowsky's version is indirect. Paraphrasing the words of Samuel in the original version, he merely declares that God is angry at Saul for his rebelliousness, and that the king and his people will die the next day.

In turning to Samuel, Saul has no hope of emerging from the sense of limitation and death which has come to overwhelm him. Samuel himself belongs to the world of the dead, and his only response to Saul is to foretell the king's impending death. In the conclusion of the poem, Saul returns to the Israelite camp plunged deeply in the despair that this experience of confronting his mortality has aroused in him. His only alternative, he now realizes, is to engage in the battle with the Philistines in which he is about to commit suicide (I Samuel 31).[10]

In his portrayal of Saul's situation and state of mind at the time that he seeks help from the woman at En-dor, Tchernichowsky conveys the dilemmas of the European Jew at the end of the nineteenth century. Like Saul facing the imminent victory of the Philistines, the late-nineteenth-century Jew is in danger of physical destruction at the hands of anti-Semitic pogromists. He feels, like Saul, that God has abandoned him, and he is no longer even certain of God's existence. Just as Saul felt extremely limited in his position as king of Israel, so the Jew resents the role which he has been asked to play since biblical times as a member of a special chosen people with many more spiritual demands placed on them than on other peoples. He longs to return to an existence in harmony with nature, which he believes his people must have had in their earliest history and thereby escape his present more limited existence.[11]

As he turns to the Jewish tradition, represented in "Be'ein-dor" by Samuel, the late-nineteenth-century Jew finds only dead forms emerging from the world of the dead. The response of the traditional Jewish religious leadership to the dilemmas of modern Jewish existence is to rebuke modern Jews for not living up to the spiritual demands of the tradition. Tchernichowsky clearly disagrees with this traditional response: if Jews are in physical and spiritual danger, he believes, it is not because they have failed to live up to the demands of the tradition, but rather because they have tried to do so. With no real solution to his dilemmas, the modern Jew is left, like Saul at the end of the poem, in a state of despair, which can only lead to self-destruction, either through the path of physical suicide chosen by Saul or through the path of spiritual suicide by abandoning one's Jewish identity. Saul's despair, which leads to his suicide, functions in much the same way as does the suicide of the captive martyrs in Bialik's "Megillat ha'esh," as a symbol of the sense of futility which both writers felt at least at certain moments as they contemplated the future of Jewish existence.

The pessimistic assessment of the future fate of the Jewish people, which Tchernichowsky conveys in "Be'ein-dor," is presented

even more bleakly at the beginning of "'Al ḥorvot beit-shan."
Although in "Be'ein-dor" Tchernichowsky portrays the situation of
the Jewish people in his day by means of the figure of Saul on the
brink of failure and death, Saul is still clinging to the hope that he
might be saved. In "'Al ḥorvot beit-shan" he portrays that situation
by means of describing the period after the death of Saul.

Tchernichowsky imagines the dead king as a restless ghost who
wanders night after night through the place where his body had been
desecrated by the Philistines. While the biblical text in I Samuel 31
makes it clear that following the desecration of Saul's body, the
inhabitants of Jabesh-gilead restored his honor by properly burying
him and his sons who died in the battle, Tchernichowsky chooses to
ignore that fact. He begins the poem with selected quotations from
I Samuel 31:8–10, which emphasize the desecration of Saul's body,
and he omits all references to Saul's subsequent burial:

> The Philistines came . . . and they found Saul . . . They cut off his
> head . . . and they impaled his body on the wall of Beth-shan (p. 23).

The poem describes the inability of Saul's soul to find eternal rest
because of his defeat in battle and because of the subsequent desecration of his body. In its restlessness, his soul keeps returning to Beth-
shan in search of the javelin he had lost in his final battle with the
Philistines.

Toward the end of the night, Saul's ghost seeks to alleviate his
humiliation by taking revenge on his enemies. Since he is unable to
find the javelin that will enable him to take his revenge, the poet
envisions him wandering until the time of the resurrection of the
dead in the messianic era. At that time he will find his lost weapon
and call his army to challenge the enemy in battle.

While in "Be'ein-dor" Saul's situation represents both the
physical and cultural dangers to which the Jewish people in Tchernichowsky's time are prey, in "'Al ḥorvot beit-shan" the focus is
primarily on the physical dangers. Like the defeated Saul of ancient
times, the Jewish pogrom victims of modern times lead a ghostly,
humiliated existence. They are restless, like the ghost of Saul in the

poem, but they are powerless to defend themselves and to right the injustices which have been perpetrated against them. The vision at the end of the poem of Saul and his army taking revenge on his enemies represents a call on the part of the poet for an angry, aggressive response by the Jewish pogrom victims, who he believed to have been overly passive.

This vision of revenge is interrupted at the end of the poem. At that point, God restrains Saul from engaging in vengeful battle and says that He forgives the enemies of Israel. Vengeance, He declares, must now be transformed into love. Some critics have considered this ending to be an ironic attack on the Jewish tradition.[12] According to this interpretation, Tchernichowsky believes in the validity of an angry, aggressive response by the Jews to their persecution, and therefore God's restraint of Saul represents for Tchernichowsky the Jewish tradition's unfortunate tendency to limit the natural aggressive drive of the people in the name of the unnatural spiritual demands of love.

Another way of understanding this ending would be to see it not as Tchernichowsky's ironic attack on the Jewish tradition, but rather as the expression of his ambivalent attitude toward the alternative responses to Jewish suffering of hatred and revenge or love and forgiveness.[13] This ambivalence calls to mind the two-sided wondrous person of Bialik's "Megillat ha'esh," who embodies the alternative responses to Jewish suffering of the revenge of the man of terror or the love and comfort of the fair youth. Bialik does not seem to hold out much hope for the viability of either response: in "Megillat ha'esh" all but one of the captives chooses revenge, and that leads only to their self-destruction. Tchernichowsky, on the other hand, seems to want to hold on to both responses as possibly viable. By concluding the poem with God's affirmation of the response of love, however, he singles it out as ultimately the higher and more valid response.

It is possible that Tchernichowsky's choice to use the death of Saul to represent the physical attacks on European Jewry was influenced by the use of Saul's suicide in medieval Hebrew liturgical poetry to represent the Jewish fathers killing their families and committing suicide during the Crusades rather than submit to forced conversion to Christianity.[14] Tchernichowsky indicates his fascination with these medieval acts of martyrdom in his poem about the Jewish response to the Crusades titled "Barukh mimagentsa" ("Baruch of Mainz") (1901).[15] In that poem, as in the Saul poems, Tchernichowsky expresses a modern discomfort with the traditional martyrological ideal that is parallel to a similar discomfort with that ideal found in Bialik's "Megillat ha᾽esh."

Saul as Prophet, Mystic, and Poet

While in the first two Saul ballads Tchernichowsky's focus was on the figure of the dying and dead king as a representation of the responses of modern Jews to their physical and cultural destruction, in "Hamelekh" he makes use of Saul for a different purpose. In keeping with Tchernichowsky's preoccupation at the time with the role of art and poetry as a regenerative force in the degenerating culture of Europe since the outbreak of World War I, Saul functions in "Hamelekh" as the embodiment of the qualities of the modern poet who has the power to achieve a visionary transcendence of the declining European civilization.

This modern poet's power is shown by retelling incidents reported in I Samuel of Saul undergoing an ecstatic prophetic experience. Most of the poem draws on the account of events that occurred at the time that Samuel anointed Saul as king of Israel (I Samuel 10). In that account Saul turns to Samuel to help him find his father's lost asses. Having been told by God that He has chosen Saul to be the new king, Samuel reassures Saul that the asses have been found, he anoints Saul, and then he tells him that a series of events will occur that will confirm that God has chosen him to lead the people. After leaving Samuel, Saul is told, he will meet two men who will inform him that the lost asses have been found and that his father is looking for him. Then, he will be met by three men on a pilgrimage to the shrine at Bethel: one will carry three kids, one will carry three loaves of bread, and one will carry a jar of wine. These men will offer Saul two loaves of bread, which he is to accept. Then he is to proceed to

Ramah, where he will meet a band of prophets descending from the shrine, led by players of musical instruments. These prophets will be undergoing an ecstatic prophetic experience, in which Saul, seized by the spirit of God, will soon find himself participating. The account goes on to relate that all of these signs came true in confirmation of God's choice of Saul as king of Israel.

The poem also alludes to another incident of ecstatic prophetic experience which Saul undergoes during the period of rivalry between David and himself (I Samuel 19:18–24). Saul is seized by an urge to kill David but is told that his rival has already escaped to Naioth, where he is staying with Samuel. Saul sends three groups of messengers to Naioth to capture David, but each time they attempt to do so the messengers come upon a band of prophets led by Samuel in ecstatic prophesy and join them in their ecstasy. Saul finally decides to go to Naioth himself. On the way, however, he too is gripped by the spirit of God and undergoes an ecstatic experience. When he arrives at Naioth, Saul takes off his clothes and continues his ecstatic prophesy before Samuel in a state of nakedness for the rest of that day and night.

In "Hamelekh" Tchernichowsky appears to be less interested in the specific contexts of these two incidents of ecstatic prophesy — the anointing of Saul as king and the rivalry between Saul and David — than in focusing on the experience of ecstasy that Saul undergoes. The poem begins at the point in I Samuel 10 when Saul meets the prophets descending from the shrine at Ramah. The prophets carry the kids, bread, and wine that the pilgrims had carried in the original version and one of the musical instruments, a harp, that the prophets had carried in the original version. As in the biblical text, the three basic ancient Middle Eastern foods — lamb, bread, and wine — and the musical instruments are to be used in a cultic sacrificial ritual accompanied by music which will celebrate and establish Saul's choice by God to be king of Israel.

Before Saul undergoes an ecstatic religious experience with the prophets, one of the prophets tells Saul of the powers he will possess now that he has become God's anointed one:

And the Spirit of God came upon a prophet,
And one of them spoke, saying: "Welcome,
Blessed among men, anointed of God,
Exalted over his brothers! Twice blessed
In the blessing of great sufferings and their joy
And in the joy of a lord of his brothers and master of his
    sorrows,
Girt in the mysteries of a ruler whose word
Decides for life or for death,
Who is drunk in great passion, that of a visionary
With eyes open to gaze on the shadow of the living God.
Even more exalted you, your heart shall be so pure
That it will absorb of the sublime light;
And if you are not holy, your soul shall hurt
From the touch of the wings of infinity, as they fleet
Through eternities pouring into eternities
To know the secret of final freedom . . ." (p. 83)!¹⁶

The portrait of Saul in the prophet's statement attributes to the
newly anointed king qualities associated with romantic poets, kings,
prophets, and mystics. In each of these roles, Saul will be fully aware
of the positive and negative extremes in human experience as well
as of the ultimate unity of existence that draws these extremes
together. As a romantic poet, he will know more than any other
human being the extremes of human suffering and joy and the
paradoxical connections between them ("Twice blessed/In the blessing of great sufferings and their joy/And in the joy of a lord of his
brothers and master of his sorrows"). As a king, he will have the God-
like power to bring to human beings the extreme experiences of both
life and death. By envisioning God, he will also know how to find
the divine source of the opposing extremes of joy and suffering, life
and death. The prophet's description of this divine revelation, which
Saul will receive, contains both the biblical idiom *laḥazot . . . 'el ḥai*
("to gaze on [or: envision] . . . the living God") and anachronistic
expressions from later Jewish mysticism: *ha'or hane'tsal* ("the sublime
[or: emanating] light") and *'ein sof* ("infinity [or: infinite God]").

These terms suggest that Saul's visionary experience will resemble both that of the prophet and the mystic. In this revelation of God, Saul will discover how to liberate himself fully from the contradictory extremes of life of which he is so fully aware.

After Saul and the prophets partake of the sacrificial meal, they begin a frenzied dance that progresses through five stages of intensity. In an allusion to the account in I Samuel 19, in which Saul strips himself of all his clothing, at each stage of the dance Saul removes some article which he is wearing until he falls to the ground naked at the end of the poem. As he removes each article, Saul symbolically removes a barrier between himself and some aspect of existence until he gradually ascends to the revelation of which the prophet had spoken before the meal. In this revelation he discovers the unity of all of existence.

In the first stage Saul and the prophets join hands in song and dance around the sacrificial altar. As they dance they experience a sense of unity among themselves. That unity, however, is not yet complete: they dance in a war-like manner, with some playing the role of the attackers and others playing the role of the attacked. In the midst of this stage of dancing Saul removes his crown, thereby symbolically removing the barrier between himself as king and the rest of the people of Israel:

> And hand in hand then the prophets pranced,
> To the right, to the left, they backed and advanced
> Then leaping ahead, now swaying, now cheering,
> As in siege of a wall, like besieged disappearing;
> From moment to moment their joy gathered might,
> As their bodies strained for the heights, for the height.
>
> Then the King put aside his coronet of gold,
> He cast away the ornament of splendor,
> And the crown fell to the ground, where it bounced
> And resounded and again rolled and rang.
> Then also fell the dividing wall
> That stood between him and all his people,
> The division erected by man for man,
> And he was as all Israel, one of his people (pp. 83–84).

In the second stage the prophets continue to be not fully united, but at those times when they do come together, they are closer than they had been in the first stage. In this stage Saul removes his harp, thereby divesting himself of the instrument that represented the barrier which God had made between him as a skilled musician and other human beings:

And arm in arm then the prophets swirled,
To the right, to the left, they yelled and they whirled,
Splitting apart, returning, uniting,
In a circle of bustle, rearing and rioting;
From moment to moment their joy gathered might,
As their hearts yearned for the heights, for the height.

Then he put aside his cypress-wood harp,
He cast his instrument of song into the bushes,
And the harp fell among the tangle of branches,
Where its strings broke. Each string with its sigh.
Then also fell the dividing wall
That stood between him and all men,
The division erected by the Creator of the world,
And he was as all men on earth (p. 84).

In the third stage the prophets are no longer divided. As they join closer and closer together in an insanely wild dance, they lose their sense of separate existence. Saul now removes his sword, thereby renouncing the tool that divides him from all living creatures who are threatened by such human weapons of destruction:

And hand in hand then the prophets went wild,
To the right, to the left, aloft now, in flight,
Embracing each other, and cleaving and cleaving,
Body to body, kissing and heaving;
From moment to moment their closeness gained might,
Their being would end in the heights, in the height.

Then he put aside his sword, the sword of his pride,
He cast his implement of war into the rocks,

> And the weapon fell upon the stone,
> Where it hit the rock, and rang out.
> Then also fell the dividing wall
> That stood between him and all life on earth,
> The division of hate between life and man,
> And he was as all that lives on the face of the earth (p. 84).

In the fourth stage the prophets are so united that it is no longer possible to see them as individuals. The king now removes his royal garment. In doing so, he removes the barrier between himself as a civilized human being and the rest of nature:

> And body to body the prophets whirled striving,
> Straining to the skies but never arriving,
> Straining in fury, to the right, to the left,
> Between body and body no difference, no cleft;
> From moment to moment their frenzy gained might,
> As their souls longed for the heights, for the height.

> And he put aside his clothes, the robe of his rule,
> He cast his raiment of monarchy to earth,
> And the cloth of his splendor fell on the path,
> Where it lay gleaming, embroidered, and white.
> Then also fell the dividing wall
> That stood between him and all of Creation,
> Erected by the forces of *In the beginning*,
> And he was as all that was wrought by God's word (p 84).

In the fifth and final stage the prophets become one body as they reach their highest level of ecstasy. The king, who shares this experience with them, finally throws himself to the ground in a state of complete nakedness and full harmony with all of existence:

> In one many-faced body the prophets united,
> Leaping right, leaping left, dancing, excited,
> Tripping on tree trunks and stray altar stones,
> Rolling on grass and down scented lawns;
> From moment to moment their union gained might,
> As their spirits rose up to the heights, to the height.

And the Spirit of God came upon His anointed;
And the King began prophesying among them,
And became one with the universe and the fullness thereof,
One tiny spark in the infinity of being,
Loving and cleaving to all of Creation.
And he fell down naked, all that day,
And all the night . . . naked . . . naked . . . naked . . . (p. 84).

The description of Saul's discovery of the oneness of existence in the prophets' dance and in his gradual divestment of his clothing links this revelation to a chain of alternative traditions which attract Tchernichowsky as a way out of the cultural degeneracy of his time. The earliest link is that of the primitive sacrificial cults and ecstatic outbursts of early prophets described in I Samuel. The next is that of the Jewish mystical tradition, the expressions of which are used by one of the prophets to describe what Saul will be able to discover. The prophets are described anachronistically as dancing a *meḥol ḥasidim* ("Hasidic dance"). It is clear from this reference to Hasidism that Tchernichowsky sees in this late manifestation of Jewish mysticism the next link in this chain of alternative traditions. Finally, Tchernichowsky has the prophet speak of the revelation of freedom *(deror)* and describe the king as becoming like one of his people *(ke'aḥad 'ammo)*. These expressions, which by Tchernichowsky's time had become secular Jewish national concepts used by Hebrew writers to express their yearning for national freedom and their identification with the folk, suggest that the poet sees modern Zionism as the most recent link in this chain of alternative traditions.

Saul's revelation is also connected to his being, in the biblical text, a man on the brink of insanity. The notion of the "spirit of God" coming upon Saul in I Samuel refers both to the ecstatic religious experiences of Saul and the prophets and to Saul's intermittent outbreaks of depression. In a similar vein, the dancing prophets, among whom Saul receives his revelation, are described with the word *hishtag'u* ("went wild [or: crazy]"). It is clear that Tchernichowsky shares in the modern romantic glorification of the insane as in possession of special insights from which the civilized sane world has been barred.

The figure of Saul as king, prophet, mystic, poet, and crazy man represents the role that Tchernichowsky seeks to play in a time of cultural and political upheaval. It is the poet who can envision the resolution of the conflicts of his time. If the world that Tchernichowsky knows has been torn apart by war, hatred, and destruction, its only hope is to turn to him as a poet who can show it where civilization has gone wrong. From the poet's point of view, the error of civilization has been to take too seriously the structures that divide human beings from each other and from nature. Only by becoming aware of the poet's discovery of the unity of existence will the peoples of Europe reconstruct their culture and build a world based on harmony and peace.

In this retelling of an event from the life of Saul when the king was at the height of his powers, Tchernichowsky presents a most positive image of Saul. Saul is transformed in this poem from a powerful king with a flawed character to one who discovers the essential truths of human existence. It is Saul, not the prophet Samuel, who is in touch with the truth. The conflict between king and prophet portrayed in "Be'ein-dor" is replaced here by the portrait of the king as a prophet whose vision is superior to Samuel's.[17] Similarly, it is Shaul Tchernichowsky, the modern poet, who is the truly proper leader of the people who through his unique sensitivity can show them the way to be liberated from the agonies of the present historical moment.

Saul's ecstatic dance in "Hamelekh" bears some resemblance to Timna's dance at the end of Frischmann's story "Meholot." In both dances the authors seek to represent their role as artists bringing a modern revelation of transcendent unity to their people. Timna's and Saul's dances are ultimately individual, and perhaps also lonely acts of self-expression, as are the attempts of these modern writers to compose works of literature. When Timna and Saul each fall to the ground in either death or exhaustion, without necessarily having had any effect on others, one senses the essentially frustrating task of the modern writer who expends his energies on an outpouring of the self without any assurance that his message has been communicated to the people or that it will transform them in the way it has transformed him.

The Death of Saul Reconsidered

Having devoted the first two Saul ballads to the death of the king, and the next one to a portrait of the king at the height of his powers, Tchernichowsky returned once more in the last two Saul ballads to the death of the king. In keeping with his preoccupation in the late 1920s and 1930s with the struggle of the Jews and Arabs over the Land of Israel, Tchernichowsky focused in these two final poems on the figure of Saul as the commander of the Israelite forces in their battle with the Philistines.

"'Al harei gilboa'" retells the account of the Philistines' victorious battle against the Israelites that followed Saul's desperate attempt to seek guidance from the ghost of Samuel at En-dor (I Samuel 31:1–7). In the course of the battle the Philistines kill Saul's three sons, Jonathan, Abinadab, and Malchi-shua. Realizing that he is about to be defeated, Saul asks his arms-bearer to kill him so that he will not be taken captive and made sport of by the enemy. The arms-bearer, unable to take upon himself the awesome task of killing the king, refuses to do so. Saul then commits suicide, as does his arms-bearer. The Israelites seeing that they have lost their leader and that their army has been defeated, flee from their towns, which are soon occupied by the victorious Philistines.

Tchernichowsky's interest in this account of Saul's last stand against the Philistines was very likely sparked by the Arab massacre of the Jews of Hebron in the Land of Israel in 1929. In the original version of the story there is an account of a complete defeat of the Israelites by their enemies, who force them to flee from their homes. In choosing this biblical account of military defeat, Tchernichowsky radically transforms the portrait of Saul. He is so disturbed by the national defeat that has occurred in Hebron that he retells the story of Saul's final battle not as one in which he gives up and commits suicide, but rather as one in which Saul refuses to give in to the overwhelming odds against him and insists on fighting heroically to the end. Although his arms-bearer repeatedly urges him to rest, Saul refuses to listen to him. When he hears of the deaths of his sons in battle, he is even more strengthened in his resolve to fight on.

Saul's declarations during the battle reflect Tchernichowsky's protest against those he feels are responsible for the modern defeat at Hebron. When Saul calls out to "those who sit on their weapons" and he condemns "the slanderers and lazy stragglers"[18] who have not joined in the fighting, Tchernichowsky is expressing his anger at those who have not fully supported the Zionist enterprise, as well as those who have actively opposed it.[19] When toward the end of the poem Saul asks rhetorically, "Is Israel a lamb to be slaughtered like sheep?!"[20] Tchernichowsky is expressing his anguish as he contemplates the weakness of the Jews of Hebron in the face of their enemies. In Saul's final call for Israelites to replace those who have fallen in battle one senses an even more blatant emergence of Tchernichowsky's voice calling for increased emigration ('aliyyah, going up) to the Land of Israel in order to strengthen the hand of the Jews there in their battle to establish Jewish sovereignty against the opposition of the Arab majority. There is a particular poignancy to Tchernichowsky's call for increased emigration to the Land of Israel, considering how much he desired to emigrate himself at the time but was kept from doing so by his inability to find proper employment.[21]

"'Al harei gilboaʿ" is written with the romantic glorification of the Zionist struggle that would be expected of a poet still living in the diaspora detached from the actual scene of the events to which he is reacting. In contrast, "ʾAnshei ḥayil ḥevel," written in Tel Aviv, reflects the more sober perspective on the Zionist struggle of one who lives in the Land of Israel and is more in touch with the full range of realities of that struggle.

The poem, dated March 11, 1936, was written during a period when tensions between Jews and Arabs in the Land of Israel had reached great heights. Although the major rioting and protest strikes by Arabs in that year did not begin until a month after the poem was written,[22] it is clear that, as in 1929, the struggle between Arabs and Jews over control of the Land of Israel brought to mind again for Tchernichowsky the biblical conflict between the Philistines and Saul.

"ʾAnshei ḥayil ḥevel" retells the accounts found in I Samuel 31 and in I Chronicles 10 of how the "stalwart men" of Jabesh-gilead carried the bodies of Saul and his sons from the place of their desecration in Beth-shan to their burial in Jabesh under either a tamarisk tree (according to the version in I Samuel) or an oak tree (according to the version in I Chronicles). As in "ʿAl harei gilboaʿ," which takes place at the time of Saul's last battle against the Philistines, "ʾAnshei ḥayil ḥevel," which takes place after Saul has died in that battle, portrays the weakness of the Israelites in the face of their enemies which Tchernichowsky associates with the struggle of the Jewish minority against the Arab majority in 1929 and 1936.[23] Tchernichowsky's assessment of the Jews' weakness in the later poem is much graver, however, than his assessment of their weakness in the earlier poem. Whereas the Jews' weakness is suggested in "ʿAl harei gilboaʿ" by means of Saul's defiant commitment to fight on even though the Israelites are outnumbered by their enemies, their weakness is indicated in "ʾAnshei ḥayil ḥevel" by the need of the bearers of the dead king's corpse to walk steathily up into the mountains in order to avoid the powerful Philistines who control the valleys.

Tchernichowsky is more concerned in "ʾAnshei ḥayil ḥevel" with the Jewish deaths that are the result of the struggle for the Land of Israel than he is in glorifying the ability of Jews to stand up against all odds. His response to those deaths is full of irony and bitterness. The poet describes the bearing of the bodies of Saul and his sons on a pole, which calls to mind the carrying of the fruit of Canaan by the spies in the days of Moses when the people were preparing themselves to enter the land (Numbers 13).[24] There is an irony to this allusion in that it points to the terrible contrast between the dream of the fruit that modern Zionism would bear and the reality of the dead bodies of Jewish settlers killed by Arabs. The modern reality would seem to confirm the truth of the ten spies' fear that Israel would not be able to prevail over the inhabitants of the land and that indeed it was a land "that devours its settlers" (Numbers 13:32). The bodies of Saul and his sons are described as being wrapped in Egyptian cloth. This image alludes to the burials of Jacob and Joseph, whose bodies were prepared in Egypt for burial but were eventually carried up and buried in Canaan. In this allusion Tchernichowsky points to the irony that for so many of the modern settlers in Zion, as for Jacob and Joseph, their return to the land has consisted of burial in the grave.

It is in "'Anshei ḥayil ḥevel" that Saul finally finds the javelin that he left behind when he went to En-dor in the poem "Beʿein-dor," that he sought in "ʿAl ḥorvot beit-shan," and that he cast aside in "Hamelekh." He has used it, according to the poem, for the purpose of killing himself and his sons. While the biblical Saul did kill himself, he did not kill his sons directly by his javelin in the way that Tchernichowsky's version suggests. By declaring that Saul used the javelin to kill himself and his sons the poet is saying that just as the battles led by Saul ended in his death and the death of his sons, so there is a suicidal and even infanticidal aspect to modern Jewish settlement in the Land of Israel, for Jews are constantly subjecting themselves and their children to the mortally dangerous violent Arab opposition to Zionism. In the Land of Israel Jews have ironically reverted to dying in a way that resembles the martyrdom of the Crusades that medieval liturgical poetry had represented in the image of Saul's death. Nevertheless, despite the dangers inherent in the Zionist enterprise, the poet declares, the Jews cannot allow themselves to abandon the Land of Israel any more than the lion can "forsake his rocky home."[25]

Until 1936, even in those poems that focused on the defeat of Saul, Tchernichowsky had never chosen to write about the final burial of Saul as recounted at the end of I Samuel. "Beʿein-dor" concludes with Saul's return to his camp in despair. "ʿAl ḥorvot beit-shan" is written as if Saul had not found his rest in a proper burial. "ʿAl harei gilboaʿ" creates the impression that Saul survived the battle in which he called on others to aid him. In writing this final ballad on Saul, Tchernichowsky was ready to put the ancient king to rest by describing his burial. As he grew closer to the time of his own death, Tchernichowsky apparently began to face the realization that most human struggles, no matter how noble, are not resolved in the lifetime of one individual, and thus not all that he had fought for in his attempts to radically transform European Jewish culture and support the Zionist movement would be accomplished while he still lived. His only comfort in this realization was the hope that others would remember and carry on the fight for the cultural renewal of the Jews to which he had been so passionately committed.

Chapter 5

Men and Women in the Bible: Yocheved Bat-Miriam

Like this before you, just as I am
Not charming, not painted with pink and blue
But wild and rebellious, very bad,
So do I wish to stand before you.

Thus and thus is the measure of my height,
And so my life upon earth must be.
A larger measure for my soul's ascent,
Wandering silent it escapes its captivity.

My words will not soar me up to the heights
My words melt, suddenly frightened away.
Is it so, is it so I will speak to you,
I who am dying from day to day?[1]

In much of the poetry of Yocheved Bat-Miriam a female speaker yearns to unite with a distant being who appears to her mainly as either a male lover or divine being. The absence of the being tends to arouse in the speaker feelings of rejection, loneliness, guilt, and worthlessness. In some poems, as in the passage quoted at the opening of this chapter, the speaker comes to doubt whether she will ever be united with the being. She therefore rebelliously declares that her sense of self-worth is independent of the acceptance or rejection of the distant being. The qualities in her that he apparently considers to be bad become for her the very ones she affirms to be worthwhile.

This cycle of distance, rejection, loneliness, guilt, worthlessness, and rebellious affirmation of self-worth operates for speakers in Bat-Miriam's poems not only in their relationship with God and with male lovers, but also in their contemplation of the mortality of their existence. In some of her poems existence itself seems to have withdrawn from the speaker and to have rejected her by denying her immortality and causing her to confront death "from day to day." God, male lovers, and death all have in common the ability and inclination to limit the speaker's desire for self-expression, self-worth, and self-fulfillment and to condemn her individual soul to oblivion. It is more difficult for the speakers, however, to affirm their self-worth in the face of death than in the face of a rejecting God or male lover.

In some of Bat-Miriam's poems, the speaker affirms her self-worth by turning from the rejecting male lover or God and imagining an accepting being who lives in a realm beyond that of everyday reality. It is this imaginary being, who may resemble a human or divine being, who finally affirms her worth. The approach toward poetry conveyed by speakers in Bat-Miriam's poems corresponds to the discovery by speakers in her poems of accepting imaginary beings. Just as some speakers feel that any attempt to define their self-worth in terms of their acceptance by a male lover or God is limiting, so there are speakers who express the feeling that in writing poetry any attempt to allow reality to determine the content of their poetry is limiting. Just as some speakers must imaginatively transcend their longing to be attached to a male lover or to God, so there are speakers who feel the need to transcend reality so that their poetry will be fully expressive. Thus in general, for speakers in Bat-Miriam's poetry it is imagination that allows the soul to successfully "escape its captivity."

Like the speakers in her poems, for Yocheved Bat-Miriam, the woman, the Jew, the mortal, and the poet, external reality would not do as a source of affirmation of worth. She needed to discover that worth in the freedom of her imagination, which reflected but also refashioned reality in her own image.[2]

This feeling of constant struggle to be liberated from the external limitations of reality may have derived from two sets of experiences: those related to her life as a woman in transition from traditional to modern society and those related to her life as an immigrant. She was born to a traditional Jewish family in Keplits, Belorussia, but she received a secular university education. Her exposure to modern society in the university must have raised questions in her mind about the role of women in traditional Jewish culture both in terms of relations between men and women and relations between Jewish women and a masculine God.[3] After emigrating to the Land of Israel in the 1920s, she was forced to deal with the new realities of the land which attracted her but also seemed to her to be strange and elusive.[4] Her marriage to the Hebrew writer Hayyim Hazaz was problematic and eventually ended in divorce.[5]

Bat-Miriam's concerns as a woman, a Jew, a mortal, and a poet found expression in "Bein ḥol veshemesh," ("Between Sand and Sun"), a cycle of poems which she published in the late 1930s and early 1940s. The poems in this cycle portray six biblical characters: Miriam, Saul, Abraham, Hagar, Adam, and Eve.[6] In Bat-Miriam's retelling of their stories these characters struggle like the poet to find fulfillment and self-worth despite the limitations inherent in their relationships with the opposite sex, God, mortality, and reality as a whole.

Miriam

Bat-Miriam's choice of the Hebrew name Bat-Miriam to replace her original family name of Zhelezniak suggests that she closely identified with the biblical character of Miriam. The poem "Miryam" ("Miriam") draws on three major events in the life of Miriam as recorded in the Bible. In each event Miriam took the initiative to do something that affected the leadership of Moses over the Israelites. In the first event (Exodus 2:1–10), she helped to save Moses from death as an infant so that he would be able to grow up to lead the Israelites out of Egypt. After her parents placed her baby brother in a basket on the Nile to avoid Pharaoh's decree to kill all Hebrew male babies, she waited by the Nile to see what would happen to him. When Pharaoh's daughter found Moses, Miriam offered her mother as a wetnurse for the baby. By making this offer, Miriam made it more certain that Pharaoh's daughter would decide to adopt Moses, and she helped assure that Moses would benefit from being nurtured by his natural Israelite mother.

In the second event (Exodus 15:20–21), she functioned as a prophetess in a role of leadership parallel to that of her brother Moses. After the miraculous crossing of the Sea of Reeds by the Israelites and the drowning of their Egyptian pursuers, the celebration of their having been saved consisted both of Moses leading the Israelites as a whole in song and Miriam leading the Israelite women in song and dance. In the third event (Numbers 12:1–16), which took place during the wandering of the Israelites in the wilderness, Miriam and her brother Aaron challenged Moses' marriage to a Cushite woman and then called into question their brother's preeminence as the leader of Israel. God was angered at their opposition to His chosen prophet, so He punished Miriam (but curiously not Aaron) by afflicting her with a leprous-like skin disease for which she was quarantined from the camp for seven days.

The poem "Miryam" begins with a portrait of Miriam standing before Moses in his basket hidden in the reeds of the Nile. As she awaits the fateful role she is to play as the one who will save Moses, the future liberator of the Israelites, Miriam symbolically inhales the limitless power of the stars of heaven and the sands of the wilderness. In doing so she connects herself with the past promise of God to Abraham that his people will be as numerous as the stars and sand as well as with the liberating experience of the future exodus of the people from Egypt to the wilderness that will take them to Canaan.

The potential for freedom, which Miriam's situation represents, is sharply contrasted by the portrait of Egypt as a land frozen by limitation. As the sun shines on the scene, it resembles the eye of the ancient Egyptian god Apis, the bull-god of the Nile, who was sometimes depicted with the sun between his horns. Apis is presented here as a sleepy god who floods Egypt with a light that casts a spell of mystery and inertia. This spell is embodied in the secretive smile of Pharaoh's daughter, the magicians' hieroglyphics frozen in stone, and the music of the royal palace, which resembles a monotonous, rhythmic marching song.

In opposition to the frozen mystery of Egypt, the Israelites, represented metonymically as Goshen, the place of their sojourn in Egypt, are beginning to awake to a dynamic liberation. In a lowly state resembling a trampled snake, the Israelite tribes emerge from the ashes of their destroyed past before slavery and recover their desire to live. This desire is portrayed to be as boundless as the instinctive drive of the poisonous viper snake to attack his enemy in order to survive. At this point, however, the Israelites have not yet achieved full liberation. Their new identity as a confederation of tribes ready to settle Canaan is still foreign to them. It is characterized as an adopted, obscure image, not a firmly established identity that has emerged naturally from them.

Goshen is portrayed in the poem by means of both masculine and feminine images. The Hebrew word for "memory" which is used, *zekher*, has the same root as the word for "masculine," *zakher*. The viper imagery has phallic connotations. At the same time, the Hebrew word for "desire" which is used, *ta'avah*, is feminine in form, and Goshen, like all place names in Hebrew, is feminine, and thus the Hebrew word for "adopted," *'imtsah*, appears in the feminine form. This latter image alludes as well to the adoption of Moses by Pharaoh's daughter at the Nile. The creative masculine and feminine energies of the people are being called forth in this period of national liberation: the reaching forward of the sexually aroused phallus, which is part of the process of procreation, and the mother's nurturing drawing of her baby toward herself.

The speaker of the poem then addresses Miriam as the figure who she believes is even more capable than Moses to liberate the ancient Israelite men and women and the speaker herself. In her imagination, the speaker joins Miriam in her dance celebrating the deliverance of the Israelites from the Egyptians at the Sea of Reeds. The dance is not portrayed, as in the biblical text, as a group dance, but rather as that of Miriam alone. Her body, extended like an ancient drum (*tof*), dances before the limitless sands of the wilderness and expresses in this way her liberation and the expansion of her perspective.

Miriam's liberation is celebrated in the dance at the Sea of Reeds, but, from the speaker's point of view, it is actually fully achieved only when she challenges the masculine authority of Moses after his marriage to the Cushite woman. The speaker identifies with Miriam, because she considers her own condition to be parallel to that of Miriam complaining against Moses. Just as Miriam was jealous of the Cushite woman and of Moses' power and was therefore punished with a skin disease by the masculine God, so the speaker portrays herself as "jealous and leprous." Unlike Miriam in the Bible, however, the speaker directs her anger not against the masculine authority, but against herself. She becomes the object of her own complaint. She has so fully accepted the masculine authority's opinion that she is worthy of punishment, that she must torture herself with the conviction that she is unworthy. In the biblical story Moses is Miriam's brother, but God also compares His anger at Miriam to the image of a father spitting in his daughter's face. The tension between the female speaker and a male figure would thus appear to encompass the experiences of sibling rivalry with a brother or a conflict between a daughter and her father. The speaker's use of the word "jealous" would extend the possibility of including the relationship of a female lover or wife to her male lover or husband who has left her for another woman.

Miriam provides the inspiration for the speaker's liberation from a stronger masculine authority, be he brother, father, lover, or husband. The speaker portrays Miriam's leprosy and isolation outside the Israelite camp as a freely chosen state of Nazirite abstention whose purpose is to declare an unyielding stance toward masculine authority. Rather than internalize the negative image forced on her by the masculine authority, Miriam has created for herself a positive self-image that will lead her to a truly liberated way of living.

Having discovered the way to personal self-liberation from dominance by masculine authority, Miriam emerges as the liberator of Israel. In the final stanza of the poem, the scene returns to Miriam standing by the infant Moses' basket in the Nile. Miriam prays for the well-being of the infant Moses and watches over him like a mother. Like a divine figure, she seeks to establish his future fate by commanding him to follow certain ways of living. The male-female relationship earlier in the poem has been radically changed. Miriam is no longer the victim of Moses' authority, but rather the parental authority and divine being teaching the male child the path to liberation.

In this retelling of the story of the exodus from Egypt, it is not Moses the man who is the leader of the people, but rather Miriam the woman. The emergence of Miriam as the true liberator of Israel comes about as a result of her personal struggle to be liberated from the power of masculine authority. Bat-Miriam declares in this poem her belief that there is an important need for the twentieth-century Jewish woman to discover her own independent sense of self-worth. Once she does, she like Miriam can point the way for both male and female Jews to be free of those forces that foster in them negative images of self-worth. These forces would include the anti-Semitism of gentile society, represented in the poem by the Israelites' enslavement in Egypt, and the guilt-inducing masculine religion of traditional Jewish society, represented in the poem by the angry male God who so cruelly punishes Miriam. When Jews are finally liberated from these forces, they will be free to discover the positive sense of self-worth which is the prerequisite for true individual and national liberation.

Saul

In the poem "Sha'ul" ("Saul"), dedicated by the poet to her brother Saul,[7] Bat-Miriam focuses on the agony of mortal human beings confronting the reality of death. To explore this issue Bat-Miriam appropriately chose to retell the story of Saul's request of the woman at En-dor to raise the ghost of Samuel so that the prophet might help him to avoid defeat and death in the battle with the Philistines (I Samuel 28). The poem begins with a description of Saul's ride to En-dor. The description alludes to experiences of failure connected with Saul's relationship with Samuel during his life. Saul rides on aimless asses that recall the lost asses of his father, which he had asked Samuel's help in finding (I Samuel 9). His clothing is scattered like the garment torn by Samuel in their confrontation over Saul's failure to fulfill the commandment to wipe out all of Amalek (I Samuel 15). As he rides, he realizes that because of his transgression of God's commandment, his descendants will not inherit his royal throne. Like a mere commoner he will not have any glory to pass on to them.

When the woman at En-dor raises Samuel from the dead, he appears to perform a ceremony in which he anoints Saul, as he had done in the past. At this anointing, however, Saul does not appear as the divinely confirmed king of Israel. Instead, he appears as a confused, guilt-ridden man who has been rejected by the angry authority of God's prophet.

In contrast to the biblical version, Samuel does not speak in the poem. Instead, Saul delivers a monologue of entreaty to Samuel which derives from his statement in the biblical version, "Woe is me" (*tsar li me'od*) (I Samuel 28:15). There is a difference, however, between that which vexes Saul in the biblical version of the story and that which vexes him in Bat-Miriam's version. Whereas Saul's vexation in the Bible comes from his being helpless in the face of the surrounding Philistine enemy as well as in the face of his rejection by God, in the poem he is vexed by the realization that his desires and longings are limitless, while his life is not.

In the poem "Sha'ul," the conflict between Saul and Samuel becomes a conflict between the human drive to imagine and desire, represented by Saul, and the limitations of mortal human existence, represented by Samuel. The king, who is capable of ecstatic prophecy as well as of defying God's commandment, represents human desire and imagination, which bring inspiration and blessing to human beings, yet are ultimately defeated by death. Bat-Miriam portrays Samuel's anointing of Saul as king and his imposition on him of responsibilities that limit his natural inclinations as, in the words of the poem, the "crowning death" of mortality which limits the creative spirit of the human being.

Significantly, this conflict between desire and death is portrayed as a female-male conflict. Saul turns to the woman at En-dor to reveal to him the way to find fulfillment for his desires. Instead he sees a vision of the man Samuel who reminds him of his mortality. The expression which refers to Saul's desire, *kelot nafshi* ("my soul's desire") and the word which refers to Saul's soul, *nafshi* ("my soul") are feminine, as are the participles and verbs which accompany them. On the other hand, the word for Saul's death, *moti* ("my death") and the expression that refers to the limited time allotted to him in life, *yomi hakavua⁽* ("my fixed time"), are masculine, as are the participle and verb which accompany them. This conflict between feminine desires and masculine limitations is emphasized by the interplay between time, which according to Saul does not *know* (in the masculine form *yeda⁽*) how to contain the soul's desire, and the soul, which, according to Saul, does not *know* (in the feminine form *teda⁽*) how to submit to death. There is in this tension between human desire and human mortality an echo of the female-male tensions expressed in the poem 'Miryam." Thus the drive to be liberated from the limiting force of mortality is associated in this poem with the rebellious impulses of women against male dominance.

In the biblical version of the story, Saul leaves the scene at En-dor to return to die in his final battle. In Tchernichowsky's version, Saul is portrayed as immersed in suicidal despair. In Bat-Miriam's version, Saul declares to Samuel at the end of the poem that while he recognizes the inevitability of his mortality, his soul will not be fully subject to the power of death. Instead, it will follow the path of the poet who enters into the world of imagination beyond this world of reality and there transforms the "splendor and suffering" of life into an aesthetic creation. That path will provide a kind of victory of the desiring soul over its fixed time on earth.

Abraham and Hagar

Given Bat-Miriam's preoccupation with the experience of a woman being rejected by a man, it is not surprising that she chose to retell the story of Abraham's expulsion of Hagar (Genesis 21). In the biblical context its main significance lies in the way that the events of the story serve the divine plan for the descendants of Abraham. When Abraham resisted fulfilling Sarah's demand to expel Hagar and her son Ishmael from their household, God commanded him to fulfill it, for it was part of His plan for Isaac to be the next patriarch of Israel and for Ishmael to be the father of a different nation. The biblical text, however, does not ignore the human significance of the story as well. For the biblical author the story is not only a link in the chain of events comprising the divine plan, but also one of jealous rivalry between Sarah and Hagar, which results in the cruel suffering of Hagar and Ishmael. This human significance is emphasized in God's response to the suffering of Hagar and Ishmael when He reveals a well to Hagar so that she and her son will have water to drink and also assures her that like Isaac, Ishmael will be rewarded by being the progenitor of a great nation.

In the poems ")Avraham" ("Abraham") and "Hagar" ("Hagar") Bat-Miriam displays little interest in the relationship of the story to the biblical divine plan. Instead, she emphasizes the human side of the story in which the focus is on Hagar's suffering. That suffering, however, is transformed from that of an ancient Middle Eastern handmaiden expelled from the patriarch's household because of a jealous wife to that of the situation of the rejection of a woman by her male lover. Bat-Miriam uses the characters of the biblical story to explore the motivation of the male lover for rejecting the woman and the ways that the rejected woman deals with the humiliation of having been rejected, recovers her dignity, and reaffirms her sense of self-worth.

")Avraham" begins with allusions to the covenant made between Abraham and God during which Abraham cut several sacrificial animals in two (Genesis 15). At night Abraham fell into a deep sleep. A flaming torch then passed through the halves of the animals, and God assured him that he would beget a son and that his descendants would inherit Canaan. The account of that covenant is followed immediately in the biblical text by the account of how Hagar came to bear the child Ishmael to Abraham with the consent of Sarah, who was barren at that time. (Genesis 16). This juxtaposition of the covenant and the story of Hagar may have suggested to Bat-Miriam a convergence of images by which she could use the character of Abraham to say something about the nature of male-female relations in her day.

At the beginning of the poem Abraham is portrayed with the

images of sleep, darkness, night, and a flaming torch related to those that accompany the biblical description of Abraham's vision at the time of the covenant. Standing on the threshold of a house of God, Abraham seeks to escape the images of light and fire that are being revealed to him. He retreats into sleep and darkness from an image of lightning, and he digs a well for cool water to relieve himself of an image of flame.

It turns out that the images of light and fire revealed to Abraham are a prelude to the more specific image that he is trying unsuccessfully to escape: Hagar. Abraham's expulsion of Hagar converges in this vision with the sacrifice he performed when he made the covenant with God. Since Hagar looks to Abraham "like a trembling turtledove," one of the animals Abraham cut into two at the time of the covenant with God, her expulsion appears in the poem to have been a kind of sacrifice. As he stands on the threshold of God's house, he addresses Hagar as "the threshold of my borrowed youth." Abraham's youthful desire for Hagar is thus opposed in his mind to his longing to commune with God. In order to enter God's house and establish a covenant with Him, Abraham must extinguish the flames of his desire by rejecting and sacrificing Hagar. Abraham is unable, however, to quell the desires aroused by seeing the vision of Hagar.

In the midst of this tension between Abraham's physical desires and his spiritual yearnings, he begins to make an important discovery. His desires had seemed to weigh on him as he was weighted down with flocks and gold (see Genesis 13:2) because he had seen them as preventing him from drawing close to God. Now he realizes that in fact those desires are *not* opposed to God, but they are actually the embodiment of the divine presence. The vision of Hagar was thus not in opposition to the vision of God he sought, but rather a revelation of the erotic as a path to God. Abraham now understands that his expulsion of Hagar was unnecessary, for in reality the erotic is intimately bound up with the divine.

Oblivious to the inner conflicts which had led to Abraham's decision to expel her, Hagar sets forth at the beginning of the poem "Hagar" from the home of Abraham and Sarah as if she were sailing on a sea voyage marked by an atmosphere of loneliness, silence, and death. One might expect that Hagar, having been expelled from her home in Canaan, would be returning to her native Egypt. She declares, however, that her voyage is not back to the land of her birth, but rather it is a voyage in which she will confront the realities of her present condition and discover an alternative imagined reality that will allow her to transcend that condition.

Rejected by Abraham, Hagar comes to believe that her only true love is an elusive being with whom she is united as she enters the world of imagination. This being, like Hagar, is homeless and persecuted, but he also is capable of beautiful visions which defy commonly held notions of reality. Hagar flies off to be adopted by this being and to help him to realize his impossible dreams. This being embodies the inspiration to create a poetic world of the imagination which is more real than the world of painful reality.

It is likely that Bat-Miriam identifies with the portrait of Hagar in the poem as a woman who has responded to the depressing circumstances of her rejection by turning to the imaginative world of artistic creation. Bat-Miriam may also identify with Hagar the Egyptian in her decision not to return to her native land, despite the tragic circumstances of her life in Canaan. As an immigrant from Europe, Bat-Miriam similarly decided that despite the difficulties she encountered as a woman and a Jew in the Land of Israel, she would remain there and dedicate herself to create a poetic world in Hebrew in which these difficulties could be transcended.

Adam and Eve

In a pair of poems on the first man and woman, Adam and Eve, Bat-Miriam wrote of the differences she sensed between the ways men and women experience the world. The biblical accounts of creation in Genesis 1 and 2 differ on the nature of the creation of Adam and Eve. Genesis 1 tells of a simultaneous creation of the first man and woman. Genesis 2 relates that first Adam was created, and then Eve was created out of Adam's rib to be a fitting helper for him. According to the first account, Adam and Eve were never alone when they were created; according to the second account, Adam was alone until the creation of Eve, but Eve was never alone. In Bat-Miriam's version of the creation of Adam and Eve in the poems "'Adam" ("Adam") and "Ḥavvah" ("Eve") both Adam and Eve are created alone and experience periods of separation from each other before meeting. With this approach Bat-Miriam draws on the biblical notion of Adam's loneliness and his need for Eve to explore how men and women relate to life as separate individuals as well as what relationships between men and women add to their lives.

"'Adam" begins with a description of the tension inherent in Adam's lonely experience of the world before he meets Eve. This tension is portrayed by a series of images associated with the seashore. On the one hand, the world that Adam views is shining with the light reflected off the green moss of the sea and the shells of the beach. He feels a sense of wholeness before the divine grace that flows to him from God through his arms as if they were conduits leading directly from heaven. On the other hand, the world outside of Adam is troubling to him. It is an inscrutable riddle with an independent existence. It hovers over him like a storm cloud over the seashore, hiding a potential eruption. Adam's face is sprinkled with his tears as he longs for distant shores on which he would feel the undisturbed tranquility that could come only from a complete understanding of the world.

When he meets Eve, Adam's view of the world is suddenly transformed. In Genesis 2 Adam named all the animals right before the creation of Eve; in the poem, Adam remembers the names of all that makes up the world when he meets Eve. It is Eve who rescues him from his lonely, perplexed relationship with the world and puts him in touch with a full understanding of it. The storm that had been lurking in the mysterious riddle of the world is revealed to Adam when he enters into his relationship with Eve. The complexity of that relationship — her desire, his sorrow, his powerfully seductive manner — mirrors that storm that Adam had perceived in the outside world. This change in Adam's understanding of the world is presented in the poem as similar to a "fiery path of God," an allusion to the fiery sword of the cherubim (Genesis 3:24) that blocked

Adam's and Eve's return to Eden after they were expelled for eating the fruit of the tree of knowledge. The grace-filled wholeness of Adam's existence alone is now replaced by a fuller, more complex but less perplexing existence in the world together with Eve.

In the poem "Ḥavvah," Eve's individual relationship to the world is similar to Adam's in certain respects. Several expressions and images in the poem "ʾAdam" are echoed in the poem "Ḥavvah." She experiences the sense of divine grace (ḥesed) that he does. At the same time she shares much of his tearful longing and his realization that the world is free and independent of him. Adam dreams of "distant shores" (ḥofav hareḥokim), and Eve's face seems to reflect a "kind of flame blooming from afar" (kelehavah nifraḥat meraḥok). Adam's tears are described as "sprinkling" (dimʿato haroseset), and Eve's silence is "like an eye with drops of tears" (keʿayin birsisei hadimʿah). Adam stands perplexed before the riddle of the world which hovers in pure freedom (beḥerut tselulah), and Eve's silence wanders before things of the world "and their proud freedom" (devarim veḥerutam hageʾeh).

There is, however, an important difference between Eve's relationship to the world and that of Adam's. On Adam's face there is a kind of cloud which is a harbinger of the storm that may erupt when the hidden riddle of things is revealed. On Eve's face there is a kind of flame which lights up her perspective and brings a smile to her lips. Whereas Adam is trying to figure out the nature of the world, Eve reaches out to touch the world. When he meets Eve, Adam can finally remember the names of the fruit trees and the beasts of the field, whereas even before meeting Adam, Eve knows how to relate to the parts of the world without calling them by name. Adam's approach to the world is a more distant one, defining the world by categories; Eve's is a closer one, relating to the world as "the mother of all the living" (ʾem kol ḥai) (Genesis 3:20), "collecting and caressing each moment," as a mother caresses her child. Nevertheless, as a mother must wean her baby, so Eve realizes she must let the world go to pursue its inherent nature of freedom, "weaned, forgiven, and escaping."

In the poem "ʾAdam" when Adam meets Eve, he touches her and thereby gains understanding of the world. In "Ḥavvah" when

Eve sees Adam, she does not reach out to him. Instead, she observes him from afar. The sight of Adam provides for Eve the inspiration to express her knowledge of the world and her feelings of dread and exultation aroused by that knowledge. When Adam and Eve are expelled from Eden, Eve's role is not like that of Adam, who names and explains the complexities of life after paradise. Her role is to create an imaginative experience of tranquility for herself and for Adam like the traditional Jewish woman who prepares for the Sabbath in order to create a peaceful respite from the week for herself and her family. This tranquility echoes but also transcends the varied realities of human existence, ranging from the thorns and mortality of Adam's and Eve's post-paradise existence (Genesis 3:17–19) to its moments of glory.

In these poems Bat-Miriam makes use of the story of Adam and Eve to present a paradigm of relations between men and women. As individuals men and women are capable of experiencing the tranquility of divine grace, yet they are also susceptible to the anxiety of longings for distant fulfillment. While they are both fascinated by the independent world outside of themselves, their relationship to it is different. Men seek to understand the world by creating categories to explain its nature; women are able to understand the world by an intuitive interaction with it. Bat-Miriam presents women's understanding as deeper than that of men. It is only through contact with women that men begin to be able to understand the world in their limited way. Women, furthermore, discover for themselves and for men the path to grace-filled tranquility in the midst of the anxieties and frustrations of mortal life. That path consists of transforming the difficulties and glories of reality into an imaginative vision of a Sabbath-like world beyond this world of human existence.

Like the speakers in so many of Bat-Miriam's poems, the biblical characters portrayed in the "Bein ḥol veshemesh" series are caught in a conflict between inner desire and a limiting force. Each character seeks to overcome the limiting force either by directly defying it or by coming to terms with it. For Miriam and Abraham, the struggle is with both God and the opposite sex. Miriam struggles to assert her inner worth and show the Israelites the true path to freedom by challenging the masculine authority of Moses and God. She is ultimately victorious in her struggle and assumes the roles of human leader and divinity. Abraham is caught between two forces: God, whose holiness seems to demand that he reject the erotic urges associated with Hagar, and Hagar, whose sexual attractiveness seems to be in opposition to divinity. At first Abraham rejects Hagar for God, but he cannot fully suppress his desire for the sexuality she represents. He resolves the conflict by discovering that divinity and eros are not opposed to each other, but that in fact eros is one aspect of God's divinity.

Although the nature of their limiting forces is different, Saul and Hagar choose a similar way to overcome limitation. Saul confronts his mortality as the force that limits the complete fulfillment of all human desire. Hagar struggles with the loneliness and depression that she feels as a result of her rejection by Abraham. Each chooses the path of poetic imagination to create a world in which boundless desires can be fulfilled.

Adam and Eve both experience the limited ability of human beings to understand all the mysteries of life and fulfill all their longings. Each has a different way of perceiving the world, and so they need each other to arrive at a full understanding of the world. Eve's more intuitive imaginative way, which is similar to the poetic path of Saul and Hagar, is portrayed as the superior one, for it provides a Sabbath-like tranquility for both of them that resolves the difficulties of their existence.

The issues with which these characters struggle are permeated by conflicts between masculine and feminine energies. These energies are portrayed in ways which may seem dangerously close to oversimplified male-female stereotyping, yet they must be taken on their own terms as Bat-Miriam's metaphoric system for portraying conflicts between men and women within society as well as conflicts within her own soul. Feminine energies tend to be associated with unlimited desire, intuition, and imagination. Masculine energies tend to be associated with limitation, categorization, and arbitrary authority. For the most part, the male characters are associated with masculine energies and the female characters are associated with feminine energies. The one exception to this rule is Saul, whose feminine desires are in conflict with the masculine limitations of mortality.

The conflicts between masculine and feminine energies are never resolved by the triumph of the masculine over the feminine. Resolution comes either by the successful assertion of the feminine over the masculine or by a synthesis of the masculine and the feminine. Bat-Miriam appears to favor a synthesis of the two whenever possible: the contributions of both masculine and feminine energies to the liberation of the Israelites from their slavery in Egypt, Abraham's synthesis of masculine holiness and feminine sexuality, Hagar's discovery of a masculine being who will join her in the world of imagination, and the union of Adam and Eve. Where such a synthesis is not possible, as in the conflict between Miriam and Moses and the conflict between Saul's desires and his mortality, then what is called for is the assertion of the feminine, which is ultimately superior to the masculine. By rewriting biblical history to reflect this point of view, Bat-Miriam points to a similar need to transform the consciousness of modern Jews to take these feminine energies more seriously and strive to synthesize them with the masculine energies that have so dominated traditional Jewish culture.

Chapter 6

The Holocaust Survivor
and the Bible:
Amir Gilboa, Abba Kovner,
and Dan Pagis

More than anyone else alive the survivors of the Holocaust
know the suffering of the Holocaust world. They therefore
have a unique role to play as intermediaries conveying that world of
the victims and survivors to those who did not experience the war
at all. As Lawrence L. Langer has noted, the great challenge for
those survivors who have chosen to write works of literature about
the Holocaust world lies in making intelligible experiences that were
so radically different from what anyone has experienced before or
since the war:

> Haunted by their private visions of disaster, they had returned
> from their varied encounters with hell ... alone, bereft of
> everything but memory and the consciousness that irrationality
> and unreality were the very essence of *l'univers concentrationnaire* and
> must somehow be incorporated into their art.[1]

In the works of these survivors one hears

> a cry from those who have returned from beyond the symbolic
> grave and wonder how to reestablish contact with the living — if
> they ever can.[2]

As the Israeli Holocaust survivor writer Aharon Appelfeld has pointed out, it is not easy for the survivor to play this role of intermediary. Once he undertakes to do so, he may find himself hiding the awful realities of the Holocaust from himself as well as from those who did not experience the war:

> And just as the [survivor] witness could not continue to stand in the space of this terror, neither could the Jew who had not experienced it. A kind of covenant of silence was created between the survivor witness and the one to whom, as it were, this testimony was directed, a covenant of silence in the path of which many misunderstandings have accumulated.[2]

One way that Holocaust survivor writers have sought to play this difficult role of intermediary between the world of the Holocaust and the world of those who did not experience it has been to retell biblical stories whose events represent those of the Holocaust. Three contemporary Israeli poets who were survivors of the Holocaust, Amir Gilboa, Abba Kovner, and Dan Pagis, have attempted to do this in their poetry. The three poets' involvement in the Holocaust varied greatly. Gilboa's involvement was the least direct. He was born in Radzywilow, Volhynia, and emigrated to the Land of Israel to work as a Zionist pioneer settler (*haluts*) at the age of twenty before World War II broke out. While he himself did not physically experience the war, he was intimately affected by it when after his emigration his parents and two brothers and four sisters, who had remained in Europe, were killed by the Nazis. Although his status as a survivor might be called into question, he has been included in this chapter because in his poetry he seems to aspire to the role of survivor-intermediary between the Holocaust and the world which did not experience the Holocaust.

Kovner and Pagis may more strictly speaking be considered survivors of the war. Kovner was born in Sevastopol, Russia, and grew up in Vilna, Lithuania. He had hoped to emigrate to the Land of Israel as a member of a Zionist youth group, but was not able to do so due to the outbreak of World War II. During the war, he became a leader of the Vilna ghetto revolt against the Nazis. Following the collapse of the revolt, he fought against the Nazis as a partisan in the forests of Vilna. He emigrated to the Land of Israel at the end of the war. Pagis's suffering in the war was the severest of the three. Born in Radutz, Bukovina, he spent three years of his childhood imprisoned in a concentration camp. He, too, emigrated to the Land of Israel after the war.[4]

In each of their poems retelling biblical stories, these writers attempt not only to communicate their own experiences as survivors but also those of the victims who cannot speak for themselves. Their re-creation of the distant yet familiar world of the Bible is analogous to their attempt to re-create the Holocaust world which is so intimately familiar to them yet so distant from them and from those who did not experience that world. Just as the biblical characters are long dead yet very much alive in the consciousness of Jews, so the survivor poets seek to revive those who experienced the Holocaust and to sustain them in their own consciousness and in that of those who did not experience it.

In so doing, they set up a significantly ironic association between the traditional world of faith of the biblical stories and the modern Holocaust world of radical doubt and meaninglessness. Nevertheless, their attempt to associate the world of the Bible with the world of the Holocaust implies a strong desire to find some continuity between the meaning of traditional faith and the meaning which might be found in the experience of the Holocaust. In several of these poems, biblical stories of actual or potential murder are used to depict the destruction of European Jewry in the Holocaust. Each poet's choice of which violent stories to retell and his method of retelling them reflects his own particular relationship to the Holocaust world and what he seeks to express to those who did not experience it.

Amir Gilboa: Saul and His Arms-bearer; Abraham and Isaac

The central issue of Amir Gilboa's experience as a Holocaust survivor was that although he was spared any suffering during the war, the members of his immediate family, from whom he had been separated during the war, all perished. By emigrating to Israel, Gilboa had saved himself, but in some sense he had abandoned his parents, brothers, and sisters to the Nazis who killed them. This situation left him vulnerable to feelings of guilt for the deaths of his relatives. In addition, since he did not directly witness the war, unlike the other two survivors who did, he needed to come to terms with what he perceived to be the shameful nature of the passive deaths of the victims.

Among the poems on biblical themes published by Gilboa, two are retold versions of biblical stories in which at first a character is commanded to kill another one but in the end he does not do so. One poem, "Sha'ul" ("Saul"), is based on the story of Saul's command to his arms-bearer to kill him and the arms-bearer's refusal to do so (I Samuel 31). The other poem, "Yitshak" ("Isaac"), is based on the story of the binding of Isaac in which God commands Abraham to slaughter his son Isaac on an altar on Mount Moriah and then at the last minute prevents Abraham from doing so (Genesis 22).[5] Gilboa takes two different approaches to the retelling of biblical stories in these poems. In one approach, adopted in the poem "Sha'ul," the speaker is a modern Israeli who magically traverses the barriers of time to enter into the biblical story as an observer. The speaker compares his own reactions to Saul's command to his arms-bearer to kill him in the final battle against the Philistines with that of the arms-bearer, and he compares his reaction to the desecration of Saul's body with that of the men of Jabesh-gilead who removed the body and buried it. In the other approach, adopted in the poem "Yitshak," the speaker is an actual participant in the story, Isaac, who is portrayed as a child who naively protests the impending sacrifice only to learn that it is Abraham, not he, who is being sacrificed.

The relatively powerless position of both the outside observer and the child fits well as a framework for the poet's expression of his relationship to the victims of the Holocaust. Whether the speaker is a modern observer or a child in a biblical story, the device allows the poet to imagine himself back in Europe, which he knew only as a child, and to contrast his own current reactions to the Holocaust that engulfed that world with those of the victims. It also allows him to communicate the childlike powerlessness of having been cut off from Europe in the Land of Israel during World War II and having been forced to observe the events of the destruction of European Jewry with virtually no ability to affect those events.

In the poem "Sha'ul" the speaker enters the biblical world and observes the body of Saul impaled on the wall of Beth-shan following his defeat by the Philistines. In great agitation, he expresses to the dead body of Saul his reaction to what has happened:

Saul

Saul! Saul!
I don't know if it was shame
or fear of a head with no body
but when I passed near the wall of Beit-She'an
I turned my head.

Then, when your boy refused you the sword you ordered,
I stood dumb, unable to speak
and blood drained from my heart.
I really can't say what I would have done
if I'd been your boy.

You are the king.
And you your majesty the king give orders.

And I really can't say what I would have done.

Saul Saul come back!
In Beit-She'an the people of Israel wait.[6]

The speaker is unable to live up to the heroic examples set by the stalwart men of Jabesh-gilead of the original biblical story, portrayed in Tchernichowsky's poem "'Anshei ḥayil ḥevel," who, on hearing that the Philistines had impaled the bodies of Saul and his sons on the wall of Beth-shan, marched through the night to the place of the king's humiliation, removed the bodies from the wall, and buried them in Jabesh. When the speaker passes by the scene of the king's humiliation, he turns away, either because he is ashamed at seeing Saul's fate as a victim of suicide whose body is impaled on a wall, or because he is afraid to face the violent reality of Saul's death. The speaker realizes that he is not unlike Saul's arms-bearer, who could not bring himself to kill the king when the king commanded him to do so. Imagining himself in the role of the arms-bearer, he feels so paralyzed by inaction that in the original Hebrew the verb "done" at the end of the ninth and thirteenth lines of the poem does not actually appear.

Just as the speaker in the poem is in historical terms far from the scene of Saul's death and humiliation, so the poet living in the Land of Israel was physically very distant from the scene of destruction in Europe. This distance makes it difficult for the poet to confront the suffering of the Holocaust victims. He speaks of his difficulty as being caused by either a fear of delving into violence of such magnitude as that of the Holocaust or by shame that the Jews were made victims of the Nazis and humiliated like the ancient king who was forced to commit suicide and then suffer the desecration of his body by the enemy.

He is able to transcend his fear and shame as he thinks of the victims' deaths by imagining himself to be in their place. Like the speaker who tries to imagine what he would have done if he had played a role in the scene of Saul's death, the poet is unsure how he would have acted if he had remained in Europe and had been faced with Nazi persecution. It is significant that while the biblical version of the story does not refer to the age of Saul's arms-bearer, the speaker in the poem refers to him as a boy (na'ar), as if Gilboa can project himself back to the scene of the destruction in Europe only by imagining himself to be the age that he was when he still lived there. In so doing he admits that given a fate similar to that of the Jewish Holocaust victims, he does not know how he would have acted. In the end, he concludes, perhaps the passive victimization of the Jews, like Saul's suicide, was the only option available to them and was therefore not shameful but heroic.

Gilboa's choice of Saul's suicide as a symbol for the victimization of European Jewry may be related (as it likely was in Tchernichowsky's poetry) to the use of that image in medieval liturgical poetry to represent the Jewish fathers at the time of the Crusades killing their families and then committing suicide rather than submit to forced conversion to Christianity. Whether this connection was intentional or accidental, it is clear that Gilboa is struggling to find a way to relate to the victimization of European Jewry that is different from the martyrological ideal advocated in medieval literature.

At the end of the poem, the speaker declares to Saul that the people of the modern State of Israel are living today in the city of his humiliation, Beth-shan. With this declaration the poet is suggesting that the repopulation of the Land of Israel by Jews in the twentieth century is in some sense an answer to the humiliation of the Jews in the Holocaust. It is as if the poet is desperately calling to his relatives who died in World War II to be reconciled with him as he is reconciled with their fate by celebrating the revival of national honor in the establishment of the modern State of Israel.

The imaginative identification of the speaker in "Sha'ul" with Saul's arms-bearer suggests another dimension of the poet's relationship to the victims of the Holocaust. The arms-bearer had been commanded by Saul to kill him, but could not bring himself to do so because of the awesome implications of the act of regicide, even when commanded by the king himself. On one level the poet may be associating regicide with patricide. His inner debate regarding his readiness to play the role of the arms-bearer may be related to an inner debate regarding his readiness to accept the guilt he feels for having left his father and the rest of his family behind in Europe to die in the Holocaust, as if he were responsible for their deaths. This assumption of guilt is expressed more explicitly in the poem "Yitshak."

In "Yitshak" Isaac tells a version of the binding of Isaac story which radically departs from the original biblical story:

Isaac

Toward morning the sun strolled in the forest
Together with me and with father,
My right hand was in his left.

Like lightning flash, a knife between the trees
And I fear the terror of my eyes opposite the blood on the
    leaves.

Father, Father, come quickly and save Isaac
That no one may be missing at the noon meal.

It is I who am slaughtered, my son,
And my blood is already on the leaves.
Father's voice choked.
His face grew pale.

And I wanted to scream, writhing not to believe
And I opened my eyes wide.
And I awoke.

Bloodless was my right hand.[7]

In Isaac's version of the story in this poem some of the elements of the biblical version have been preserved: the father and son go off together to the sacrifice early in the morning, and Isaac sees the sacrificial knife before him. Isaac's perspective, however, is very different from that of the narrator of the biblical version: it is that of a child who naively believes that all is well with the world. He describes an idyllic scene of walking in the forest holding his father's hand. In his childish imagination he believes the sun is joining them on their walk. Suddenly, this idyllic scene is shattered by Isaac's view of the sacrificial knife which has already shed blood. Horrified at the sight of the blood, Isaac assumes, in accordance with the biblical version of the story, that he is the one who is being slaughtered. His cry to his father to save him so that "no one may be missing at the noon meal" reflects the continuation of his naive, childlike view of what is happening.

It turns out that in contrast to the biblical version of the story, there really is a human victim, only it is not Isaac but Abraham. Isaac is overwhelmed by the sight of his dying father, and he immaturely tries to escape this reality by refusing to believe it. At the end of the poem he wakes up from what he now realizes was all a nightmare. This realization does not bring him much relief. The draining of blood from his right hand as a result of having slept on it reminds him of his inability to reach out with the same right hand, which his father had held, to prevent the slaughter of his father. In a certain sense, like his father Abraham, Isaac has been a sacrificial victim. His hand drained of blood corresponds to the pale face of his choked father drained of blood. As he writhes on his bed unable to escape the horror of witnessing his father's death, his experience is like that of a sacrificial victim bound on the altar.[8]

In "Yitshak" Gilboa attempts to come to terms with his feelings of guilt as the only member of his family to survive the Holocaust. In some sense he is responsible for the slaughter of his father by leaving him behind in Europe to become a victim of the Nazis. The realization that when his father was in danger in World War II the poet was powerless to help him is one which the poet would rather see as only a child's nightmare from which he can awake. Burdened by the knowledge that it really did happen, he wishes he had played the original role of Isaac, the potential victim who was saved by the intervention of God. Instead, there have been two victims, the father who has been slaughtered and the son who must bear the guilt of this slaughter, and there is no angel of God to intervene to save either the father or the son from their fate.

Although the poems "Sha'ul" and "Yitshak" are personal statements about the poet's relationship to the victims of the Holocaust, they may also be read as a critique of the response of the Jews of the Land of Israel to the events of the Holocaust. The speaker's shame and disgust at confronting the fate of the victims not only suggests the deficiencies of Gilboa's attitude toward the victim, but also that of the Jews of Israel as a whole, who in the early days of the state were embarrassed by the victims, whom they could characterize only as having been led like sheep to the slaughter. In addition, the speaker's inability to accept that his naive idyllic dream has been turned into a nightmare tells us not only about Gilboa's difficulty in grasping the reality of his father's death, for which he feels responsible, but also about the passive, dreamlike lack of action on the part

of the Jews of Israel to save the Jews of Europe when there was still
time to do so.[9]

Abba Kovner: Cain and Abel

It is not surprising that survivors of the Holocaust would turn
to the story of Cain and Abel (Genesis 4:1–16) as a vehicle for exploring issues related to the destruction of European Jewry in World War
II. Even though God's direct involvement in the story is not typically
found in most violent events, the story of the first murder in human
history contains the basic elements of murder and therefore provides
a framework for evaluating all acts of murder since its occurrence.
There is the motivation of the murderer Cain, who is jealous of what
he perceives as God's favoring of Abel over him. This is followed by
the murder's acknowledgment of guilt and his subsequent punishment by God, who banishes him to wander the earth. It is significant
that God not only punishes the murderer, but also protects him from
random acts of vengeance. His protection establishes a model in
which justice carried out by a central authority transcends the more
primitive vengeance by individuals against a murderer.

Kovner retells the story of Cain and Abel in a two-part poem
titled "Mikarov" ("Near" [or:"Nearby"]).[10] The title of the poem implies that a firsthand account of the events of the poem is being given
to those who are more distant from them. Cain and Abel represent
those who experienced the war attempting to convey its significance
to those who did not. Unlike Gilboa's speakers, who can only imaginatively transport themselves or dream themselves back to the
biblical world which stands for the world of the Holocaust, the
speakers in Kovner's poem, Abel and Cain, appear as eyewitnesses
of biblical events that stand for the events of the Holocaust.

In the poem Cain and Abel are portrayed not as the individual
murderer and victim; instead, they speak as members of a community that has been violently attacked, who are recalling what happened and are describing the after effects of the violent events:

Near

1. Abel
Light the candle I will return   to you: morning
rises and smoke on the face of the deep and I

                                                        in the field
alone   heaps of feathers
flutter under the sky and I can't   tell
if the birds   dropped them all when they died
                                        or the quilt and pillows
when they were torn to shreds (I heard

                                                        the wind
hissing) lost their entrails   outside
at dawn
                                very white feathers whine there
between water and sky   if You have any
mercy put them   my God where the birds are

2. Cain
I swore I didn't hear You   all day
calling Where are you
                        it's not You I feared when I escaped
but all the terrible noises   I remember a voice
from a shed like broken sounds of the shofar
                                (my house   stood
between stables and eucalyptus)
                                and her small braided head.
                        Your day did not open   her eyes
Now a continent rises around me   perfumed
        a guilt offering of incense for the whole world
            its innocence shines like the sky's radiance
                on the desert of stone the pillar of man
                in the image of a mushroom cloud.
                Light the candle we will return
                    to You: morning rises
                    there's no other
                    messenger but
                    You where are
                    You and
                    I[11]

These accounts have some similarities that reflect the brothers' shared experience of the violence; yet the perspective of each brother is very different. This difference in perspective is the result of the different fates of the two brothers. Abel, the victim in the biblical story, represents, in the poem, the victim who actually died in the Holocaust, while Cain, the murderer who lived on after his act of violence in the biblcial story, represents the survivor who lived on after the war. Both present a few very specific images that convey the horror of the events even more powerfully than would an attempt to portray the violence in its entirety.[12] Abel refers to the spilled human entrails of the victims as the feathers of pillows torn open and of birds slaughtered. Cain recalls the broken sounds of the voice of a girl with a small braided head crying out from an animal shed. These images used by the brothers reflect the way the Jewish victims were treated like animals or objects by the Nazis.

Abel has a closer view of the events than Cain does. As the victim in the biblical story, who was slain and abandoned "in the field" (Genesis 4:8), he has stayed at the scene of the violence and can testify to its effects. Nevertheless, the images Abel uses have a more ethereal quality to them, as would befit the victim who is no longer of this world. The feathers are now floating between heaven and earth like dead souls yearning to be reunited with the bodies from which they were taken. The images that Cain uses provide a much more vivid expression of human suffering. The voice he hears is like a shofar call awakening the people to repentance. It also calls to mind the voice of Abel's blood which cried out to God after Cain murdered him (Genesis 4:10). Cain, like the murderous brother of the biblical story, has fled the scene and is haunted by feelings of guilt from not having saved the others and from being the one who lived while others died.

While Abel, the victim, seems to be concerned with the effect of the violence on the victims' souls, Cain, the survivor, is more concerned with the effect of the violence on himself and on the postwar world. Both concerns are expressed through images from other stories in Genesis, as well as by means of the prayers each one directs to God. Abel's reference to "smoke on the face of the deep" alludes to the period before the creation of the world when there was "darkness on the face of the deep" (Genesis 1:2). The presence of the feathers "between water and sky" alludes to God's creation of the sky to separate the lower waters from the upper waters (Genesis 1:6–8). There is a sense in Abel's allusions that the Holocaust brought the world back to the chaos (*tohu vavohu*) that preceded creation. Abel's prayer to God to restore the feathers to the birds, or the souls of the victims to their bodies, is a plea to create the world anew, as He had done in Genesis 1, in order to restore the moral order of the universe which had been destroyed in the war.

The relationship of Cain, the survivor, to God is a more complicated one. The biblical imagery to which he alludes expresses his feeling of guilt before God, while at the same time it conveys his feeling that he is more powerful than God. Cain arrogantly appropriates for himself the expression *bi nishba'ti* (I swore), which is used by God in the Bible. When God calls Cain to acccount with the expression *'ayyekah* (where are you) used by God in addressing Adam after he and Eve ate of the forbidden fruit (Genesis 3:9), Cain does not hear him. Unlike Adam, who at first tries to hide out of fear of God, Cain flees out of fear of the violence around him. The violent acts of human beings have almost completely eclipsed God in Cain's consciousness.

Cain's image of dry land rising from the sea calls to mind the new beginning for mankind following the flood in the days of Noah (Genesis 8). Just as the flood came to destroy the world for its sins, so the new postwar world must come to terms with its guilt. Postwar humanity offers a guilt offering for the sins of contributing to the violence or of not doing enough to counter the violence. Humanity's repentance is difficult, however, because it has been numbed by the awful events, and so it resembles a hard stone. It has been created not *betselem* '*elohim* (in the image of God) (Genesis 1:27), but rather *betselem pitri-yyah*, a play on the words *tselem* (image), *tsel* (shadow), *pitriyyah* (mushroom), and *ya* (God). Humanity lives now in the shadow of the mushroom cloud which gives to people the God-like power to destroy the world with the atomic bomb. It will not be easy for postwar humanity, which appears to be so much stronger than God, to re-establish the relationship it had had with God before the war.

Despite the vast chasm between them, Cain, the survivor, calls for a reconciliation between God and himself. In a play on the expression from the traditional prayer book, '*ein lanu melekh* '*ella*' '*attah* (there is no king but you), he declares to God '*ein davar ba*'*arets* '*ella*' '*attah*. If the word *davar* had been spelled with the letter *vet*, Cain's declaration would have been that of simple traditional faith: "there is nothing [of worth] on earth but you." Instead, the word is spelled with the letter *vav*, making the meaning of the declaration, "there is no *postman* [translated here as messenger] on earth but you." Just as the modern postman plays the role of intermediary carrying letters between people, so Cain hopes that God might play the role of re-establishing communication between the scattered members of humanity alienated from each other.

Cain the survivor, however, is not sure where he can find God. Like Adam and Cain in the Bible, God, too, has sinned by not protecting His people from the Nazi enemy. The human being must therefore call to Him with the same word that God used to call Adam to account: '*ayyekah* (where are you). In so doing, however, the post-war human being realizes that he, too, is guilty. His sins are his Cain-like responsibility for the deaths of the victims and his Adam-like yearning to gain knowledge and power which more appropriately belong to God. The question "where are you" must therefore of necessity be addressed to himself as well.

Dan Pagis: Cain and Abel

While much of Pagis's early poetry of the 1950s and 1960s reflects his world view as a Holocaust survivor, it does not make explicit reference to his experiences in the Holocaust. It is only in the collection *Gilgul* (*Transformation*) (1970) that Pagis began to directly address the issues which concerned him as a survivor. In that collection and the later collection *Moah* (*Brain*) (1975), Pagis published poems which retell the Cain and Abel story with the purpose of expressing his attitude toward the Holocaust.

In the poem "Katuv beʿipparon bakaron heḥatum" ("Written in Pencil in the Sealed Railway-Car")[13] Eve and Abel are being transported in a cattle car to a concentration camp. The poem is presented as Eve's last desperate attempt to communicate with the world by writing a note before her death:

Written in Pencil in the Sealed Railway-Car

here in this carload
i am eve
with abel my son
if you see my other son
cain son of man
tell him that i[14]

Abel, who, in this poem, represents the victims of the Holocaust, is being brought to his death by Cain, who represents the Nazi murderers. As Cain denied all responsibility for his brother Abel, so the Nazis have seen fit to destroy their human brothers, the Jews.

The Nazis' act of genocide is presented as a crime even greater than that of Cain's murder of his brother. They are attacking not only their fellow human beings, but also life itself, represented here by Eve (*Ḥavvah*), "the mother of all living" (*'em kol ḥai*) (Genesis 3:20), who is also being transported to the concentration camp. Eve is greatly disturbed that her son Cain has cut himself off from her, and she wants somehow to re-establish contact with him. When she refers to him as "son of man" (*ben 'adam*) she uses an expression which can literally mean "son of Adam" or "human being." The message which she seeks to convey to him is the call of the life-force to the Nazis to cease their acts of barbarous inhumanity. Only then will they recover their identity as human beings (*benei ʾadam*) in the fullest sense of the word.

This message never gets conveyed to the Nazi murderers. The train arrives at the concentration camp, and Eve is forced to stop her writing in midsentence. The message does however survive to be read by the postwar world. Even though Eve's message to Cain is not stated, there is still a message from Eve to those who have survived the war. Since in Hebrew there is no verb form of "to be" in the present tense, the last word of the poem, "i" (*ʾani*) may be followed immediately by the first word of the poem "here" (*kaʾn*) to mean that the message is contained in the image of: "I, Eve, am here in this carload." In this image of the Nazis' inhumane actions in the war there is a message, not for the Nazis who were never willing to hear it, but for the postwar world: what the Nazis did must never be repeated.

The poem "ʾAḥim" ("Brothers")[15] retells the Cain and Abel story as the paradigm of all murderous acts in human history:

Brothers

1
Abel was pure and woolly
and somewhat modest
like the smallest kid
and full of ringlets like the smoke of the offering
inhaled by his Master.
Cain was straight. Like a knife.

2
Cain is amazed. His big hand gropes
inside the butchered throat before him:
from where does the silence burst?

3
Abel stayed in the field. Cain stayed Cain. And since
it's decreed that he be a wanderer, he wanders diligently.

Each morning changing one horizon for another. One day
he discovers the earth tricked him over the years. It
moved, while he, Cain, marked time in one place. Marked
time, marched, ran only on a single scrap of dust, exactly
as big as the soles of his sandals.

4
One evening of grace he stumbles
on a fine haystack.
He dives in, is swallowed by it, rests.
Hush, Cain sleeps.
He's happy. He dreams that he is Abel.

5
Don't worry. Don't worry.
It's already decreed for the one who might kill you
that your vengeance shall be taken sevenfold.
Your brother Abel guards you from all evil.[16]

Portrayed here as types, Cain and Abel represent all murderers and
victims throughout history. The nature of the relationship between
murderers and victims has remained essentially the same from the
time of the first murder in human history through the destruction
of European Jewry by the Nazis in World War II. Abel is the pure,
innocent, flexible person who is loved by God but ultimately
becomes the victim whose God cannot protect him. Cain is the
strong, inflexible murderer whose resemblance to a knife suggests
that his very essence is the act of destruction he inflicts on the victim.
When Cain examines the throat he has slit, he is amazed and
fascinated at the power he has to take a human life.[17] Once he has
murdered Abel, he makes it possible for his descendants to conceive
of making use of that power in a way that human beings were in-
capable of imagining until that moment.

Human beings think they have progressed since the time of
Cain and Abel, but in fact, like Cain in the poem, they have "marked
time in one place." They have always been Cain the potential murderer. Cain's happy dream that he is Abel represents the attempts by

human beings throughout history to rationalize their aggressive tendencies and actions by seeing themselves as the powerless victims of other people's acts of aggression.

At times human beings are like Abel. Just as God protected Cain from murder by vengeance after he murdered Abel, so the Abel-like sensitivity of humanity has saved it from treating Cain in the aggressive and murderous way he treated Abel. In terms of the most horrible acts of murder committed by the Nazis, this Abel-like sensitivity of humanity ironically saves the Cain-like Nazis from being condemned to the same inhumane suffering which they directed toward their victims. Even if the Nazis did not live up to their obligation to be sensitive to their fellow human brothers, postwar humanity will live up to that obligation and will refuse to take murderous revenge against the Nazis. Those Nazis who were caught had the benefit of a trial of law, while other Nazis were allowed to escape without sufficient effort being made by the postwar world to bring them to justice.

Abel himself retells the story of Cain and Abel in the poem "ʾOtobiyyografyah" ("Autobiography").[18] Like the speaker in "ʾAḥim," Abel approaches Cain's act of murder from an historical point of view, examining its effects on the development of humanity:

Autobiography

I died with the first blow and was buried
in the stony field.
The raven showed my parents
what to do with me.

If my family is famous, not a little of the credit
goes to me.
My brother invented murder,
my parents — crying,
I invented silence.

Afterwards, those well-known events took place.
Our inventions were perfected.
One thing led to another.

And there were those who
killed in their own way,
cried in their own way.

I am not naming names
out of consideration for the reader,
since at first the details horrify,
though in the end they bore.

You can die once, twice, even seven times,
but you cannot die a thousand times.
I can.
My underground cells reach everywhere.

When Cain started to multiply on the face of the earth,
I started to multiply in the belly of the earth.
For a long time now, my strength has been greater than his.
His legions desert him and go over to me.
And even this is only half a revenge.[19]

As in "ʾAḥim," Cain's murder of Abel is a startling new type of action
of which humanity was not aware until that time. Adam and Eve do
not even know what to do with the dead body of Abel until the raven
shows them how to bury it.[20] Following this invention of murder,
death, and grief, humanity has developed technologically, but, as in
"ʾAḥim," these developments have not brought about the moral pro-
gress of humanity. Technology has been used by the murderous
descendants of Cain to develop various ways to kill. The increasing
capacity of human beings to re-enact Cain's act of murder has not
led to greater sensitivity to the suffering of victims. On the contrary,
by the time of the Holocaust people have heard so much about and
have witnessed so many acts of violence that they have been numbed
to this reality and treat it as a tiresome subject.

Abel sees the ongoing history of murder as a constant struggle
between the murderers living on earth and the dead victims buried
in the ground. In the course of history there have gradually come to
be more dead people than alive people. All those living on earth,
whether murderers or victims, have eventually had to die and join

Abel in the grave, thereby bringing to Abel a kind of triumph over Cain. The deaths of the murderers, however, do not really compensate the victims for their suffering. Instead of the seven-fold vengeance which protects Cain in the biblical story, Abel, in the role of Holocaust victim, receives here only half a revenge (*ḥatsi nekamah*), a play on the Hebrew expression *ḥatsi neḥamah* (half a comfort). The eventual deaths of the Nazis, whether by natural causes or by capital punishment, can never compensate the victims for their cruelly inhumane deaths in World War II.

Each of the relationships portrayed between murderer and victim or potential victim in the biblical stories of Saul and his arms-bearer, the binding of Isaac, and Cain and Abel have been transformed by the Holocaust survivor poets Gilboa, Kovner, and Pagis into a representation of one set of relationships between the major actors in the tragedy of the Holocaust: the murderers, the victims, or the survivors. Each poet's way of presenting a set of relationships says a great deal about his relationship to the two worlds for which he serves as intermediary: the world of the Holocaust victims and the world of those who were not directly affected by the war.

Of the three poets, Gilboa has the most ambiguous relationship to the Holocaust. It is fitting therefore that he chooses to tell stories in which a murder was commanded and then not committed. Saul's command to his arms-bearer to murder him, the arms-bearer's refusal to do so, Saul's subsequent suicide, and the desecration of his body by the Philistine enemy, as well as the inexplicable command by God to Abraham to slaughter his son and the subsequent rescinding of that command are used by Gilboa to represent the desperate lack of alternatives faced by the victims caught in the Holocaust world, as well as his own confusion as to what his relationship to that world should be. Of the two worlds, that of the Holocaust victims and that of those not directly affected by the war, he is closer to the latter. He cannot identify with the victims represented by Saul and his arms-bearer, except in an imaginative or dreamlike way, because he was not in Europe during the war. His attitude toward the victims is not unlike that of those not involved in the war. Like them he turns away from the fate of the victims in shame and disgust. Only to the extent that he can begin to empathize with their situation and face the guilt he feels for not sharing their fate as victims and for not doing more to save them can he begin to play a constructive role as the poet-intermediary between the world of those who were victims and the world of those who were not.

Having spent the war living in the Vilna ghetto and then fighting as a partisan, Kovner is closer to the world of the victims than Gilboa. Nevertheless, when he uses the story of the murder of Abel by Cain to portray the fate of the victims and the survivors, there is an ethereal quality to his portrait of Abel's concerns that derives from his inability to identify fully with the fate of the victims. Like Gilboa, he, too, seeks to flee from the reality of the victims' fate. Although he, too, feels guilty for having survived while others died, he seems more sure than Gilboa of his role as intermediary between the victims and those who were not in the war. The guilt he feels is not just a personal one, but one which he insists must be shared by all of humanity and even by God. If there is any meaning to his having survived, it would appear to be in his ability to draw humanity and God together, so that people will forgive God for allowing so much evil to occur, and so that God will forgive people for appropriating for themselves the power of life and death which properly belongs only to God. The Genesis imagery to which he alludes suggests some hope for a new beginning for the world after the war, although it remains unclear whether the necessary reconciliation between God and humanity will take place.

Although Pagis did not die in the war, there is something about his experience of having been in a concentration camp that allows him to speak with the authority of the victim. Of the three poets, he writes with the greatest empathy and in the most direct way about the fate of the victims. He feels no guilt for having survived. It is as if he did die like the victims but was resurrected for the purpose of reminding the world of its moral breakdown during the Holocaust. His approach to the telling of the Cain and Abel story suggests that he believes the Nazis' act of genocide reflects a tendency toward violence which has been a part of human nature since that first murder. Although his message to the world is that it must cease to act like

Cain, he does not appear to be very hopeful that in the long run the Abel-like sensitivity of the victims will be able to hold its own against the Cain-like destructiveness of the murderers.

Chapter 7

Uses and Abuses of Power in Ancient and Modern Israel: Nissim Aloni, Moshe Shamir, and Amos Oz

When I was nine years old the British left the Land of Israel, and Jewish Jerusalem withstood a prolonged siege in the War of Independence. Everyone believed that after the victory a free Hebrew state would arise in which nothing would be as it was before. Three years after the fall of Hitler these survivors thought that they really were conducting a last battle in the war of the sons of light against the sons of darkness and that the independence of the Jews would be a clear sign of the salvation of all the world.

The War of Independence ended with a great military victory. More than a million Jewish refugees came to Israel within a period of a few years. However, the siege and the suffering did not cease, a general salvation did not occur, and the trivial troubles of a very little state also surfaced.[1]

As Amos Oz makes clear in this passage from an autobiographical essay, within a few years of the establishment of the State of Israel in 1948, a crisis of confidence in the Zionist accomplishment of establishing Jewish political sovereignty in the Land of Israel began to develop among certain elements of the Israeli population. This crisis of confidence profoundly affected some of the Hebrew

writers of the 1950s, who came to be known as the "Palmach" generation, named after the Jewish fighting force of the Israeli War of Independence, to which some of these writers had belonged. These writers, who had set the cultural tone of Jewish life in the period before
and during the Israeli War of Independence, began to wonder
whether statehood had brought about the fulfillment of their dream
to transform the physically and spiritually destroyed Jewish culture
of the diaspora into a vibrant Hebrew culture of the Land of Israel
or had created a new cultural and political nightmare from which
they would want to escape. This questioning by some Palmach writers of what Zionism had accomplished was continued by writers of
what Gershon Shaked has termed the "New Wave," who began
publishing in the late 1950s and early 1960s, including Oz, who had
been children during the War of Independence.

The dream of Zionism had been to restore in modern times the
political sovereignty that the ancient Israelites had held over the
Land of Israel in biblical times. In the service of that dream, the
ancient period of political sovereignty became the model of what the
modern Zionist settlers were trying to accomplish. One effective way
for writers of the Palmach and New Wave generations to call into
question the validity of the fulfillment of that dream was to retell
biblical stories from the early period of settlement in the land when
the ancient Israelites were ruled first by the judges and later by the
kings. They retold these stories in such a way as to emphasize possible connections between what went wrong with political sovereignty
in biblical times and what was going wrong in modern times.

Three works will serve as illuminating examples of the retelling
of biblical stories by contemporary Israeli writers who questioned the
fulfillment of the Zionist dream. The first is a play by Nissim Aloni,
who began writing toward the end of the Palmach period. The play,
titled 'Akhzar mikol hamelekh (Most Cruel the King) (1953), is based on
the story of Kings Rehoboam and Jeroboam (I Kings 11:26-14). The
second is the novel Kivsat harash (The Poor Man's Ewe Lamb) (1956), by
one of the leading writers of the Palmach generation, Moshe Shamir,
based on the story of King David, Uriah the Hittite, and Bathsheba
(II Samuel 11-12). The third is by one of the most important mem-

bers of the New Wave generation, Amos Oz. It is the story "'Al ha'adamah hara'ah hazot" ("Upon This Evil Earth") (1966; 1974-1975), based on the story of Jephthah the judge and his daughter (Judges 11-12). All three works portray political leaders of ancient Israel who were either the exercisers or the victims of abusive power. They therefore serve as useful vehicles for each writer to explore the relationship between the uses and abuses of political power in ancient and modern Israel.

Nissim Aloni: Rehoboam and Jeroboam

The biblical story of Rehoboam and Jeroboam, on which Aloni's play '*Akhzar mikol hamelekh* is based, recounts the events that led to the division of ancient Israel into two kingdoms. According to the biblical story, this division came about because King Solomon displeased God by engaging in idolatrous worship. God decided to punish Solomon by having the rule of most of Israel taken from his son Rehoboam. The prophet Ahijah of Shiloh informed a man named Jeroboam, the son of Nebat, that he would be the one to wrest the rule of Israel from Solomon's family. Jeroboam thereupon began a revolt against Solomon. When Solomon tried to put Jeroboam to death, the latter fled to Egypt, where he remained until Solomon's death.

When Solomon's son Rehoboam was about to be proclaimed as the inheritor of his father's throne, Jeroboam returned from Egypt to challenge his leadership. He led Israel in a call to Rehoboam to lighten the harsh rule that had characterized Solomon's reign. The elders who had served Solomon advised Rehoboam to respond kindly to the Israelites' request to insure that they would serve him as loyal subjects. The young men who had grown up with him and who were then serving him gave him the opposite advice. They recommended that he declare to the Israelites that his rule would be even harsher than that of his father. Rehoboam decided to take the young men's advice.

The narrator presents Rehoboam's insistence on following the advice of his younger advisers as serving God's plan to take the rule of most of Israel from the house of Solomon. Rehoboam's declaration of harsh rule resulted in the revolt of ten of the twelve tribes of Israel, who set up a separate northern kingdom under the rule of Jeroboam. Only the tribes of Judah and Benjamin remained loyal to Rehoboam's rule over the remaining southern kingdom.

After the division of Israel into two separate kingdoms, both kingdoms began to indulge in the same kinds of idolatrous practices for which Solomon had been punished by God. Jeroboam established idolatrous sacrificial altars at Bethel and at Dan so that the people would not worship at the Temple in Jerusalem, where they might be swayed to return to the rule of Rehoboam. These idolatrous acts angered God, who declared through his prophet Ahijah that Jeroboam would be deposed and the northern kingdom punished for its sins. At the same time, the southern kingdom, under the rule of Rehoboam, also committed acts of idolatrous worship. During the reigns of Jeroboam and Rehoboam the two kingdoms continued their idolatrous practices and were engaged in constant warfare with each other.

The biblical story portrays Rehoboam and Jeroboam as two less-than-ideal kings carrying out the intention of God to punish Solomon for his idolatry. In his play, which focuses on a twenty-four hour period at the time of Jeroboam's initial challenge to Rehoboam's rule, Aloni makes use of the characters of the two kings to represent two opposing visions of the nature and purpose of political sovereignty in the newly founded State of Israel in his day.

In 'Akhzar mikol hamelekh, as Jeroboam leads his rebellion against Rehoboam, he finds himself struggling not only with Rehoboam, but also with two other characters: his mother Zeruah (the name of Jeroboam's widowed mother according to I Kings 11:26) and his former lover Maacah (the name of Rehoboam's wife according to I Kings 15:2), who had married Rehoboam. Zeruah is a fervent supporter of the rebellion against Rehoboam. She sees it as the culmination of her desire for revenge against Solomon for the death of her husband as a cutter of cedars in Lebanon when he served the late king. She considers the rebellion to be a religious act as well because it was sanctioned by God and His prophet Ahijah. Maacah, on the other hand, seeks to convince Jeroboam to flee with her from the

Land of Israel to a life dedicated not to political struggle but to pleasure. The struggle between Zeruah and Maacah for the soul of Jeroboam is portrayed on two levels. On a psychological level, Jeroboam is a man caught between the affections of his mother and those of his lover. On a political level, Jeroboam is involved in an inner struggle between pursuing a life of political commitment to change his country or fleeing that life to pursue personal pleasure.

Jeroboam has an extremely ambivalent attitude toward the responsibility that his mother believes God and His prophet have thrust on him. He cannot support the rebellion against Rehoboam as wholeheartedly as his mother does. On the one hand, he is afraid to flee the God who has called on him to challenge Rehoboam's rule, and he does not want to abandon his country for a life of exile in foreign lands. On the other hand, however, he feels that to engage in the rebellion against Rehoboam means to be committed to a path that pursues an ideal at the expense of life. Those who participate in the rebellion will have to deny the fulfillment of their individual needs, and in some cases even have to give up their lives. In a stormy argument with his mother, he tells her that he cannot share her fervent support of the rebellion as a matter of pure good against pure evil, because he is so beset by moral qualms about the inevitable deaths of many of those who will participate in the rebellion. Zeruah argues against Jeroboam's sensitivity to the human suffering which the rebellion will create by declaring that it is a war sanctioned by God for a special people "who dwells alone" (an allusion to Numbers 23:9).

In the end, Jeroboam overcomes his moral qualms and accepts his mother's belief in the superior purposes of the political struggle. He challenges Rehoboam as being too preoccupied with the aggrandizement and abuse of royal power and not sufficiently concerned with the ideal of justice and the needs of the people. He tells the king that he has returned to the Land of Israel to help the people recover the simpler way of life that once existed but was destroyed during the reign of Solomon and Rehoboam:

> I love my land. I have no more power to wander. I have a plot of land in Ephraim and also people like me, pursuers of peace, who

seek to live the life that God gave to them. At dawn they rise to
work their land with love; in the evening they gather by the gate
as in bygone days (p. 22).[2]

In response to Jeroboam's challenge, Rehoboam declares that
his use of power is the only conceivable way to rule Israel. He
believes that the way to achieve justice is to make use of all the trap-
pings of power of a kingdom, even if it is inevitable that this will
eventually lead to the abuse of power. He also believes that as a
relatively weak country, the kingdom of Israel needs a strong government to defend the nation against its enemies, even if the development of that government's strength is at the expense of the well-being
of the people:

> There is no justice, Jeroboam! . . . What is justice, Jeroboam? Do
> you know its meaning? You — wouldn't you collect taxes to in-
> crease and strengthen justice? And wouldn't you assemble soldiers
> to keep the justice? And wouldn't you appoint a general over the
> soldiers who keep the justice? And what about drink for the
> soldiers so they won't betray you? And parties, gifts, and lands for
> the ministers? . . . And wouldn't you build palaces to house
> justice? And if Shishak [King of Egypt] were to command you to
> fill his storehouses with grain — what would you do? Would you
> take this whole nation out to war, or starve it, wrap it in rags, send
> it to roll around in the dung of the street? What would you do,
> hero! A small land is in our hands, and both Assyrians and Egyp-
> tians desire it. At times we will bow our heads, at times wink to
> this one, at times lean on the neck of that one until they fall asleep
> once more. That is our fate, an old prostitute beautifying herself
> in vain (pp. 23–24).

Eventually, Ahijah withdraws his support from Jeroboam and
becomes a supporter of Rehoboam. Jeroboam then finds himself as
an opponent not only of the political establishment but also of the
religious establishment that has been so corrupted that it is willing
to side with the injustices of the king. In his last major speech of the
play, Jeroboam makes clear to his followers that he rejects the cynical
power-hungry rule of Rehoboam as well as the divine sanction which

Ahijah has granted it. In this speech Jeroboam responds to an accusation that had been made several times in the play by a number of characters, that he had become too influenced by his stay in Egypt after his flight from Solomon to be considered a true Hebrew. As an outcast challenging the authority of the political and religious establishments of his country, he feels the need to assert that the values which form the basis of his rebellion are not foreign to Hebrew culture and are, furthermore, in the best moral interests of the people. He declares that if the establishment chooses to view his values as non-Hebrew then he would just as soon not be considered a Hebrew, because his values transcend the narrower one of loyalty to corrupt rule:

> For if the person who speaks in Israel of a holy nation and a kingdom of priests is a Hebrew, then I am an Egyptian, for I speak of bread. If the person who closes his eyes from seeing all the lands around him is a Hebrew, I am an Egyptian, for I see the peace of Jerusalem in the city of Damascus. If Ahijah the Shilonite, who cries we are a people who dwells alone, is a Hebrew, I Jeroboam son of Nebat am an Egyptian, for I seek to find allies in foreign lands, from the Euphrates to the river of Egypt. It is true, I will not deny it, I am an Egyptian. Rehoboam is a Hebrew, so I am an Egyptian. Rehoboam is ready to lean on the necks of Egypt and Assyria, to acquire tranquility and pleasures for the members of his household — for the members of his household! — by means of the efforts and toil of the people, and thus to bear the burden of our being a small people, like a worn out prostitute beautifying herself in vain. And Ahijah the Shilonite did not condemn him saying he is an Egyptian, he is an Assyrian. No, he is a Hebrew. Only I am an Egyptian, for I seek to give peace to this people, even if it is a small people (p. 36).

Nevertheless, Jeroboam is troubled by his decision to assume the leadership of the rebellion against Rehoboam. He realizes that in the battle between his mother Zeruah and his former lover Maacah for his soul, it is his mother who has won. When he informs his mother that he is now committed to following her path of political engagement, however, he declares to her that he is still reluctant to suppress the escapist, hedonistic leanings of his heart and is filled with moral qualms about the cruel effects of such political engagement on the individuals involved in it.

In an interview published over a decade after he wrote ʾAkhzar mikol hamelekh, Aloni discusses the political reality of Israel in the early 1950s, when he wrote the play. From this discussion it becomes clear that Jeroboam's rebellion against Rehoboam in the play reflects the opposition of Aloni and his leftist political associates to the ruling moderate socialist party Mapai at the time:

> And suddenly I think to myself how in 1951, after the War [of In-
> dependence], the word Mapai was for us a kind of abomination!
> But at that time [this attitude] had a great deal of validity, because
> there was a certain bitterness toward the government. Apparently
> the bitterness was because they conquered the land. For suddenly
> the land became small. . . . They conquered [the land]. The land
> had become theirs, and everyone was singing in Jerusalem, "Alts
> is drek! — Everything is drek [crap]!" Yes, that was the famous song.
> Why? Because all the great "one hundred percenters," all the strong
> fighters, saw suddenly that that's it! It's finished! Now it's begin-
> ning like in every place, like let's say: Jesus has died, Paul is begin-
> ning. Paul is making a church structure, concerns, worries . . . ³

For Aloni, the institutionalization of power in the State of Israel had been difficult to accept, because it meant that from that time on there would be ruling parties like Mapai who, like the leaders of any established political institution, would become preoccupied with the day to day concerns of maintaining the state. In so doing, they would inevitably depart from the original limitless dreams, ideals, and beliefs of the revolutionary period that made possible their rise to power.

While the logic of Rehoboam's arguments in defense of his exercise of power suggests that Aloni understood at the time that he wrote the play that there was a need to develop a strong central government to establish a just and secure state, he portrays Jeroboam's moral critique of that government much more sympathetically. Jeroboam's disdain for the pursuit of self-gain by the politicians of his day, for the departure of the government from a commitment to the simple life of the individual citizen, and for the government's cynical, fawning, and unproductive power-plays with foreign governments all reflect Aloni's disillusionment at the time with what he considered to be similar actions on the part of the government of modern Israel.

Like Jeroboam, however, Aloni appears to have been unsure in the early 1950s as to whether he was really committed to engaging in politics to the degree that would be necessary to transform the State of Israel into a political entity more in keeping with his ideals. Just as in the biblical version of the story, in which both Jeroboam and Rehoboam returned to the idolatrous sins of Solomon, so in Aloni's play there is the suspicion that he who engages in the political struggle for power will eventually be corrupted by the same disdain for the needs of the individual that Aloni finds in the Israeli political establishment. The temptation is great to flee political involvement or even, as Maacah keeps tempting Jeroboam to do, flee the country altogether. This temptation is intensified by Aloni's view that the political and religious establishments of Israel insist on defining Israeli identity in terms of corrupt values which he cannot support. Like Jeroboam, who keeps being accused of being more Egyptian than Hebrew, Aloni appears to feel so alienated from what is going on politically and culturally in the new state that he begins to wonder whether there is any point for him to continue to identify with it. In the end, he seems to resolve this conflict not by leaving the state, but by committing himself to staying and fighting for a vision of Israel that affirms the ideals of caring equally for the welfare of all the citizens of the state and pursuing a true and lasting peace between Israel and its Arab enemies.

Moshe Shamir: David, Uriah, and Bathsheba

While Aloni had chosen to represent the abuse of power in the State of Israel through the story of Jeroboam's challenge to the overly harsh rule of Solomon's son Rehoboam, Shamir chose to represent the same abuse of power through the story of the sins of adultery and murder committed by Solomon's father David when he had sexual relations with Bathsheba and arranged for the death of her husband Uriah. The biblical narrator's ironic attitude toward David is clear and serves as a basis for Shamir's disillusioned ironic attitude toward Israel in the 1950s.[4] The portrait of David as the heroic fighter against Israel's enemies in the earlier biblical stories about him is undermined at the beginning of the story of David, Uriah, and Bathsheba. This later biblical story portrays David as having withdrawn from leading Israel in battle and as prepared to delegate his authority to others. During a war between the Israelites and Ammonites, David chose to remain in the capital city of Jerusalem when his army, under the leadership of Joab, was besieging the enemy capital of Rabbah. One afternoon, while walking on the roof of the royal palace David noticed a beautiful woman, Bathsheba, bathing. He arranged to have her sent to the palace and there he had sexual relations with her.

When Bathsheba, whose husband, Uriah the Hittite, was then participating in the siege of Rabbah, informed him that she was pregnant, David realized that he needed to find a way to cover up his sin of adultery. He called Uriah back to Jerusalem so that he would have sexual relations with her and the child born to her would be presumed to have been fathered by Uriah. Uriah, however, refused to sleep in his own house out of respect for the men in the field of battle (in ironic contrast to David who has remained in his palace). Thereupon, David decided he must have Uriah killed so that he could marry Bathsheba and legitimate the forthcoming birth. David sent a letter to Joab ordering him to place Uriah on the front line of the battle and then withdraw from him so that he would be killed. After Joab made such an arrangement and Uriah was killed in battle, David married Bathsheba and a son was born to them.

God then sent Nathan the prophet to rebuke David for his sins of adultery and murder. The prophet did so by telling David a parable about a rich man who takes the one ewe lamb of a poor man to serve a guest rather than take a ewe lamb from his own large flocks. When David expressed his anger at the rich man's unjust act, Nathan declared that the act of the rich man in the parable stood for the stealing of Uriah's only wife by David, the possessor of so many wives. The prophet declared to David that he would be punished for his sins. Although David repented of his sins and God forgave him, the child born from the adulterous union of David and Bathsheba died soon after childbirth. Despite the evil means by which David acquired Bathsheba as a wife, she subsequently bore him a son, Solomon, who succeeded David as king of Israel.

In his novel *Kivsat harash* Shamir tells the story from the point of view of Uriah the Hittite. While the biblical version of the story reveals little of the inner world of this victim of David's crimes, Shamir's novel consists of a series of entries in Uriah's diary during the days between his return to the battlefield from Jerusalem until his death. The novel then concludes with an epilogue by a fellow Hittite who tells of Uriah's death and offers reflections on the meaning of the events of the story.

In his diary Uriah relates that he left his native city to learn more about the nature of power so that he could understand why the Hittites had twice been defeated by enemies and were being threatened by a third defeat. He had come to believe that the ideal form of power was that of a nation on the rise which had not yet reached the height of its powers. Once such a nation does reach the height of its powers, it must reject the exercise of the typically destructive power of other nations. If it succeeds in doing so, it will remain strong and be able to resist its enemies; if it does not, it will decline and be vulnerable to its enemies.

Uriah discovered such a nation on the rise in the band of men that supported David when he challenged Saul for the royal throne. He saw the spirit of David's rise to power as a pure one that still had the potential to avoid the excesses of power that lead to a people's downfall. Uriah was impressed with David's selfless and effective way of leading his people. He was convinced that David was seeking power not for personal gain but for the greater welfare of Israel.

Uriah's initial idealized view of David represents the belief of Shamir and his Palmach generation that in fighting to establish the State of Israel they were involved in a pure struggle to strengthen the Jewish people by establishing their sovereignty over the ancient homeland of Israel. Like the high hopes which Uriah held out for an uncorrupted Davidic reign that would always remain loyal to the pure values of the struggle against Saul, so Shamir and his generation believed that they would not establish a typical state that abused its power, but a just and independent political entity that would morally surpass the ruling British Mandatory government and all other world powers. David's betrayal of Uriah by committing adultery with his wife and arranging for his murder, which in the biblical version was a sign of the moral degeneracy of David's rule, represents in Shamir's novel the disillusioning inability of the State of Israel to rule by the idealistic Zionist principles of those who struggled to establish it.

It is not clear in the biblical version of the story how aware Uriah was of what David was doing to him. Shamir makes use of this ambiguity in the biblical text to portray Uriah as attempting to understand what is happening to him. Much of the dramatic tension of the novel derives from Uriah's search for the truth regarding David's personal actions against him as well as the truth regarding the nature of David's leadership. Uriah's prolonged reluctance to accept the truth of David's sinful corruption reflects Shamir's desperate efforts to preserve his steadfast faith in the purity of the Zionist dream. By the end of the novel, however, Uriah is forced to conclude that the king he has so loyally served has slept with his wife and is trying to kill him. Similarly, Shamir felt forced to conclude that the course of events in the State of Israel in the 1950s had changed his relationship to Zionism from that of unqualified loyalty to that of pained disillusionment.

As evidence of David's corruption mounts, Uriah recalls a number of events in his life that in retrospect increasingly seem to have foreshadowed the king's moral decline. These events represent four areas in which Shamir had come to believe the newly founded State of Israel had failed him: the concentration and centralization of state power, the lack of commitment to social justice, the inability to negotiate a lasting peace with Israel's Arab enemies, and the killing of Israel's youths in wars with those enemies.[5]

Shamir's alienation from the growing centralization of state power in Israel is represented by Uriah's reflections on his and David's relationships with Bathsheba. While nothing is told in the biblical version of the story about the nature of Uriah's relationship with Bathsheba, in Shamir's version Uriah dwells at length on the history of their relationship, which had been problematic from the beginning. When Uriah was interested in marrying Bathsheba, she resisted the idea at first. After she agreed to marry him, she went to great lengths to resist Uriah's sexual advances. The one son who was born to them died before he was weaned.

In reviewing his marriage to Bathsheba in light of his growing awareness of David's corruption, Uriah concludes that Bathsheba had withheld herself from Uriah because her true desire was for David. This leads him to believe that Bathsheba had knowingly enticed the king to commit adultery with her. Instead of feeling angry at his faithless wife and king, Uriah blames himself for David's success in stealing Bathsheba from him. There is in him, he feels, an inner weakness and an overly cautious fear of sinning which made it impossible for Bathsheba to be attracted to him and which led her to seek a more manly lover, David.

As Dan Miron has noted, the failure of Uriah's relationship with Bathsheba to whom he refers in one passage as "my plot of ground in the fields of Judah" (p. 9),[6] makes it clear to Uriah that he has failed in "his attempt to strike roots in [Judah] and establish his seed."[7] This analogy between Bathsheba and Judah suggests that Uriah's relationship with Bathsheba represents Shamir's relationship with the State of Israel. Bathsheba's strong preference for David over Uriah represents the attractiveness of the powerful new state to the people of Israel. Just as Bathsheba longs for David the strong, manly king, so the Jews of modern Israel long for strong political leadership. Uriah is cut off from his relationship with Bathsheba, and Shamir, likewise, feels that he is unable to identify with the new state which he lovingly helped to create because it embodies the values of excessive abuse of power which are so foreign to him. In Uriah's characterization of himself as a weak, fearful, guilt-ridden man unable to attract Bathsheba, Shamir expresses his own sense of frustration that the hearts and minds of the citizens of the new state have been won over by the decisive, morally obtuse political leadership of Israel. As an opponent of the insensitive abuse of power in Israel, Shamir is bitter that he is powerless to attract the people of Israel to his own values, which represent the only way to avoid the decline of Israel into moral disaster.

Shamir expresses his concern for the decline in commitment to social justice in the State of Israel by combining two stories of David into one: the conflict between David and Nabal (I Samuel 25) and the parable told by Nathan to David to rebuke him for his crimes against Uriah. In the biblical version of the Nabal story, during David's struggle with Saul, he sought contributions of food for his men from a wealthy man named Nabal. When Nabal refused to aid David, he prepared to attack Nabal. Nabal's wife Abigail, however, persuaded him not to do so. In the end, God struck Nabal dead in punishment for spurning David, and David married Abigail.

In Shamir's novel Uriah recalls the visit of David and his men to Nabal's household in a story that follows the plot of Nathan's parable. During the visit the wealthy Nabal serves his guests a ewe lamb that he has stolen from a poor shepherd dwelling on his lands. When David learns of this unjust act, he is indignant (as David had been in the biblical story on hearing Nathan's parable), and he rebukes Nabal. David then leaves Nabal's household, vowing to the poor shepherd that justice will be done. After this incident, David becomes despondent and castigates himself before Uriah for not having fought the unjust Nabal on the spot. This image of David in agony over a moral issue contrasts significantly with the image of David in later times, who thinks nothing of stealing Uriah's wife and arranging for his murder. Having begun to suspect that David had stolen Bathsheba from him, Uriah starts to realize that when David took his enemy Nabal's wife, he was already demonstrating a potential for immorality that would be more fully actualized in his later life. Uriah's growing realization of Bathsheba's longing for the strong, manly David represents Shamir's sense that all along the people of Israel have yearned for a strong concentration of power in a central government. Similarly, Uriah's realization that David's earlier commitment to social justice was flawed in the past and is now nonexistent represents Shamir's understanding that the earlier Zionist commitment to social justice had not been strong enough to withstand the established government's inclination to abandon an idealistic approach to establishing social justice in Israeli society.

Shamir explores the failure of the State of Israel to negotiate a lasting peace with its enemies by means of Uriah's account of a meeting between representatives of David and the king of Ammon that eventually led to the outbreak of war between Israel and Ammon, during which David committed adultery with Bathsheba. The story of this meeting is based on the account found in II Samuel 10. In the biblical version of the story the king of Ammon died, and David sent messengers to the king's son Hanun to convey his condolences. Suspecting that the Israelites had been sent as spies, Hanun seized them and humiliated them by cutting off half of their beards and half of their garments and then sent them away. David was so incensed at what Hanun had done that he declared war against Ammon.

In Shamir's novel, Uriah recalls the arrival of the Israelite delegation, headed by Uriah and David's brother Eliab, at the gates of Rabbah, where they find a mob of people waiting outside the city. Eliab explains to Uriah that these people are refugees from Moab. As the guards of the city open the gates just enough to let in the members of the delegation, it is clear that the Ammonites do not want any of the Moabite refugees to enter the city. Uriah learns from this scene that "the Ammonites loved their Moabite brothers, as long as they were outside the gates" (p. 11).

While the Israelite delegation awaits its audience with Hanun, who is portrayed as a youthful and relatively weak king, Uriah and Eliab become involved in a discussion of the intentions of the Ammonites. Their assessments are almost diametrically opposed. Eliab suspects that the delay in granting the audience may indicate that the Ammonites see themselves as the enemies of Israel. Uriah in turn offers the suggestion that their inhospitable treatment expresses the Ammonites' reaction to the defeat of Moab by Israel. Eliab then angrily challenges Uriah's suggestion that the Ammonites' hostility is justified because of what Israel did to Moab. Uriah, who is more understanding of the Ammonites' hostility to Israel, believes, however, that in the end they can be trusted, while Eliab, who can find no reason to understand the Ammonites' hostility, is convinced that they cannot.

Once Uriah and Eliab enter into discussions with Hanun, it becomes clear to Uriah that there is greater hostility toward the Israelites in the court of Hanun than he had suspected and that Eliab's assessment of the Ammonites had been closer to the truth than his own. Although Uriah has come to accept Eliab's negative appraisal of the Ammonites' intentions, he insists on responding to the situation not in the mistrusting manner of Eliab, but in such a way as to attempt to convince the Ammonites that the Israelites really want peace.

Now that Uriah has grown increasingly skeptical toward David, he begins to realize that an earlier suspicion he had had at the time of the discussions with Hanun might have been true: David had not sent the delegation to make peace, but rather to create a pretext for Israel to make war on Ammon.

Uriah's assessment of ancient Israel's relations with Ammon represents Shamir's assessment of modern Israel's relations with Jordan, which today occupies the lands of ancient Ammon. The portrayal of Hanun as a young king alludes to King Hussein of Jordan, who rose to power as a youth and whose strength had not been fully tested in the early 1950s when Shamir wrote the novel. The Moabite refugees huddled outside the gates of Rabbah represent the Palestinian Arab refugees of Israel's War of Independence, who have served as the ostensible motivation for the hostility of Jordan and the other Arab nations toward Israel, but have not in Shamir's opinion been adequately cared for by the Arab countries to which they have fled.

The debate between Uriah and Eliab over how to handle the Ammonite hostility toward Israel expresses Shamir's understanding of the division within Israeli society regarding the question of whether the Arab enemies of Israel can ever be trusted to make a lasting peace with Israel. In presenting the points of view of Uriah and Eliab, Shamir appears to be more sympathetic to that of Uriah, the hero of the novel. Eliab's assumption that the Ammonites are never to be trusted comes across as self-defeating. Shamir appears to be saying that such an attitude toward the Arabs in his own day is also not a productive one. Uriah's more trusting attitude toward Ammon, however, is based on a realistic assessment of the situation. He realizes that the Ammonites are not eager for peace, but he blames their attitude on the negative influence of the Moabite refugees. Similarly, Shamir appears to be saying that the bitterness of the Palestinian refugees made homeless by the Israeli War of Independence is the root cause of the state of war between Israel and the Arabs, and that the only hope for peace is for modern Israel to attempt to undo the negative image it has received as a result of the plight of the Palestinian refugees. Just as Uriah feels that ancient Israel should keep making offers of peace to its enemy, despite Ammonite hostility, so Shamir feels that modern Israel should keep making offers of peace to its enemy.

Shamir is not convinced that the government of Israel is as committed to pursuing peace as he is. He expresses this concern through Uriah's doubts as to whether David really wanted to make peace with Ammon. Now that the State of Israel is engaged in what might be a prolonged state of war with the Arabs, it begins to appear to Shamir that the Zionist dream of building a Jewish state that would be a harmonious part of the Middle East has been abandoned by a government whose policies further war, not peace.

For Shamir the worst consequences of the state of war maintained between Israel and the Arabs appears to be the death of the young Israeli soldiers and the turning of those young soldiers into the killers of their enemies. As Dan Miron has pointed out, Shamir saw this issue to be a central one of Israeli existence. In Shamir's essay ")Edipus ve'avraham" ("Oedipus and Abraham"), for example, Shamir argues that the story of the binding of Isaac, in which the father is called on to kill the son (in contrast to the story of Oedipus, in which the son kills the father) is *the* story of his generation, in which the fathers seek salvation by sending their sons off to die in war.[8] Uriah's growing sense in the novel that his life is being cruelly sacrificed to enhance David's power leads him to the conviction that war is absurd and contrary to the innermost yearnings of the human soul. Uriah's attitude reflects Shamir's own growing doubts about life in a state that keeps denying its young men the fulfillment of the desires of their life for the sake of maintaining the existence of the state.

Joab, in an act of disobedience to David's order which is not found in the biblical version of the story, saves Uriah from death in battle and gives Uriah an opportunity to flee the war. Although by this point in the novel Uriah is fully aware of David's betrayal of him, he chooses not to flee but willingly to accept the role of the victim of David's war and of the moral decay of Israel in order to bear witness to the vision of peace and brotherhood that David has abandoned. As he goes to his death in the battle, Uriah comes to the conclusion that the price that Israel has paid for its rise to power under the leadership of David has been too great. By gaining power at the expense of others, Israel will never know true peace, strength, or freedom:

> And if a man say to you: "Here are the strong on this side, and over there, down below, we the weak," ask him: Which is the strong, and which the weak? Shall the man who cannot stay alive without killing be called strong? He is the weakest of all. And the man who does not die, though others live, multiply, are fruitful and grow great — shall he be called weak?
>
> Not by war shall truth be tested. They will say: "The victor has conquered the vanquished." Ask them, then: Who is the victor and who is the vanquished? For the victor returns to his house, his mind on great matters, and he finds his field a wasteland. To his women's beds he brings the bodies of dead warriors who will no longer plant their seed in women's bodies. Few and exhausted, his sons will ask: Where is our victory? They will seek it, and will not find it. The rains will not come in season, and the fish of the sea will not spawn. Famine will come to the land, slaying and bringing pestilence. But the vanquished man returns to his home, hoards his remaining strength and life, and toils, his mind on small matters. He will sow and will reap. He will mourn his dead, and life will give him others in their stead. He will strive for little, and that little he will attain (p. 213).

In Uriah's thoughts on the relationship between the victor and the vanquished it is possible to discern Shamir's deep concern for the moral consequences of what the State of Israel has done to its citizens and its enemies. It is a terrible burden for the Israeli to serve a state that is constantly at war. In such a situation the people have come to assume that victory in war is the ultimate goal of the nation, and so they spend all their strength on war and the maintenance of the power they have gained in victory. Meanwhile, the vanquished Arabs may be better off than the victorious Israelis, for the former are not preoccupied with the maintenance of power; they, instead, can concentrate on getting the most pleasure out of life.

The conclusion Uriah reaches before his death about the true nature of David's rule suggests an attitude of despair on the part of Shamir about the moral failures of the Zionist struggle to which he had been so passionately committed. Shamir does not, however, conclude the novel with the death of Uriah. In the epilogue to the novel, Ahimelech the Hittite, a friend of Uriah who witnessed Uriah's death and rescued his diary from oblivion, interprets Uriah's thoughts in such a way as to convey to the readers of the novel a way out of concluding that Zionism must be rejected because it lacks moral purity. Writing at the time of the rule of Solomon, Ahimelech considers the paradoxical situation of the king. He is considered to be a good king, yet his origins lie in the sinful manner by which his father David acquired his mother Bathsheba as a wife. He understands from this situation and from thoughts expressed by Uriah in his diary that God makes use of evil as well as good to further his ends:

> An idea that Uriah almost summoned up comes into my mind now: not only does good serve the will of God, but evil also; not only do the righteous carry out the divine purpose, but the unrighteous as well. In truth, this is the Lord's way and this His power, that He does not wait for men to worship Him in the path of righteousness, but with His vast and miraculous powers, He contrives that even those who toil against Him and turn from His path serve Him and serve His ends (pp. 218–19).

This point of view allows Shamir and his readers to see that the Zionists' establishment of the State of Israel does serve a greater moral purpose, even if some of the state's deeds have been evil. Nevertheless, Shamir makes it clear to his readers that such a view of Israel's establishment does not exonerate it from the moral condemnation of the state's evil acts when they are committed. As Ahimelech declares:

> An evil deed is evil, even though the loftiest motives engendered it, even if it results in the greatest good. Even the man who is forced to sin, sins: even the man who saves life by his sin, sins. Should you seek to save a life by sinning, save it; but you cease to be numbered among the righteous in the land (pp. 219–20).

Since Israel was created by acts of less than moral purity, there is for Shamir the constant danger that it will suffer some form of retribution in the future which will be its downfall. He expresses this concern through the words of Ahimelech, who wonders whether the greatly successful Israel of Solomon's day may yet pay the price for David's sins against Uriah:

> Perhaps David's sin did not end in Uriah. Perhaps it is only outwardly that the deed is praised together with Solomon, and together with him is included in the blessing of all who knew him. Somewhere in the inmost being of the royal house the curse of the betrayed man may tremble still, flowing in the blood of each generation; the end of the great and terrible punishment may still be to come (p. 219).

In an essay written shortly after the publication of *Kivsat harash*, Shamir responded to the reactions of a number of readers of the novel who were troubled by what they perceived to be his negative portrayal of King David. Shamir argued that he was not trying to portray David as an evil king, for he believed that as far as kings go,

> David was a good king. Without a doubt he was a king who conquered, united, built a nation, stabilized a kingdom and a state, a wise king, who maintained religion, spread Torah, increased wealth and property. He was a king in the full meaning of the

word, and there has been no king among the nations of the world at any time and in any state who could not have learned something from him about kingship.[9]

The problem with David, according to Shamir, was not that he was a bad king, but that every good king who seeks to rule his people successfully inevitably chooses some evil means to do so. There is, therefore, a basic conflict between the demands of history and the demands of morality. That for Shamir is the terrible choice facing the Jews of Israel in his day. If they wish to continue to exist they must be involved in a less than morally perfect state. If they wish to be morally perfect, they will cease to exist, for there will be no state to protect them from their enemies.[10] In the final analysis, Shamir chooses to cast his lot with the reality of David's rule, even as he continues to judge it by the idealism of Uriah.

Amos Oz: Jephthah and His Daughter

At the beginning of the biblical story of Jephthah, on which Oz's story "ʿAl haʾadamah haraʿah hazot" is based, Jephthah, who had been born as a result of his father Gilead's relations with a prostitute, was driven out of Gilead's household by Gilead's other sons. Jephthah then settled for a while in the land of Tob among men of low character. When the Ammonites went to war against Israel, the elders of the region of Gilead went to Tob to convince Jephthah, who had a reputation as a good warrior, to return to lead the fight against the Ammonites. Jephthah agreed to do so on condition that if they were victorious in battle, he would become their leader. Jephthah then engaged in an exchange of messengers with the Ammonites in an attempt to convince them to cease their war against Israel. When the king of the Ammonites explained that he had begun the war against Israel because the Israelites had seized his land after their exodus from Egypt, Jephthah replied that whatever land Israel possessed was given to it by God and therefore no one had the right to fight Israel for having seized that land. The king of the Ammonites refused to accept Jephthah's argument, so Jephthah went on the offensive against Ammon.

Before his final battle with Ammon, Jephthah vowed to God that if He granted him victory over the Ammonites, Jephthah would make a burnt offering to God of whatever greeted him first at his house when he returned home from battle. Jephthah was victorious, but when he returned home it was his only child, his daughter, who greeted him. Both he and his daughter agreed that he could not violate his vow to God, but he acceded to her request to be allowed to go for two months with some companions to the hills and lament her fate of dying without ever having had relations with a man. Jephthah's sacrifice of his daughter later captured the imagination of the maidens of Israel for generations to come, and they instituted a custom to spend four days each year mourning the fate of Jephthah's daughter.

Oz focuses in his version of the story on Jephthah's relationship with three peoples: the Israelites, their enemies the Ammonites, and the people of the land of Tob, who are presented as indiscriminate raiders of both the Israelites and Ammonites alike. Jephthah is portrayed as a skillful leader whose leadership is sought after not only by the Israelites, but also by the Ammonites and the people of the land of Tob. Although at various points in the story Jephthah develops a special relationship with each of these peoples, he remains throughout the story an individualist who refuses to commit himself deeply to any one group.

As a leader of Israel for six years from the time of his victory over the Ammonites, Jephthah is portrayed by the narrator as willing to fulfill his responsibilities to the nation. During this period, however, he refrains from getting caught up in the nationalist feelings of love of country, hatred toward enemies, and triumphant celebration of military victory. Instead, he seeks his true fulfillment within his own soul.

Oz's story compares Jephthah's ambivalent relationship with Israel to his earlier involvement with Ammon, where he flees in Oz's version after his brothers drive him out of his father's house. Jephthah goes to Ammon with the notion that he will join them in an attack on his father's household. According to the story, Jephthah already has a connection to the Ammonites, for his prostitute mother had come from that people. When he arrives in Ammon, the leaders of the Ammonites are at first very attracted to him, for they see in him great qualities of leadership. As time goes on, Jephthah develops a special relationship with Gatel the king of Ammon. As in *Kivsat harash*, the portrait of the king of ancient Ammon alludes to the youthful King Hussein of modern Jordan. He is described as a boy who yearns to be a great king but is prevented from becoming one because of his childish personality.

In his weakness Gatel turns to Jephthah to tell him stories and advise him on his decisions. The special relationship that develops between Gatel and Jephthah arouses suspicion and jealousy on the part of the elders of Ammon. They are concerned because Gatel has allowed himself to be so subservient to Jephthah and because they feel he is too involved in his own concerns to be trusted to serve the national interests. When Gatel hears that the elders are suspicious of Jephthah's loyalty to Ammon, he tests Jephthah by calling on him to join the Ammonites in battle against Gilead. Although Jephthah had originally planned to be involved in such an attack when he had fled to Ammon, he decides at this point instead to flee from Ammon to the land of Tob.

By inserting a flight by Jephthah to Ammon (which does not appear in the biblical version) before Jephthah's flight to the land of Tob (which does appear in the biblical version), Oz emphasizes the dichotomy in Jephthah's soul between Israel and Ammon. In the land of Tob Jephthah joins "desert nomads who . . . were all malcontents or outcasts" (p. 129),[11] who are parallel to the men of low character with whom Jephthah lived in Tob in the biblical version. The flight to Tob represents an escape by Jephthah from choosing between loyalty to Israel and loyalty to Ammon. The nomads of Tob live in opposition to the civilizations of Israel and Ammon and therefore arouse the hatred of both peoples. After an initial period of suspicion, the leaders of Tob accept Jephthah to be their leader in the attacks on the Ammonites and the Israelites. In this role Jephthah deals with the dichotomy in his soul between loyalty to

Israel and loyalty to Ammon by attempting to destroy both peoples. Jephthah, however, does not continue his involvement with the nomads, and, as in the biblical version of the story, he eventually agrees to return to Israel to lead it in the war against the Ammonites.

The reasons behind Jephthah's vacillation between loyalty to the Israelites and loyalty to the Ammonites are made clear in Jephthah's relationship with the deities worshiped by his Israelite father Gilead and his Ammonite mother, named Pitdah in the story. The two deities are presented to Jephthah by Pitdah as Milcom, the pleasure-loving god of the Ammonites, and the stern moral God of Israel who brings little pleasure to His people:

> And she would speak to him of Milcom, whom the Ammonites worshiped with wine and silk. Not like your father's god, a barren god who afflicts and humiliates those who love him. No, Milcom loves marauders, he loves those who are merry with wine, he loves those who pour out their hearts in song, and the music that blurs the line between ecstasy and rage.
>
> Of the God of Israel Pitdah said: Woe to those who sin against him and woe to those who worship him in faith; he will afflict them both alike with agonies because he is a solitary god (p. 199).

It is clear from his dreams that Jephthah often feels greatly attracted to Milcom and the affirmation of physical pleasure that he represents and most frightened of the God of Israel:

> At night Jephthah dreamed of God coming heavy and shaggy, a bear-God with rapacious jaws who growled at him panting and gasping and panting as though he were throbbing with lust or boiling rage . . . .
>
> Milcom, too, crept into Jephthah's dreams on those summer nights. Warm currents coursed luxuriantly through his veins as the silken fingers touched his skin and sweet juices washed through him to the soles of his feet (pp. 199–200).

Jephthah realizes, however, that as attractive as Milcom is and as easy as it is for him to relate to that god, he really yearns much more for the more forbidding God of Gilead.

Jephthah's escape to Ammon provides him with an opportunity to flee the stern and frightening God of Israel and engage in the physical pleasures of Milcom, in which he finds the Ammonites indulging. Nevertheless, Jephthah's participation in the pleasures of Milcom is always qualified by an attitude of detachment that never allows him to fully immerse his soul in them.

Just as Jephthah had attempted to resolve his conflict of loyalties between Israel and Ammon by fleeing to the land of Tob, so does he resolve the tension in his soul between the God of Israel and Milcom by developing for himself the notion of a god of the desert who shares the wild qualities of the marauding people of the land of Tob. The qualities that Jephthah attributes to this god are closer to those of Gilead's God than to those of Pitdah's god. In this god's endorsement of marauding, however, he bears some resemblance to Milcom. In an address to this god it is clear that although Jephthah does not feel much closer to him than he did to Gilead's God, he is attracted to him because he gives him a sense of purpose:

> O Lord of the asp in the desert, do not hide yourself from me. Call me, call me, gather me to you. If I am not worthy to be your chosen one, take me to be your hired assassin: I shall go in the night with my knife in your name to your foes, and in the morning you may hide your face from me as you will, as if we were strangers. You are the lord of the fox and the vulture and I love your wrath and I do not ask you to lift up the brightness of your countenance toward me. Your wrath and barren sorrow are all I want. Surely anger and sadness are a sign to me that I am made in your image, I am your son, I am yours, and you will take me to you by night, for in the image of your hatred I am made, O Lord of the wolves at night in the desert. You are a weary and a desperate God, and whomsoever you love, him will you burn with fire, for you are jealous (p. 214).

As an act of devotion to this god of the wild Jephthah vows to sacrifice his daughter, who is presented in the story as having been born from licentious sexual relations that Jephthah had in Ammon. Jephthah had drawn very close to his daughter, whom he had named Pitdah after his mother. He became so close to her that he was consumed with jealousy whenever he thought of her marrying a man. The sacrifice is compared in the story to the binding of Isaac (Genesis 22). Jephthah's expectation is that the sacrifice is a test of loyalty to his god and that like Abraham, he will be instructed by his god at the last minute not to sacrifice his offspring. Unlike Abraham's God, however, Jephthah's god of the wild does not intervene to stop the sacrifice of his daughter. If Jephthah is to prove his faith in this god, he must sacrifice the pleasure-seeking way of life that his daughter and her mother represent.

Jephthah's inner conflict between loyalty to Milcom and Ammon and loyalty to the people and God of Israel conveys the conflict in the soul of Oz and his sabra generation of first-born native Israelis whose parents are of European origin. On the one hand, that generation had been reared in the morally demanding Jewish tradition and its secular transformation into loyalty to the fulfillment of the Zionist dream, represented in the story by the God of Israel. On the other hand, it had been born in a Middle Eastern setting in which its Arab neighbors seem to have a greater appreciation for the pleasures of life, represented by Milcom.

By presenting Jephthah as the offspring of Gilead, an Israelite, and Pitdah, an Ammonite, Oz suggests that the sabra generation feels itself as strongly tied to its Middle Eastern cultural influences as it is to its European Jewish cultural influences. Oz's use of the biblical detail that Jephthah's mother was a prostitute, however, points to the sabra generation's sense that its inclination to seek pleasure rather than a life committed to Jewish and Zionist values is somehow illegitimate. The sabra is so torn within between these two tendencies that when he fulfills his national obligations to Israel and when he seeks physical pleasure, he can never be fully committed to either set of actions, just as Jephthah could never be fully trusted to be loyal either to Israel or to Ammon.

Jephthah's conception of a god of the wild as a way out of his inner conflict between the God of Israel and Milcom the god of Ammon represents Oz's understanding of the existential situation of the sabra. Jephthah's image of himself as the hired assassin fighting the enemies of the god of the wild is the key to understanding with what the sabra most authentically identifies. It is his role as a soldier in the army of Israel, called upon to kill the enemies of God's people Israel. This is not presented by Oz as completely fulfilling an identity as that of the European Jew or the Middle Eastern Arab. Indeed there are two disturbing aspects to it. One is in the image of Jephthah as hired assassin that suggests the tragedy of the sabra having been turned into the killer of his enemies. The other is in the image of Jephthah's sacrificing his daughter that suggests the tragedy of the parents of the sabra and of the sabra himself, when he becomes a parent, of having to sacrifice his children, who represent the affirmation of life, in order to defend the state. Oz's portrayal of the sacrifice of Jephthah as a binding of Isaac story gone wrong suggests how troubled he is by the role which the Israeli of his and later generations has been called on to play in a test that is so much crueller than any Abraham had to withstand.

There is a clear generational difference between the nature of the discomfort with the State of Israel felt by the writers Nissim Aloni and Moshe Shamir, who wrote during the Palmach period and were adults at the time of the establishment of the state, and the nature of the discomfort felt by the New Wave writer Amos Oz, who became an adult after the establishment of the state. Aloni and Shamir can vividly remember the prestate period when the Jewish community of the Land of Israel lived without the full range of moral dilemmas that accompany political sovereignty. As they witness abuses of power in the state they helped to create, they raise in their works the memory of that relatively morally pure prestate period as a model to be followed even after the acquisition of political sovereignty.

In their portrayals of Jeroboam and Uriah as representatives of themselves as moral critics of the state, they express the agony they feel as Israelis who want to remain loyal to their state but find it acting in ways that they cannot condone. By the end of their works, both Aloni and Shamir express their awareness that the moral purity of the past can never be fully recovered. Jeroboam begins the rebellion against Rehoboam with the knowledge that he, like the harsh king he opposes, will cause the suffering of at least some of those whom he leads because they will die in the rebellion. Uriah concludes before his death that the ideal of an established government maintaining uncorrupted power may be impossible to attain.

For Oz the issue is not disillusionment with the state he helped to create, but rather his difficulty in accepting the role of maintaining and defending the state that the previous generation had established in his childhood. He feels pulled between what he perceives to be the stern morality of the European Jewish culture of his parents' generation and what he perceives to be the more pleasure-oriented culture of the Arabs native to the Middle Eastern region in which he was born. His identity as a soldier fighting to defend Israel may provide him with his least problematic identity, but it is not one that allows him to participate as fully as he would like to in the European Jewish and Middle Eastern Arab cultures that have influenced his life. It turns him instead into a killer and potential victim in the war to preserve Israel's existence.

The heroes of all three retold versions of biblical stories by these Israeli writers are portrayed as foreigners of some sort. Much is made in Aloni's play of the Egyptian influences on Jeroboam that are considered by the other Israelites to be foreign to the true spirit of Israel. Uriah in Shamir's novel is a Hittite. In Oz's story, Jephthah is the rejected brother, half-Israelite and half-Ammonite. By identifying with these foreign heroes the authors of these works are saying something about the nature of their Israeli identities. In so doing they raise the question of what it means to be an Israeli. Does it mean to fit in to all that the society and government has established as the moral norms of the nation, always to do what the government wants you to do, and always to accept what the government is doing to you? Or does it mean to allow yourself to be a moral gadfly, running the risk of being accused of disloyalty to the state, as if you really had the interests of Israel's neighboring enemies in mind rather than those of the state?

Aloni, Shamir, and Oz seem to express some degree of inner debate about whether it is worth their while to cast their lot with the society and government of Israel when their lives there are so difficult for them to accept. Each of their biblical heroes is portrayed in their works as tempted at a certain point to abandon ancient Israel. Maacah constantly tempts Jeroboam to flee Israel for a life of pleasure in foreign lands. Just before Uriah's death Joab offers him the option of fleeing the Israelite army. Jephthah is attracted to the hedonistic pleasures of Ammonite society.

Despite these temptations, each hero chooses not to flee, even though he knows that by not fleeing he will be involved in a personal sacrifice. By staying in Israel to challenge Rehoboam's rule, Jeroboam must make use of the cruel means of Rehoboam in direct violation of his inner moral instincts. When he chooses to remain in the battle, Uriah allows himself to be the victim of David's abuse of royal power. Jephthah's choice to remain loyal to a god who calls on him to fight Israel's enemies forces him to sacrifice his daughter. Aloni, Shamir, and Oz do not appear to be fully happy with what they must give up in individual fulfillment and moral purity to remain a part of the State of Israel, but they affirm in their works their commitment to do so in order to preserve this reality that is the product of the Zionist dream.

Conclusion:
Traditional Heroes
for Modern Times

In their choices of which traditional Jewish narratives to retell, the modern midrashic Hebrew writers of the twentieth century have at times expressed the sense that this period in Jewish history is one of renewal and have at other times expressed the sense that it is one of destruction. These conflicting senses have persisted among these writers in both Europe and Israel throughout the century and are found among Jewish writers in other cultural contexts as well. On the one hand, the modern midrashic Hebrew writers have displayed a particular interest in narratives that tell of new beginnings: the biblical stories of Genesis, the exodus from Egypt, the early period of Israelite settlement in Canaan and the establishment of new political institutions there; legends of the return to Zion in the days of Ezra and Nehemiah; and tales of religious revival at the time of the rise of Hasidism. On the other hand, they have been equally fascinated with aspects of these narratives of renewal and other narratives that portray violent struggles and desolate failures: the biblical stories of the expulsion of Adam and Eve from the Garden of Eden, the murder of Abel by Cain, Abraham's banishment of Hagar, the attempted sacrifice of Isaac by Abraham, the conflicts between God and the Israelites in the wilderness, the battles of Jephthah and Saul against the enemies of Israel, and the power struggles between David and Uriah and between Rehoboam and Jeroboam; as well as legends of the destructions of the First and Second Temples.

The heroes of these retold versions of traditional Jewish narratives represent modern Jews who struggle to triumph over some force that threatens to deny their existence on either a physical or a cultural level. On a physical level, the gentiles constitute a violent force that attacks and seeks to destroy the Jews, beginning with the pogroms of Eastern Europe in the late nineteenth and early twentieth centuries and culminating with the Holocaust and the Arab attempts to deny Jews the right to gain political sovereignty in the Land of Israel. On a cultural level, Jewish culture seeks to limit the fulfillment of the Jews' individual needs, placing restraints on their intellectual freedom, moral instincts, natural physical drives, and contact with non-Jewish culture. It is interesting that the same kinds of complaints of European Jews against the limitations of traditional Jewish culture are found among Israeli Jews who feel that the State of Israel has limited the fulfillment of their individual needs.

The heroes that represent responses to the problematic nature of modern Jewish existence have a variety of relationships to the traditional heroes on which they are based. In some cases there is a strong resemblance between what the hero does in the traditional narrative and what he does in the retold version. In other cases there is some aspect of the traditional hero's situation or actions that suggests the usefulness of this character as a representative of modern struggles, although what the modern hero struggles with is not exactly what the traditional hero struggles with. Finally, in some cases the modern hero of the retold version seems to do almost the exact opposite of what the hero in the traditional version does.

In response to the physical threats to Jewish existence we find both heroes who fight and those who are destroyed before they have a chance to fight. The two major examples of fighter heroes are, significantly, based on traditional heroes who are defeated victims of gentile power. In Bialik's "Megillat ha'esh" from among the captive martyrs of ancient legend emerges the man of terror who calls for vengeance on the oppressors. In Tchernichowsky's "'Al ḥorvot beit-shan" the defeated Saul, who in the Bible commits suicide, is transformed into a spirit who in messianic times will summon his army to take revenge on the gentiles who defeated the Jews. In Tchernichowsky's "'Al harei gilboa'" that same Saul is portrayed as the tireless fighter setting an example for the Jews not to abandon their struggle to settle the Land of Israel even in the dark days of 1929. By turning the victims of the past into fighter heroes, these authors deliberately challenge the traditional martyrological ideal of dying for the sanctification of God's name.

And yet even as they challenge that ideal, neither Bialik nor Tchernichowsky is very comfortable with the violent alternative of fighting for one's existence. In the end the man of terror leads the captive youths to their deaths in the river Abaddon. He thus proves to have contributed no more positively to the physical existence of the people than did the traditional notions of martyrdom that lead the captive maidens to their death in the river Abaddon. Tchernichowsky's ghost of Saul is prevented by God at the end of days from taking revenge on the gentiles and instead is instructed to respond to them in love. The Saul who fights to defend the Jews of the Land of Israel in "'Al harei gilboa'" is eventually killed and buried in "'Anshei ḥayil ḥevel," thereby calling into question the worth of the Zionist struggle that has claimed so many Jewish lives.

In the context of the Holocaust there are two kinds of heroes: the victims who died and the survivors who lived to tell the rest of the world what happened. In portraying the victims as the defeated Saul (in Gilboa's "Sha'ul") or the slain Abel (in Kovner's "Mikarov" or in Pagis's "Katuv be'ipparon," "'Aḥim," and "'Otobiyyografyah,") no judgment is made of the victims' response (although at first Gilboa appears to be somewhat ashamed of it). The survivors have a particular role to play after the war. The speaker in Gilboa's poem "Sha'ul," who identifies with Saul's arms-bearer, Isaac in Gilboa's poem "Yitsḥak," Cain in Kovner's poem "Mikarov," and Abel in Pagis's poem "'Otobiyyografyah" all serve as mediators between the Holocaust and the postwar world, challenging the world to live up to higher ideals than it did in the war.

A variety of heroes suffer from limitations placed on them by Jewish culture. Some of these characters actively rebel against Jewish culture. The gatherer of wood on the Sabbath and the rebellious son of biblical law become in Frischmann's stories "Hamekoshesh" and "Sorer umoreh" models of heroes who challenge the arbitrary nature of Jewish law and Jewish communal leaders' lack of commitment to social justice. In Bialik's "Megillat ha'esh" one of the captive victims of ancient legend is the fair youth who chafes at the limitations placed on him by the old Nazirite, who represents the traditional Jewish restrictive approach to sexuality. Similarly, Saul's struggle with the ghost of the prophet Samuel is transformed in Tchernichowsky's "Be'ein-dor" into the life-affirming struggle of the Jew against the life-denying forces of traditional Jewish culture. Abraham's expulsion of Hagar ends in Bat-Miriam's poem "'Avraham" with his rejection of his earlier assumption that he needed to deny his sexual needs in order to experience the holy.

Another way that some of these heroes challenge Jewish culture is to leave it for a time and enter into a gentile culture that appears to be an attractive alternative. Berdyczewski uses the captivity of Eliezer in the original Hasidic tale to portray in his story "Shnei 'olamot" a heroic break with the ascetic life of traditional Judaism and an escape into involvement in European culture. In Frischmann's story "Meḥolot," Put of the mixed multitude that left Egypt with the Israelites represents the temptations of European culture. Similarly, Jeroboam's sojourn in Egypt after his attempt to rebel against Solomon in Aloni's 'Akhzar mikol hamelekh provides a critical perspective on the abuse of power in Israel. Oz makes use of Jephthah's rejection by his brothers to transform him in "'Al ha'adamah hara'ah hazot" into a half-Ammonite and half-Israelite who flees to Middle Eastern ways of life that allow him to experience sensuality freely without the constraints of religion or national duty.

It is important to note, however, that each of these heroes eventually returns to the Jewish culture from which he or she fled. The hero then makes use of the wider perspective that gentile culture offered to transform Jewish culture into something new and more relevant to his or her needs. Eliezer's entrance into gentile culture paves the way for what Berdyczewski hoped would be the birth of a neo-Hasidic generation that would transcend the limitations of traditional Judaism and the Haskalah. As a result of her love affair with Put of the mixed multitude, Timna presents an alternative revelation of a God of all the earth to the Israelites that corresponds to Frischmann's dream of a synthesis of the Jewish and gentile cultures. Jeroboam's insistence that the supposedly Egyptian values that he wants Israel to live by are in fact a return to the pure uncorrupted values of the past reflects Aloni's wish that his fellow Israelis would widen their cultural horizons so that they could escape the narrow corruption into which Israel has slipped. Jephthah's god of the wild, who combines cultural elements of the Israelites, Ammonites, and people of the land of Tob, represents Oz's attempt to forge for Israelis a self-understanding that is based on both European Jewish influences and Middle Eastern Arab influences.

It is not surprising that given the nature of the formidable struggles that these old/new heroes undertake, most are really not successful in what they set out to do. The fighters against gentile enemies never achieve the revenge or victory that secures the tenuous physical existence of the Jews in the world. The survivors of the Holocaust do not appear to be convinced that the moral message they bear to the postwar world will really be heeded. The rebels against Jewish culture generally die having been defeated by the cultural establishment. Those who leave Jewish culture and then return do not have much success in converting their fellow Jews to the wider perspective that exposure to gentile culture might afford them.

The heroes with whom these writers most closely identify are those who serve as models for the modern artist. The achievement of these heroes is to perceive hidden truths and know how to embody and communicate them to the rest of the Jews in works of art. The storytelling Nachman of Bratslav represents in Peretz's "Ha'ofot vehagevilim" the neoromantic author himself who knows how to show the modern alienated Jew how to return to a more positive relationship with his tradition. In "Megillat ha'esh" Bialik transforms the priests who discover the holy fire of the sacrificial cult into the modern poet/collector of legends who serves as the only source of truth and connection to the vitality of the past that is left for the Jewish people. The lonely, rejected Hagar in Bat-Miriam's poem "Hagar" represents the poet herself who can show the way to transcend the limitations of existence in this world by entering into the world of poetic imagination. Uriah, the keeper of a diary in Shamir's novel

Kivsat harash, becomes the contemporary Israeli writer searching for the truths about abuses of power that the leaders of the state are hiding from the citizens.

The most inspiring of these heroes-turned-artists are the dancers. Dancing allows each of these heroes to be liberated from the constraints of culture and to communicate to his or her fellow Jews a revolutionary new cultural path. Miriam's dance after the crossing of the Sea of Reeds becomes in Bat-Miriam's poem "Miryam" a dance of the liberation of Jewish women from their limitation by Jewish men. Out of the dances around the golden calf emerges Timna in Frischmann's story "Meḥolot," who reveals a new gentile-Jewish cultural synthesis that is more in touch with God than a narrowly based Jewish culture. The ecstatic prophetic experiences of Saul become in Tchernichowsky's "Hamelekh" a mad dance that uncovers for those weary of the degenerate European civilization insights into the unity of existence.

Even though, like their artist heroes, these retellers of traditional narratives express truths that are not always heeded by their people, they persist in making use of their artistic powers to teach Jews what will set them free from the forces that threaten to destroy them. Their way is, to borrow Bialik's phrase, that of *tikkun yetsiri*, the creative restoration of the narratives of the past by writing works of modern midrash on those narratives. These writers use characters, plot structures, images, and themes of traditional narratives to point to new directions for Jewish culture in the twentieth century. What makes modern midrash so important is that it creates that link between the insights of the past and present which is so essential for achieving the national and cultural revival of the Jews.

Notes

Introduction

1. *Bereshit Rabbah* 55; 56. See Moshe Aryeh Mirkin, ed., *Midrash Rabbah* (Tel Aviv: Yavneh, 1957), 2:260, 273.

2. See the analysis of this liturgical poem in Shalom Spiegel, *The Last Trial: On the Legends and Lore of the Command to Abraham to Offer Isaac as a Sacrifice: The Akedah,* trans. Judah Goldin (Philadelphia: Jewish Publication Society of America, 1967).

3. Alan Mintz, *Ḥurban: Responses to Catastrophe in Hebrew Literature* (New York: Columbia University Press, 1984), 99–100.

4. For discussions of the development of the midrashic tradition in the biblical and postbiblical periods, see the following essays in Geoffrey H. Hartman and Sanford Budick, eds., *Midrash and Literature* (New Haven: Yale University Press, 1986): Michael Fishbane, "Inner Biblical Exegesis: Types and Strategies of Interpretation in Ancient Israel," 19–37, which draws upon the author's work, Michael Fishbane, *Biblical Interpretation of Ancient Israel* (Oxford: Clarendon Press, 1985); Joseph Heinemann, "The Nature of the Aggadah," 41–55, which is a translation of the first chapter of the author's work, Joseph Heinemann, *'Aggadot vetoldoteihen* (Jerusalem, Keter, 1974); and James L. Kugel, "Two Introductions to Midrash," 77–103.

5. Henry A. Murray, "The Possible Nature of a 'Mythology' to Come," in Henry A. Murray, ed., *Myth and Mythmaking* (1960; reprint, Boston: Beacon Press, 1968), 337.

6. Northrop Frye, *The Secular Scripture: A Study of the Structure of Romance* (Cambridge: Harvard University Press, 1976), 161–88.

7. Harry Slochower, *Mythopoesis: Mythic Patterns in the Literary Classics* (1970; reprint, Detroit: Wayne State University Press, 1973), 34.

8. See David Biale, *Gershom Scholem: Kabbalah and Counter-History* (Cambridge: Harvard University Press, 1979).

9. Jonathan Culler, *The Pursuit of Signs: Semiotics, Literature, Deconstruction* (Ithaca: Cornell University Press, 1981), 107.

10. Harold Bloom, *A Map of Misreading* (New York: Oxford University Press, 1975), 19. See also Harold Bloom, *Kabbalah and Criticism* (New York: The Seabury Press, 1975).

11. See the discussion of the analogous relationship of midrash and modern literary theory in Susan A. Handelman, *The Slayers of Moses: The Emergence of Rabbinic Interpretation in Modern Literary Theory* (Albany: State University of New York Press, 1982).

12. For discussions of the period of modern Hebrew literature to which these writers belong, see Simon Halkin, *Modern Hebrew Literature: From the Enlightenment to the Birth of the State of Israel: Trends and Values* (1950; reprint, New York: Schocken Books, 1970); Dan Miron, "Hasifrut ha'ivrit bereshit hame'ah ha'esrim: perakim mitokh massah," *Me'asef ledivrei sifrut, bikkoret, vehagut* 2 (1961): 436-64; and Dan Miron, "Lereka' hamevukhah basifrut ha'ivrit bereshit hame'ah ha'esrim" in Boaz Katz and Menahem Perry, ed., *Sefer hayovel leShim'on Halkin* (Jerusalem: Reuben Mass, 1975), 419-87.

13. For discussions of this shift in the center of modern Hebrew literature from Europe to the Land of Israel, see Zohar Shavit, *Hahayyim hasifrutiyyim be'erets yisra'el, 1910-1933* (Tel Aviv: Tel Aviv University, 1982); and Zohar Shavit, "Hashorashim halkhu vehitma'atu," *Hasifrut* 32 (1983): 45-50.

14. For discussions of the period of modern Hebrew literature to which these writers belong, see Gershon Shaked, *Gal hadash basipporet ha'ivrit: massot 'al sipporet yisra'elit tse'irah* (Merhavia and Tel Aviv: Sifriat Poalim, 1971); Nurith Gertz, *'Amos 'Oz: monografyah* (Tel Aviv: Sifriat Poalim, 1980), 9-43; and Nurith Gertz, *Hirbet Hiz'eh vehaboker shelemohorat* (Tel Aviv: Hakibbutz Hameuchad, 1983). An English translation of an extract from the latter work may be found in Nurit Gertz,"'Hirbet Hiz'eh' and the Morning After," *Modern Hebrew Literature* 11 (1985): 16-21.

15. As Gershon Shaked notes, S.Y. Agnon wrote "a great many stories which *appear* to be sacred texts or 'quasi-sanctified' texts . . . , stories in which the author, by various devices, hints that his text is indeed a link in the chain of sacred texts." Although Agnon's mythopoetic works are beyond the scope of this study, there is an affinity between the quasi-sanctified texts

that Agnon wrote and the works of secular scripture written by Berdyczewski, Peretz, Bialik, and Frischmann discussed in this study. See Gershon Shaked, "Midrash and Narrative: Agnon's 'Agunot'" in Hartman and Budick, *Midrash and Literature*, 285-303. For a more comprehensive discussion of mythopoetic works by Agnon, see Arnold J. Band, *Nostalgia and Nightmare: A Study in the Fiction of S.Y. Agnon* (Berkeley and Los Angeles: University of California Press, 1968).

Chapter 1. Neo-Hasidic Tales: Micha Yosef Berdyczewski and Y.L. Peretz

1. Martin Buber, *The Legend of the Baal-Shem*, trans. Maurice Friedman (1955; reprint, New York: Shocken Books, 1969), 10.

2. For a discussion of the development of the publication of such narratives, see Yosef Dan, *Hasippur hahasidi* (Jerusalem: Keter, 1975).

3. In 1904, the Hebrew writer Yehuda Steinberg also published in Warsaw two collections containing neo-Hasidic stories, titled *Sippurei hasidim (Stories of Hasidim)* and *Sihot hasidim (Discourses of Hasidim)*.

4. *Encyclopaedia Judaica*, s.v. "Berdyczewski, Micha Yosef" and s.v. "Peretz, Isaac Leib;" G. Kressel, *Leksikon hasifrut ha'ivrit badorot ha'aharonim* (Merhavia: Sifriat Poalim, 1965-1967), 1: 332-25; 2: 693-99.

5. My analysis is based on the version of the essay in Micha Yosef Bin-Gorion (Berdyczewski), *Kitvei Micha Yosef Bin-Gorion (Berdyczewski): Ma'amarim* (1952; reprint, Tel Aviv: Dvir, 1966), 29-30.

6. Ibid., 29.

7. See Aliza Klausner-Eshkol, *Hashpa'at Nietzsche veSchopenhauer 'al M.Y. Bin-Gorion (Berdyczewski)* (Tel Aviv: Dvir, 1954).

8. Bin-Gorion (Berdyczewski), *Kitvei Micha Yosef Bin-Gorion (Berdyczewski): Ma'amarim*, 30.

9. Ibid. The English translation of this passage is from Simon Halkin, *Modern Hebrew Literature From the Enlightenment to the Birth of the State of Israel: Trends and Values* (1950; reprint, New York: Schocken Books, 1970), 93-94.

10. Samuel Z. Fishman, "The Dimensions and Uses of Jewish History

in the Essays of Micha Yosef Berdichevsky (Bin-Gorion)" (Ph.D. Diss. University of California, Los Angeles, 1969), 159.

11. "Nishmat Ḥasidim" was first published in *Mimizraḥ umima‘arav* 4 (1899): 55–64. Berdyczewski mentioned the essay in a letter to David Frischmann in 1897. See Dan Almagor and Shmuel Z. Fishman, *Naḥalat Micha Yosef Berdyczewski: mafteaḥ bibliyyografi liytsirot Micha Yosef Berdyczewski (Bin-Gorion) uleḥibburim ‘al ʾodotav* (Tel Aviv: Hakibbutz Hameuchad, 1982), 21.

12. Micha Yosef Berdyczewski, *Sefer ḥasidim* (Warsaw: Tushiyyah, 1900), 11.

13. Ibid., 14.

14. Ibid., 17–18. Berdyczewski appears to have been attracted to the Hasidic doctrine, which has been characterized by Louis Jacobs as "panentheisim," according to which the apparent separateness of the world from God is an illusion, for in actuality "all is *in* God." See Louis Jacobs, *Hasidic Prayer* (New York: Schocken Books, 1973), 9. This doctrine, which had its origins in the teachings of the Baal Shem Tov, was particularly stressed by the school of the Maggid of Mezhirech. See Rivka Schatz-Uffenheimer *Haḥasidut kemistikah* (Jerusalem: Magnes Press, 1968). In the essay "Nishmat ḥasidim" Berdyczewski quotes a number of times from the writings of the Ḥabad school of Rabbi Shneur Zalman of Lyady, a disciple of the Maggid of Mezhirech.

15. *He‘atid* 5 (1913): 151–71.

16. "Shnei ʾolamot" was first published in *Hamaggid* 8 (1899). An English translation of the story by Pamela Altfeld Malone was published in Howard Schwartz, ed., *Gates to the New City: A Treasury of Modern Jewish Tales* (New York: Avon, 1983), 570–74. This anthology provides many examples of mythopoetic works by modern Jewish writers. Two later retold versions of the first story in *Shivḥei habesht* by Berdyczewski, both titled "Beʾerets reḥokah," can be found in Micha Yosef Bin-Gorion (Berdyczewski), *Tsefunot veʾaggadot* (1957; reprint, Tel Aviv: Am Oved, 1967), 307–308, and Micha Yosef Bin-Gorion (Berdyczewski), *Mimekor yisraʾel: ma‘asiyyot vesippurei ‘am* (Tel Aviv: Dvir, 1966), 306. An English translation of the latter story can be found in Micha Yosef Bin-Gorion, *Mimekor Yisrael: Classical Jewish Folktales*, trans. I. M. Lask (Bloomington: Indiana University Press, 1976), 2:925–27. Shmuel Werses has made the observation that

these later versions reflect Berdyczewski's developing commitment to render the Hasidic text in a more literal manner than he had in *Sefer ḥasidim.* See Shmuel Werses, *Sippur veshorsho* (Ramat Gan: Massada, 1971), 114.

17. See Shmuel Abba Horodetzky, ed., *Shivḥei habesht* (1947; reprint, Tel Aviv: Dvir, 1968), 39-41. An English translation of the story may be found in Dan Ben-Amos and Jerome R. Mintz eds. and trans., *In Praise of the Baal Shem Tov* (1970; reprint, Bloomington: Indiana University Press, 1972), 7-11.

18. Ben-Amos and Mintz, *In Praise of the Baal Shem Tov,* 308.

19. See Northrop Frye, *The Secular Scripture: A Study of the Structure of Romance* (Cambridge: Harvard University Press, 1976), 129.

20. Dan, *Hasippur haḥasidi,* 56.

21. See Gershom Scholem, *Major Trends in Jewish Mysticism* 3d ed. (1954; reprint, New York: Schocken Books, 1961), 265-68.

22. The page references are from Berdyczewski, *Sefer ḥasidim.*

23. See Marcus Jastrow, *A Dictionary of the Targumim, The Talmud Babli and Yerushalmi and the Midrashic Literature* (New York: Pardes Publishing House, 1950), 941.

24. Y. L. Peretz, *Kol kitvei Y. L. Peretz* (Tel Aviv: Dvir, 1966), 8: 247-48. See Yehuda Friedlander, *Bein havayyah leḥavayyah: Massot ʿal yetsirato shel Y. L. Peretz umivḥar miyetsirato ʾasher loʾ kunsu bekhol kitvei.* (Ramat Gan and Tel Aviv: Bar Ilan University and Dvir, 1974), 11-33.

25. "Bein shnei harim" was published in Y. L. Peretz, *Ketavim: temunot, tsiyyurim, sippurim, veshirim yeshanim gam ḥadashim* (Warsaw: Tushiyyah, 1901) 4:161-175. It can be found in Y. L. Peretz, *Kol kitvei Y. L. Peretz* (Tel Aviv: Dvir, 1966), 2:11-24. Peretz also published a Yiddish version of the story, "Tsvishn tsvey berg," which can be found in Y. L. Peretz, *Ale verk fun Y. L. Peretz* (New York: "Yiddish," 1920) 6:7-23. An English translation of the Yiddish version of the story, by Nathan Halper, from which the quotations are taken, can be found in I. L. Peretz, *Selected Stories,* ed. Irving Howe and Eliezer Greenberg (1974; reprint, New York: Schocken Books, 1975), 83-95. See also the introduction by Howe and Greenberg to Peretz, *Selected Stories.*

26. Peretz, *Selected Stories*, 94.

27. Ibid., 94–95.

28. "Ha'ofot vehagevilim" was first published in *Hashiloah* 12 (1903). It may also be found in Peretz, *Kol kitvei Y. L. Peretz*, 2: 83–97. The page references are from the latter. In the original version of the story published in *Hashiloah* in 1903, this passage concludes with the word *ha'ashpah* ("the trash"). Later versions, including the one published in *Kol kitvei Y. L. Peretz* in 1966, read *hahol* ("the sand"). Peretz also published a Yiddish version of the story, "Dos blondzhn in midber" ("The Wandering in the Wilderness"), which can be found in Peretz, *Ale verk fun Y. L. Peretz*, 6: 164–80.

29. Arthur Green, "Bratslav Dreams," *Fiction* 7 (1983): 185–86.

30. The dream-tale may be found in Nathan of Nemirov Sternharz, *Hayyei moharan* (New York: R. Eliezer Shomo Bratslaver, 1965), 1:36. An English translation of the story by Arthur Green, from which the quotations are taken, can be found in *Fiction* 7 (1983), 188–89.

31. Arthur Green, *Tormented Master: A Life of Rabbi Nahman of Bratslav* (1979; reprint, Schocken Books: 1981), 169.

32. Ibid.

33. Ibid., 164.

34. Ibid., chap. 5

35. Ibid., 209.

36. Ibid., 212.

37. I thank Arthur Green for suggesting this interpretation to me.

Chapter 2. The Creative Restoration of Legends

1. "Megillat ha'esh" was first published in *Hashiloah* 15 (1905): 443–65. It may be found in Chaim Nachman Bialik, *Kol kitvei Ch. N. Bialik* (1938; reprint, Tel Aviv: Dvir, 1958), 88–94. A transcript of Bialik's talk titled "Mashehu 'al megillat ha'esh" ("Something About The Scroll of Fire") was first published in *Moznayim* 2 (1934): 348–59.

2. Bialik, "Mashehu 'al megillat ha'esh," 353–54.

3. My interpretation of "Megillat ha'esh" draws on the following critical works: Fishel Lahower, *Bialik: hayyav viytsirotav* (1944; reprint, Jerusalem and Tel Aviv: Mosad Bialik and Dvir, 1964), 538–77; 601–602; Jacob Fichmann, *Shirat Bialik* (1946; reprint, Jerusalem: Mosad Bialik, 1953), 197–226; Yonatan Ratosh, "Shirat ha'ahavah hazarah 'etsel Bialik," *'Alef* (September 1951), included in Gershon Shaked, ed., *Bialik: yetsirotav lesugeha bere'i habikkoret* (Jerusalem: Mosad Bialik, 1974), 261–65; Ephraim Urbach, "Bialik ve'aggadat hazal," *Molad* 17 (1959): 266–74; Aryeh Ludwig Strauss, *Bedarkhei hasifrut: 'iyyunim besifrut yisra'el uvesifrut ha'ammim* (Jerusalem: Mosad Bialik, 1965), 137–44; Baruch Kurzweil, *Bialik vetcher-nichowsky: mehkarim beshiratam* 3d ed. (Jerusalem and Tel Aviv: Schocken, 1967), 23–51; and Aharon Mazya, *Bialik ha'ehad: besovkhei parshanut umehkar* (Tel Aviv: Reshafim, 1978). 60–98. None of these critics, however, has delved as deeply into the nature of Bialik's creative restoration of legends in "Megillat ha'esh" and its meaning in the context of the work as I do in this study.

4. Bialik, "Mashehu 'al megillat ha'esh," 354.

5. *Encyclopaedia Judaica*, s.v. "Bialik, Hayyim Nahman;" G. Kressel, *Leksikon hasifrut ha'ivrit badorot ha'aharonim* (Merhavia: Sifriat Poalim, 1965–1967), 199–219.

6. Bialik, "Mashehu 'al megillat ha'esh," 351.

7. Fichmann, *Shirat Bialik*, 348.

8. Lahower, *Bialik: hayyav viytsirotav*, 538–43.

9. In his discussion of "Megillat ha'esh" in *Bialik: hayyav viytsirotav*, Lahower refers to both versions of each legend as sources for "Megillat ha'esh." Though I have not found conclusive proof that Bialik worked from both versions of each legend when composing "Megillat ha'esh," there is evidence to suggest a strong probability that he did. In his talk on "Megillat ha'esh" Bialik refers to the existence of several versions of the hidden fire legend, which would lead one to conclude that he was aware of the two main sources, II Maccabees and *Josippon*, on which I base my comparison. It may also be safely assumed that he was well acquainted with the talmudic and midrashic sources in *Gittin* and *'Eikhah Rabbah*, both of which texts serve as sources for *Sefer ha'aggadah* by Bialik and Rawnitzky.

10. *Encyclopaedia Judaica*, s.v. "Josippon."

11. For the Hebrew text of the legend, see David Flusser, ed., *Sefer Yosifon* (Jerusalem: Mosad Bialik, 1978), 1:44–45.

12. The sources of the two versions of the legend consulted for this study were *Talmud Bavli: Massekhet Gittin* (Vilna: Moshe Hillel Cohen, n.d.), 57b and Solomon Buber ed., *Midrash ʾeikhah rabbah* (Vilna: Romm, 1899), 81–82.

13. The translations of passages from "Megillat haʾesh" are from Chaim Nachman Bialik, *Selected Poems: Bilingual Edition*, trans. Ruth Nevo (Tel Aviv: Dvir and Jerusalem Post, 1981). Nevo's rendition of *yehatsu — veyikafel massaʾ ʾasonam* as: "if they cross over their calamity will be doubled" should be changed, according to the interpretation offered here, to: "may they be divided and their calamity doubled."

14. Kurzweil, *Bialik veTchernichowsky*, 23–51.

15. Nevo translates the expressions *shadmoteihem, ginnatam,* and *pesel maskitam* as "your fields," "your garden," and "your sculptured contrivance." Based on the literal meaning of the possessive suffix of each expression, the translation should read "their," rather than "your," in each case.

16. As Joseph Heinemann points out in his article, "ʿAl darko shel Bialik baʾaggadah hatalmudit," *Molad* 31 (1974): 83–92, Bialik's modern lack of commitment to scripture as a source of ultimate truth led to the frequent omission of the original scriptural prooftexts in legends which he collected together with Y. Rawnitzky in *Sefer haʾaggadah*. In general, Heinemann's critique of *Sefer haʾaggadah* in the article demonstrates that even the legends collected in *Sefer haʾaggadah*, which are considered to be closer in form and content to their original sources than those in such a work as "Megillat haʾesh," underwent creative restoration to a considerable extent.

17. See David C. Jacobson, "Religious Experience in the Early Poetry of Yocheved Bat-Miriam," *Hebrew Annual Review* 5 (1981): 47–64, in which I discuss a similar reaction by Yocheved Bat-Miriam to the separation between the holy and the erotic in traditional Jewish culture.

18. Bialik, "Mashehu ʿal megillat haʾesh," 358.

19. Lahower and Urbach suggest that Bialik's use of Nazirite imagery at this point in the work alludes to the legend of Simon the Righteous and the Nazirite in *Nazir* 4b and in other rabbinic sources.

Chapter 3. Biblical Tales of the Wilderness

1. David Frischmann, *Shiv*ʿ*ah mikhtavim ḥadashim* ʿ*al devar hasifrut* (Berlin: Dvir, 1923), 133.

2. Ibid., 134.

3. Ibid., 167.

4. For detailed analyses of the critical works of Frischmann, see Menuha Gilboa, *Bein re*ʾ*alizm leromantika:* ʿ*al darko shel David Frischmann bebikkoret* (Tel Aviv: Hakibbutz Hameuched, 1975) and Shalom Kramer, *Frischmann hamevaker* (Jerusalem: Mosad Bialik, 1984).

5. *Encyclopaedia Judaica,* s.v. "Frischmann, David;" G. Kressel, *Leksikon hasifrut ha*ʿ*ivrit badorot ha*ʾ*aḥaronim* (Merhavia: Sifriat Poalim, 1965-1967), 667-75.

6. Kramer, *Frischmann hamevaker,* 25.

7. Frischmann, *Shiv*ʿ*a mikhtavim ḥadashim* ʿ*al devar hasifrut,* 95-96.

8. Ibid., 123.

9. Ibid., 177.

10. The stories that constitute the *Bamidar* series were originally published as follows: "Meḥolot," *Sifrut: me*ʾ*asef lasifrut hayafah uvikoret* 1 (1909); "ʿEved ʿivri" (later titled "Bamartsea"'), *Hatsefirah* no. 28 (1913); "Neḥash hanehoshet," *Hatekufah* 1 (1918); "ʿIr hamiklat," *Hatekufah* 2 (1918); "Behar sinai," *Hatekufah* 4 (1919); "Sotah," *Hatekufah* 6 (1920); "ʿEglah ʿarufah," *Hatekufah* 8 (1921); "Sorer umoreh," *Hatekufah* 9 (1921); and "Hamekoshesh," *Hatekufah* 12 (1922). The series was published as a whole after Frischmann's death in David Frischmann, *Bamidbar: ma*ʿ*asiyyot bibliyyot, sippurim, ve*ʾ*aggadot* (Berlin: Hasefer, 1923). A translation of "Meḥolot" (titled "The Dance") by Yosef Shachter may be found in S. Y. Penueli and A. Ukhmani, eds., *Hebrew Short Stories* (Tel Aviv: Institute for the Translation of Hebrew Literature and Megiddo, 1965), 1:68-74. My interpretation draws on the following critical studies, in addition to the works by Gilboa and Kramer already mentioned, but it reveals a more complex vision in *Bamidbar* than has been recognized by these previous studies: Baruch Kurzweil, *Sifrutenu haḥadashah: hemshekh* ʾ*o mahpekhah* 2d ed. (Jerusalem and Tel Aviv: Schocken, 1965), 11-146; Avraham Shaanan, *Hasifrut ha*ʿ*ivrit hahadashah lezerameha* (Tel

Aviv: Massada, 1973), 2:243–49; and Gershon Shaked, *Hasipporet haʿivrit 1880-1970* (Tel Aviv: Hakibbutz Hameuched and Keter, 1977), 1:124–27.

11. Frischmann, *Bamidbar*, 17.

12. David Biale relates Frischmann's *Bamidbar* series to a number of what he calls counter-histories conceived by such modern Jewish writers as Micha Yosef Berdyczewski, Martin Buber, and Gershom Scholem. See David Biale, *Gershom Scholem: Kabbalah and Counter-History* (Cambridge: Harvard University Press, 1979), 236.

13. Frischmann's use of biblical law to reveal the life of the Israelites in the wilderness is paralleled by Bialik's notion in his essay "Halakhah veʿaggadah" that the laws of the Mishnah are sources that reveal the life of the Jewish people in rabbinic times. See Chaim Nachman Bialik, *Kol Kitvei Ch. N. Bialik* (1938; reprint, Tel Aviv: Dvir, 1958), 207–213.

14. The page references are from David Frischmann, *Bamidbar maʿasiyyot bibliyyot, sippurim veʾaggadot* (Berlin: Hasefer, 1923).

15. See Shaked, *Hasipporet haʿivrit 1880-1970*, 1:124–25.

16. Stanley Nash, *In Search of Hebraism: Shai Hurwitz and His Polemics in the Hebrew Press* (Leiden: E. J. Brill, 1980), 311.

17. Shaanan, *Hasifrut haʿivrit hahadashah lezerameha*, 2:247.

18. Shaked, *Hasipporet haʿivrit 1880-1970*, 1:126.

19. Shaanan, *Hasifrut haʿivrit hahadashah lezerameha*, 2:258; Shaked, *Hasipporet haʿivrit 1880-1970*, 1:126.

Chapter 4. The Life and Death of King Saul

1. Shaul Tchernichowsky, "ʾAvtobiyyografyah," *Hashiloah* 35 (1918): 103.

2. Yosef Klausner cites an example of Tchernichowsky's dislike for the figure of David in a passage in his poem "Perek baʾanatomyah" (1933) in which Tchernichowsky dwells on the excessive involvement of David in acts of violence. Klausner claims that Tchernichowsky's dislike of David was motivated less out of a hatred of David and more out of a great love of Saul, whose rule David challenged. See Yosef Klausner, *Shaul Tchernichowsky: haʾadam vehameshorer* (Jerusalem: Hebrew University Press Association, 1947), 293.

3. The five ballads on Saul were originally published as follows: "Be'ein-dor" in *Hatsevi* 14 (1897); "'Al ḥorvot beit-shan" in *Sefer sha'ashu'im* 6 (1897); "Hamelekh" in *Ha'olam* 14 (1926); "'Al harei gilboa'" in *Ha'olam* 17 (1929); and "'Anshei ḥayil ḥevel" in *Ha'arets* 19 (1936). See Ziva Golan and Haviva Yonay, eds., *Shaul Tchernichowsky: bibliyyografyah* (Tel Aviv: Tel Aviv University, 1980). The dates of each poem that are referred to in this chapter are those found at the end of each poem as it appears in Shaul Tchernichowsky, *Shirei Shaul Tchernichowsky* 2d ed. (Tel Aviv: Dvir, 1968).

4. *Encyclopaedia Judaica*, s. v. "Tchernichowsky, Saul;" G. Kressel, *Leksikon hasifrut ha'ivrit badorot ha'aharonim* (Merhavia: Sifriat Poalim, 1965–1967) 2:44–58; Klausner, *Shaul Tchernichowsky.*

5. Shaul Tchernichowsky, *Shirei Shaul Tchernichowsky* , 25.

6. For a description of the personal suffering of Tchernichowsky and the suffering he witnessed during this period, see Klausner, *Shaul Tchernichowsky*, chaps. 10, 14.

7. Tchernichowsky, *Shirei Shaul Tchernichowsky*, 59.

8. The opening passage of "Be'ein-dor" provides a good example of the influence of German and English ballads and nineteenth-century European romantic literature in general on Tchernichowsky at that time. In addition, as has been noted by critics, Tchernichowsky's portrayal of the house of the woman at En-dor most likely draws on the opening scene of the weird sisters in Shakespeare's play *Macbeth*, which reportedly fascinated Tchernichowsky as a youth, and which he later translated into Hebrew. See Avraham Shaanan, *Hasifrut ha'ivrit hahadashah lezerameha*, 3: 281; Avraham Shaanan, *Shaul Tchernichowsky: monografyah* (Tel Aviv: Hakibbutz Hameuchad and Sifriat Poalim, 1984), 142; Yeshayahu Rabinovich, "Shaul Tchernichowsky: shnei perakim," *Moznayim* 27 (1968): 350; Klausner, *Shaul Tchernichowsky*, 16–17.

9. Baruch Kurzweil, *Bialik veTchernichowsky: mehkarim beshiratam* 3d ed. (Jerusalem and Tel Aviv: Schocken, 1967), 258.

10. Eisig Silberschlag, *Shaul Tschernichowsky: Poet of Revolt* (Ithaca: Cornell University Press, 1968), 53.

11. Kurzweil, *Bialik veTchernichowsky*, 254.

12. Ibid., 258–60; and Yaakov Bahat, "Sha'ul hamelekh biytsirato shel Shaul Tchernichowsky," *Hahinnukh* 36 (1963): 11.

13. Avraham Shaanan points out that there is a tension in Tchernichowsky's poetry between his attraction to natural and irrational aspects of human existence and his attraction to ethical and rational aspects of human existence. This tension may be seen to correspond to Tchernichowsky's ambivalent response to Jewish suffering of an irrational hatred and a desire for revenge on the one hand and a more ethical attitude of love and forgiveness on the other hand found in the poem "'Al ḥorvot beit-shan." See Shaanan, *Hasifrut ha'ivrit haḥadashah lezerameha*, 3: 285, 290.

14. See the reference to the use of the image of Saul's suicide in medieval literature responding to the Crusades in David G. Roskies, *Against the Apocalypse: Responses to Catastrophe in Modern Jewish Culture* (Cambridge: Harvard University Press, 1984), 44.

15. See the discussion of "Barukh mimagentsa" in Alan Mintz, *Ḥurban: Responses to Catastrophe in Hebrew Literature*: (New York: Columbia University Press, 1984), 123-29.

16. The translations of passages from "Hamelekh" are from the translation of the poem by Richard Flantz in S. Y. Penueli and A. Ukhmani, eds., *Anthology of Modern Hebrew Poetry* (Jerusalem: Institute for the Translation of Hebrew Literature and Israel Universities Press, 1966), 76-79. The page number references are from the Hebrew version in Tchernichowsky, *Shirei Shaul Tchernichowsky*.

17. Kurzweil, *Bialik véTchernichowsky*, 259-60.

18. Tchernichowsky, *Shirei Tchernichowsky*, 90.

19. Kurzweil, *Bialik véTchernichowsky*, 261.

20. Tchernichowsky, *Shirei Tchernichowsky*, 90.

21. *Encyclopaedia Judaica*, s.v. "Tchernichowsky, Saul."

22. Ibid., s.v. "Israel, State of (Historical Survey)."

23. Eliezer Schweid and Baruch Kurzweil offer interpretations of "'Anshei ḥayil ḥevel" which focus more on what Tchernichowsky is saying in the poem about the biblical Saul, particularly regarding his struggle with David and Samuel. While I believe that they present valid readings of the poem, I consider its main thrust to be a statement about the contemporary situation of the Jews of the Land of Israel.

24. Silberschlag, *Saul Tschernichowsky*, 56.

25. Tchernichowsky, *Shirei Tchernichowsky*, 109.

Chapter 5. Men and Women in the Bible

1. "Kazot lefanekha" ("Like This Before You"), the poem from which these stanzas were excerpted, was published in *Musaf Davar* 7 (1932). It was included in the collection Yocheved Bat-Miriam, *Meraḥok* (Tel Aviv: Agudat Hasofrim, 1932), 182–83. See the bibliography of works by and about Bat-Miriam in Ruth Kartun-Blum, *Barmerḥak haneʿlam: ʿiyyunim beshirat Yocheved Bat-Miriam* (Ramat Gan: Agudat Hasofrim and Massada, 1977), 165–75. The translation is by Ruth Finer Mintz in Ruth Finer Mintz, ed. and trans., *Modern Hebrew Poetry: A Bilingual Anthology* (Berkeley and Los Angeles: University of California Press, 1966), 160, 162.

2. For a more detailed analysis of this theme in the poetry of Bat-Miriam, see David C. Jacobson, "Religious Experience in the Early Poetry of Yocheved Bat-Miriam," *Hebrew Annual Review* 5 (1981): 47–64. See also Fishel Lahower, "Shirei Bat-Miriam," *Moznayim* 4 (1932): 10–12; Dan Miron, "Shiratah shel Yocheved Bat-Miriam," *Haʾarets* (February 22, 1963); and Kartun-Blum, *Bamerḥak haneʿelam*.

3. In some of her poetry Bat-Miriam expresses her dissatisfaction with the male-dominated nature of traditional Judaism, and she indicates how uncomfortable Jewish women are in attempting to pray from prayer books that reflect only the male religious perspective. See Jacobson, "Religious Experience in the Early Poetry of Yocheved Bat-Miriam."

4. See the cycle of poems by Bat-Miriam titled "ʾErets Yisraʾel" (1937) in Bat-Miriam, *Demuyyot meʾofek* (Tel Aviv: Machbaroth Lesifrut, 1941), 151–65 and in Bat-Miriam, *Shirim* (Merhavia: Sifriat Poalim, 1963), 39–53.

5. *Encyclopaedia Judaica*, s.v. "Bat-Miriam, Yokheved;" G. Kressel, *Leksikon hasifrut haʿivrit badorot haʾaharonim* (Merhavia: Sifriat Poalim, 1965–1967), 1: 391; and Warren Bargad, *Ideas in Ficton: The Works of Hayim Hazaz* (Chico: Scholars Press, 1982), 7.

6. Five of the poems appeared originally in periodicals under the title "Bein ḥol veshemesh" as follows: "ʾAvraham," "Miryam," and "Shaʾul" in *Musaf Davar* 14 (1939); "ʾAdam" and "Ḥavvah" in *Maḥbarot lesifrut* 1 (1940). The five poems together with the sixth poem, "Hagar," were published under the title "Bein ḥol veshemesh" in the collection Bat-Miriam, *Demuyyot meʾofek*, 86–97, and again in the collection Bat-Miriam, *Shirim*, 179–90. See the bibliography of works by and about Bat-Miriam in Kartun-Blum, *Bamerḥak haneʿelam*, 165–75.

7. This dedication appears in Bat-Miriam, *Demuyyot meʾofek*, 88. It does not appear in Bat-Miriam, *Shirim*, 181.

Chapter 6. The Holocaust Survivor and the Bible

1. Lawrence L. Langer, *The Holocaust and the Literary Imagination* (New Haven: Yale University Press, 1975), 20.

2. Ibid., 27.

3. Aharon Appelfeld, *Massot beguf rishon* (Jerusalem: World Zionist Organization, 1979), 20.

4. *Encyclopaedia Judaica*, s.v. "Gilboa, Amir;" "Kovner, Abba;" G. Kressel, *Leksikon hasifrut haʿivrit badorot haʾaharonim* (Merhavia: Sifriat Poalim, 1965–1967), 1: 481; 2: 568, 731–732; Dan Pagis, *Points of Departure*, trans. Stephen Mitchell (Philadelphia: The Jewish Publication Society of America, 1981), 124.

5. "Yitsḥak" and "Shaʾul" were published in the collection of Gilboa's poetry titled *Shirim baboker baboker* (1953). They may be found in the collection *Keḥullim vaʾadummim* (1963; reprint, Tel Aviv: Am Oved, 1971), 213, 216.

6. This translation of the poem by Shirley Kaufman may be found in Howard Schwartz and Anthony Rudolf, eds., *Voices Within the Ark: The Modern Jewish Poets* (New York: Avon, 1980), 82–83. A more accurate translation of the final word of the poem, *yoshvim* would be "dwell" rather than "wait."

7. This translation by Ruth Finer Mintz may be found in Ruth Finer Mintz, ed., *Modern Hebrew Poetry: A Bilingual Anthology* (Berkeley and Los Angeles: University of California Press, 1966), 256.

8. See the interpretation of the poem "Yitsḥak" by Arieh Sachs in Stanley Burnshaw, T. Carmi, and Ezra Spicehandler eds., *The Modern Hebrew Poem Itself* (New York: Holt, Rinehart and Winston, 1965), 136–38.

9. Hillel Barzel, *ʾAmir Gilboaʿ: monografyah* (Tel Aviv: Sifriat Poalim, 1984), 26.

10. "Mikarov" was published in the collection Abba Kovner, *Mikol haʾahavot* (Merhavia: Sifriat Poalim, 1965), 69–70.

11. This translation of the poem by Shirley Kaufman may be found in Abba Kovner, *My Little Sister and Selected Poems 1965–1985*, trans. Shirley Kaufman (Oberlin: Oberlin College, 1986). The graphic representation of the poems in their original Hebrew version was preserved by the translator.

12. See the discussion of a similar technique used by Bialik in describing the after effects of the Kishinev pogrom of 1903 in his poem "Beʿir haharegah" ("In the City of Slaughter") (1904) in Alan Mintz, *Ḥurban: Responses to Catastrophe in Hebrew Literature* (New York: Columbia University Press, 1984), 145–46.

13. "Katuv beʿipparon bakaron heḥatum" was published in the collection Dan Pagis, *Gilgul* (Ramat Gan: Massada, 1970), 22.

14. This translation of the poem by Stephen Mitchell may be found in Pagis, *Points of Departure*, 23.

15. "ʾAḥim" was published in the collection Dan Pagis, *Moaḥ* (Tel Aviv: Hakibbutz Hameuchad, 1975), 5–6.

16. This translation of the poem by Shirley Kaufman may be found in Schwartz and Rudolf, *Voices Within the Ark*, 131.

17. The image of the amazement of the murderer derives from the rabbinic legend which tells of Cain's repeated wounding of Abel because, as the first murderer in human history, he did not know how to take his brother's life (*Sanhedrin* 37a).

18. "ʾOtobiyyografyah" was published in the collection Pagis, *Moaḥ*, 7–8.

19. This translation of the poem by Robert Friend may be found in Schwartz and Rudolf, *Voices Within the Ark*, 132.

20. The image of the raven teaching Adam and Eve how to bury Abel is derived from the rabbinic legend which tells that the fowl and the ritually clean animals buried Abel (*Bereshit Rabbah* 22:18).

Chapter 7. Uses and Abuses of Power in Ancient and Modern Israel

1. Amos Oz, *Be'or hatekhelet ha'azzah: ma'amarim ureshimot* (Tel Aviv: Sifriat Poalim, 1979), 206.

2. The page references are from Nissim Aloni, *'Akhzar mikol hamelekh* (reprint, Tel Aviv: University of Tel Aviv, 1968/1969; date of original publication not indicated). The play was first staged in 1953.

3. Moshe Natan, "Sihot 'im Nissim 'Aloni," *Keshet* 32 (1966): 26. This interview is referred to in Zephyra Porat, "The Tragi-Comedy of Fulfillment in Nissim Aloni's Plays," *Ariel* 32 (1973): 177–187.

4. My interpretation of the story of David, Uriah, and Bathsheba draws on Menahem Perry and Meir Sternberg, "Hamelekh bemabat 'ironi: 'al tahbulotav shel hamesaper besippur David uVat Sheva ushetei haflagot late'oryah shel haprozah," *Hasifrut* 1 (1968): 263–92.

5. Dan Miron, "'Al sippurei Moshe Shamir," in Dan Miron, *'Arba' panim basifrut ha'ivrit bat yamenu: 'iyyunim biytsirot 'Alterman, Ratosh, Yizhar, Shamir* (Jerusalem and Tel Aviv: Schocken, 1975), 439–71.

6. The quotations are from the English translation of the novel, Moshe Shamir, *The Hittite Must Die* (originally titled *David's Stranger*), trans. Margaret Benaya (1964; reprint, New York: East and West Library, 1978). The Hebrew text consulted was Moshe Shamir, *Kivsat harash: sippur 'Uriyyah hahitti*: 4th ed. (Merhavia: Sifriat Poalim, 1959).

7. Miron, "'Al Sippurei Moshe Shamir," 452.

8. Ibid., 453. See the essay by Shamir in Moshe Shamir, *Bekulmos mahir* (Merhavia: Sifriat Poalim, 1960), 329–33.

9. Shamir, *Bekulmos mahir*, 326.

10. Miron, *'Arba' panim basifrut ha'ivrit bat yamenu*, 466–69.

11. Quotations are from the English translation of the story by Nicholas de Lange in Amos Oz, *Where the Jackals Howl* (1981; reprint, New

York: Bantam, 1982), 185-239. The Hebrew text consulted may be found in Amos Oz, *ʾArtsot hatan* (1976; reprint, Tel Aviv: Am Oved, 1982), 200-43.

Selected Bibliography

Agnon, Shmuel Yosef. *Sifreihem shel tsaddikim: me'ah sippurim ve'ehad 'al sifreihem shel talmidei habesht zal veshel talmidei talmidav.* Jerusalem and Tel Aviv: Schocken, 1961.

Almagor, Dan and Shmuel Z. Fishman. *Nahalat Micha Yosef Berdyczewski: mafteah bibliyyografi liytsirot Micha Yosef Berdyczewski (Bin-Gorion) ulehib-burim 'al 'odotav.* Tel Aviv: Hakibbutz Hameuchad, 1982.

Aloni, Nissim. *'Akhzar mikol hamelekh.* n.d. Reprint. Tel Aviv: University of Tel Aviv, 1968/1969.

Appelfeld, Aharon. *Masot beguf rishon.* Jerusalem: World Zionist Organization, 1979.

Bahat, Yaakov. "Sha'ul hamelekh biytsirato shel Shaul Tchernichowsky." *Hahinnukh* 36 (1963): 1–13.

Band, Arnold J. *Nostalgia and Nightmare: A Study in the Fiction of S. Y. Agnon.* Berkeley and Los Angeles: University of California Press, 1968.

Bargad, Warren. *Ideas in Fiction: The Works of Hayim Hazaz.* Chico: Scholars Press, 1982.

Barzel, Hillel. *'Amir Gilboa': monografyah.* Tel Aviv: Sifriat Poalim, 1984.

Bat-Miriam, Yocheved. *Demuyyot me'ofek.* Tel Aviv: Machbaroth Lesifrut, 1941.

———. *Merahok.* Tel Aviv: Agudat Hasofrim, 1932.

———. *Shirim.* Merhavia: Sifriat Poalim, 1963.

Ben Amos, Dan and Jerome R. Mintz, eds. and trans. *In Praise of the Baal Shem Tov.* 1970. Reprint. Bloomington: Indiana University Press, 1972.

Biale, David. *Gershom Scholem: Kabbalah and Counter-History.* Cambridge: Harvard University Press, 1979.

Bialik, Chaim Nachman. *Kol kitvei Ch. N. Bialik.* 1938. Reprint. Tel Aviv: Dvir, 1958.

―――. "Mashehu ʿal megillat haʾesh." *Moznayim* 2 (1934): 348–359.

―――. *Selected Poems: Bilingual Edition.* Translated by Ruth Nevo. Tel Aviv: Dvir and Jerusalem Post, 1981.

Bialik, Chaim Nachman and Yehoshua Hana Rawnitzki, eds. *Sefer haʾaggadah: mivḥar haʾaggadot shebatalmud uvamidrashim.* 3d ed. 1948. Reprint. Tel Aviv: Dvir, 1962.

Bin-Gorion (Berdyczewski), Micha Yosef. *Kitvei Micha Yosef Bin-Gorion (Berdyczewski): Maʾamarim.* 1952. Reprint. Tel Aviv: Dvir, 1966.

―――. *Mimekor yisraʾel: maʿasiyyot vesippurei ʿam.* Tel Aviv: Dvir, 1966.

―――. *Mimekor Yisrael: Classical Jewish Folktales.* Edited by Emanuel bin Gorion. Translated by I. M. Lask. Bloomington: Indiana University Press, 1976.

―――. *Sefer ḥasidim.* Warsaw: Tushiyyah, 1900.

―――. *Tsefunot veʾaggadot.* 1957. Reprint. Tel Aviv: Am Oved, 1967.

Bloom, Harold. *Kabbalah and Criticism.* New York: The Seabury Press, 1975.

―――. *A Map of Misreading.* New York: Oxford University Press, 1975.

Buber, Martin. *The Legend of the Baal-Shem.* Translated by Maurice Friedman. 1955. Reprint. New York: Schocken Books. 1969.

―――. *ʾOr haganuz: sippurei ḥasidim.* Jerusalem and Tel Aviv: Schocken, 1976.

―――. *The Tales of Rabbi Nachman.* Translated by Maurice Friedman. 1956. Reprint. New York: Avon, 1970.

Buber, Solomon, ed. *Midrash ʾeikhah rabbah.* Vilna: Romm, 1899.

Burnshaw, Stanley, T. Carmi, and Ezra Spicehandler, eds. *The Modern Hebrew Poem Itself.* New York: Holt, Rinehart and Winston, 1965.

Culler, Jonathan. *The Pursuit of Signs: Semiotics, Literature, Deconstruction.* Ithaca: Cornell University Press, 1981.

Dan, Yosef. *Hasippur haḥasidi.* Jerusalem: Keter, 1975.

Fichmann, Jacob. *Shirat Bialik.* 1946. Reprint. Jerusalem: Mosad Bialik, 1953.

Fishbane, Michael. *Biblical Interpretation of Ancient Israel.* Oxford: Clarendon Press, 1985.

_____. "Inner Biblical Exegesis: Types and Strategies of Interpretation in Ancient Israel." In *Midrash and Literature,* edited by Geoffrey H. Hartman and Sanford Budick, 19–37. New Haven: Yale University Press, 1986.

Fishman, Samuel Z. "The Dimensions and Uses of Jewish History in the Essays of Micha Yosef Berdichevsky (Bin-Gorion)." Ph.D. diss., University of California, Los Angeles, 1969.

Flusser, David, ed. *Sefer Yosifon.* Vol. 1. Jerusalem: Mosad Bialik, 1978.

Friedlander, Yehuda. *Bein havayyah leḥavayyah: masot ʿal yetsirato shel Y. L. Peretz umivḥar miyetsirato ʾasher loʾ kunsu bekhol kitvei.* Ramat Gan and Tel Aviv: Bar Ilan University and Dvir, 1974.

Frischmann, David. *Bamidbar: maʿasiyyot bibliyyot, sippurim, veʾaggadot.* Berlin: Hasefer, 1923.

_____. *Shivʿa mikhtavim ḥadashim ʿal devar hasifrut.* Berlin: Dvir, 1923.

Frye, Northrop. *The Secular Scripture: A Study of the Structure of Romance.* Cambridge: Harvard University Press, 1976.

Gertz, Nurith. *ʿAmos ʿOz: monografyah.* Tel Aviv: Sifriat Poalim, 1980.

_____. *Ḥirbet ḥizʿeh vehaboker shelemoḥorat.* Tel Aviv: Hakibbutz Hameuchad, 1983.

_____. "'Hirbet Hiz'eh' and the Morning After." *Modern Hebrew Literature* 11 (1985): 16–21.

Gilboa, Amir. *Keḥullim vaʾadummim.* 1963. Reprint. Tel Aviv: Am Oved, 1971.

Gilboa Menuha. *Bein reʾalizm leromantikah: ʿal darko shel David Frischmann bebikkoret.* Tel Aviv: Hakibbutz Hameuchad, 1975.

Golan, Ziva and Haviva Yonay, eds. *Shaul Tchernichowsky: bibliyyografyah.* Tel Aviv: Tel Aviv University, 1980.

Green, Arthur, "Bratslav Dreams." *Fiction* 7 (1983): 185–202.

————. *Tormented Master: A Life of Rabbi Nahman of Bratslav.* 1979. Reprint. New York: Schocken Books, 1981.

Halkin, Simon. *Modern Hebrew Literature: From the Enlightenment to the Birth of the State of Israel: Trends and Values.* 1950. Reprint. New York: Schocken Books, 1970.

Handelman, Susan A. *The Slayers of Moses: The Emergence of Rabbinic Interpretation in Modern Literary Theory.* Albany: State University of New York Press, 1982.

Heinemann, Joseph. *ʾAggadot vetoldoteihen.* Jerusalem: Keter, 1974.

————. "ʿAl darko shel Bialik baʾaggadah hatalmudit." *Molad* 31 (1974): 83–92.

————. "The Nature of the Aggadah." In *Midrash and Literature,* edited by Geoffrey H. Hartman and Sanford Budick, 41–55. New Haven: Yale University Press, 1986.

Horodetzky, Shmuel Abba, ed. *Shivḥei habesht.* 1947. Reprint. Tel Aviv: Dvir, 1968.

Jacobs, Louis. *Hasidic Prayer.* New York: Schocken Books, 1973.

Jacobson, David C. " Religious Experience in the Early Poetry of Yocheved Bat-Miriam." *Hebrew Annual Review* 5 (1981): 47–64. ·

Kartun-Blum, Ruth. *Bamerḥak haneʿlam: ʿiyyumin beshirat Yocheved Bat-Miriam.* Ramat Gan: Agudat Hasofrim and Massada, 1977.

Klausner, Yosef. *Shaul Tchernichowsky: haʾadam vehameshorer.* Jerusalem: Hebrew University Press Association, 1947.

Klausner-Eshkol, Aliza. *Hashpaʿat Nietzsche veSchopenhauer ʿal M. Y. Bin-Gorion (Berdyczewski).* Tel Aviv: Dvir, 1954.

Kovner, Abba. *Mikol haʾahavot.* Merhavia: Sifriat Poalim, 1965.

————.*My Little Sister and Selected Poems 1965–1985.* Translated by Shirley Kaufman. Oberlin: Oberlin College, 1986.

Kramer, Shalom. *Frischmann hamevaker.* Jerusalem: Mosad Bialik, 1984.

Kressel, G. *Leksikon hasifrut haʿivrit badorot haʾaharonim.* Merhavia: Sifriat Poalim, 1965–1967.

Kugel, James L. "Two Introductions to Midrash." In *Midrash and Literature*, edited by Geoffrey H. Hartman and Sanford Budick, 77–103. New Haven: Yale University Press, 1986.

Kurzweil, Baruch. *Bialik veTchernichowsky: mehkarim beshiratam.* 3d ed. Jerusalem and Tel Aviv: Schocken, 1967.

_____. *Sifrutenu hahadashah: hemshekh ʾo mahpekhah.* 2d ed. Jerusalem and Tel Aviv: Schocken, 1965.

Lahower, Fishel. *Bialik: ḥayyav viytsirotav.* 1944. Reprint. Jerusalem and Tel Aviv: Mosad Bialik and Dvir, 1964.

_____. "Shirei Bat-Miriam." *Moznayim* 4 (1932): 10–12.

Langer, Lawrence L. *The Holocaust and the Literary Imagination.* New Haven: Yale University Press, 1975.

Mazya, Aharon. *Bialik haʾehad: besovkhei parshanut umehkar.* Tel Aviv: Reshafim, 1978.

Mintz, Alan. *Ḥurban: Responses to Catastrophe in Hebrew Literature.* New York: Columbia University Press, 1984.

Mintz, Ruth Finer, ed. and trans. *Modern Hebrew Poetry: A Bilingual Anthology.* Berkeley and Los Angeles: University of California Press, 1966.

Mirkin, Moshe Aryeh, ed. *Midrash Rabbah.* Vol. 2. Tel Aviv: Yavneh, 1957.

Miron Dan. *ʾArbaʿ panim basifrut haʿivrit bat yamenu: ʿiyyunim biytsirot ʾAlterman, Ratosh, Yizhar, Shamir.* Jerusalem and Tel Aviv: Schocken, 1975.

_____. "Hasifrut haʿivrit bereshit hameʾah haʿesrim: perakim mitokh massah." *Meʾasef ledivrei sifrut, bikkoret, vehagut* 2 (1961): 436–464.

_____. "Lerekaʿ hamevukhah basifrut haʿivrit bereshit hameʾah haʿesrim." In *Sefer hayovel leShimʿon Halkin bemeleʾot lo shivʿim shanim,* edited by Boaz Katz and Menahem Perry, 419–487. Jerusalem: Reuben Mass, 1975.

_____. "Shiratah shel Yocheved Bat-Miriam." *Haʾarets* (February 22, 1963.)

Murray, Henry A. "The Possible Nature of a 'Mythology' to Come." In *Myth and Mythmaking,* edited by Henry A. Murray, 300–353. 1960. Reprint. Boston: Beacon Press, 1968.

Nachman of Bratslav. *Sefer Sippurei Ma'asiyyot.* Jerusalem: Hasidei Bratslav, 1965.

Nash, Stanley. *In Search of Hebraism: Shai Hurwitz and His Polemics in the Hebrew Press.* Leiden: E. J. Brill, 1980.

Natan, Moshe. "Sihot 'im Nissim 'Aloni." *Keshet* 32 (1966): 5–39.

Oz, Amos. *'Artsot hatan.* 1976. Reprint. Tel Aviv: Am Oved, 1982.

———. *Be'or hatekhelet ha'azzah: ma'amarim ureshimot.* Tel Aviv: Sifriat Poalim, 1979.

———. *Where the Jackals Howl.* Translated by Nicholas de Lange and Philip Simpson. 1981. Reprint. New York: Bantam, 1982.

Pagis, Dan. *Gilgul.* Ramat Gan: Massada, 1970.

———. *Moah.* Tel Aviv: Hakibbutz Hameuchad, 1975.

———. *Points of Departure.* Translated by Stephen Mitchell. Philadelphia: The Jewish Publication Society of America, 1981.

Penueli, S. Y. and A. Ukhmani, eds. *Anthology of Modern Hebrew Poetry.* Jerusalem: Institute for the Translation of Hebrew Literature and Israel Universities Press, 1966.

———. *Hebrew Short Stories.* Tel Aviv: Institute for the Translation of Hebrew Literature and Megiddo Publishing Co., 1965.

Peretz, Y. L. *Ale verk fun Y. L. Peretz.* Vol. 6. New York: "Yiddish," 1920.

———. *Ketavim: temunot, tsiyyurim, sippurim, veshirim, yeshanim gam hadashim.* Vol. 4. Warsaw: Tushiyyah, 1901.

———. *Kol kitvei Y. L. Peretz.* Vols. 2, 8. Tel Aviv: Dvir, 1966.

———. *Selected Stories.* Edited by Irving Howe and Eliezer Greenberg. 1974. Reprint. New York: Schocken Books, 1975.

Perry, Menahem and Meir Sternberg. "Hamelekh bemabat 'ironi: 'al tahbulotav shel hamesaper besippur David uVat Sheva ushetei haflagot late'oryah shel haprozah." *Hasifrut* 1 (1968): 263–292.

Porat, Zephyra. "The Tragi-Comedy of Fulfillment in Nissim Aloni's Plays." *Ariel* 32 (1973): 177–187.

Rabinovich, Yeshayahu. "Shaul Tchernichowsky: shnei perakim." *Moznayim* 27 (1968): 350–355.

Ratosh, Yonatan. "Shirat ha'ahavah hazarah 'etsel Bialik." In *Bialik: yetsirotav lesugeha bere'i habikkoret,* edited by Gershon Shaked, 261–265. Jerusalem: Mosad Bialik, 1974.

Roskies, David G. *Against the Apocalypse: Responses to Catastrophe in Modern Jewish Culture.* Cambridge: Harvard University Press, 1984.

Schatz-Uffenheimer, Rivka. *Hahasidut kemistikah.* Jerusalem: The Magnes Press, 1968.

Scholem, Gershom G. *Major Trends in Jewish Mysticism.* 3d ed. 1954. Reprint. New York: Schocken Books, 1961.

Schwartz, Howard, ed. *Gates to the New City: A Treasury of Modern Jewish Tales.* New York: Avon, 1983.

Schwartz, Howard and Anthony Rudolf, eds., *Voices Within the Ark: The Modern Jewish Poets.* New York: Avon, 1980.

Shaanan, Avraham. *Hasifrut ha'ivrit hahadashah lezerameha.* Vols. 2, 3. Tel Aviv: Massada, 1973.

———. *Shaul Tchernichowsky: monografyah.* Tel Aviv: Hakibbutz Hameuchad and Sifriat Poalim, 1984.

Shaked, Gershon. *Gal hadash basipporet ha'ivrit: massot 'al sipporet yisra'elit tse'irah.* Merhavia and Tel Aviv: Sifriat Poalim, 1971.

———. *Hasipporet ha'ivrit 1880–1970.* Vol. 1. Tel Aviv: Hakibbutz Hameuchad and Keter, 1977.

———. "Midrash and Narrative: Agnon's 'Agunot.'" In *Midrash and Literature,* edited by Geoffrey H. Hartman and Sanford Budick, 285–303. New Haven: Yale University Press, 1986.

Shamir, Moshe. *Bekulmos mahir.* Merhavia: Sifriat Poalim, 1960.

———. *The Hittite Must Die.* Translated by Margaret Benaya 1964. Reprint. New York: East and West Library, 1978.

———. *Kivsat harash: sippur 'Uriyyah hahitti.* 4th ed. Merhavia: Sifriat Poalim, 1959.

Shavit, Zohar. *Haḥayyimn hasifrutiyyim be'erets yisra'el. 1910–1933*. Tel Aviv: Tel Aviv University, 1982.

———. "Hashorashim halkhu vehitma'atu." *Hasifrut* 32 (1983): 45–50.

Silberschlag, Eisig. *Shaul Tschernichowsky: Poet of Revolt*. Ithaca: Cornell University Press, 1968.

Slochower, Harry. *Mythopoesis: Mythic Patterns in the Literary Classics*. 1970. Reprint. Detroit: Wayne State University Press, 1973.

Spiegel, Shalom. *The Last Trial: On the Legends and Lore of the Command to Abraham to Offer Isaac as a Sacrifice: The Akedah*. Translated by Judah Goldin. Philadelphia: The Jewish Publication Society of America, 1967.

Steinberg, Yehuda. *Siḥot ḥasidim*. Warsaw: Tushiyyah, 1904.

———. *Sippurei ḥasidim*. Warsaw: Tushiyyah, 1904.

Sternharz, Nathan of Nemirov. *Ḥayyei moharan*. Vol. 1. New York: R. Eliezer Shlomo Bratslaver, 1965.

Strauss, Aryeh Ludwig. *Bedarkhe hasifrut: 'iyyunim besifrut yisra'el uvesifrut ha'ammim*. Jerusalem: Mosad Bialik, 1965.

Talmud Bavli: Massekhet Gittin. Vilna: Moshe Hillel Cohen, n.d.

Tchernichowsky, Shaul. "'Avtobiyyografyah." *Hashiloaḥ* 35 (1918): 97–103.

———. *Shirei Shaul Tchernichowsky*. 2d ed. Tel Aviv: Dvir, 1968.

Urbach, Ephraim. "Bialik ve'aggadat ḥazal." *Molad* 17 (1959): 266–274.

Werses, Shmuel. *Sippur veshorsho*. Ramat Gan: Massada, 1971.

Zweifel, Eliezer. *Shalom 'al yisra'el*. Edited by Avraham Rubenstein. Jerusalem: Mosad Bialik, 1972.

Index